European Monographs in Social

Situation cognition and c

European Monographs in Social Psychology

Executive Editors:
J. RICHARD EISER and KLAUS R. SCHERER
Sponsored by the European Association of Experimental Social Psychology

This series, first published by Academic Press (who will continue to distribute the numbered volumes), appeared under the joint imprint of Cambridge University Press and the Maison des Sciences de l'Homme in 1985 as an amalgamation of the Academic Press series and the European Studies in Social Psychology, published by Cambridge and the Maison in collaboration with the Laboratoire Européen de Pychologie Sociale of the Maison.

The original aims of the two series still very much apply today: to provide a forum for the best European research in different fields of social psychology and to foster the interchange of ideas between different developments and different traditions. The executive Editors also expect that it will have an important role to play as a European forum for international work.

Other titles in this series:

Unemployment by Peter Kelvin and Joanna E. Jarrett
National characteristics by Dean Peabody
Experiencing emotion by Klaus R. Scherer, Harald G. Wallbott and Angela B. Summerfield
Levels of explanation in social psychology by Willem Doise
Understanding attitudes to the European Community: a social-psychological study in four member states by Miles Hewstone
Arguing and thinking: a rhetorical approach to social psychology by Michael Billig
Non-verbal communication in depression by Heiner Ellgring
Social representations of intelligence by Gabriel Mugny and Felice Carugati
Speech and reasoning in everyday life by Uli Windisch
Account episodes. The management or escalation of conflict by Peter Schönbach
The ecology of the self: relocation and self-concept change by Stefan E. Hormuth

SUPPLEMENTARY VOLUMES

Politics, power, and psychology: views from working-class youth in Britain by Kum-Kum Bhavnani

Situation cognition and coherence in personality

An individual-centred approach

Barbara Krahé

Heisenberg Fellow, University of Sussex

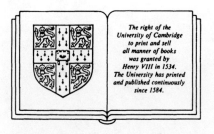

The right of the
University of Cambridge
to print and sell
all manner of books
was granted by
Henry VIII in 1534.
The University has printed
and published continuously
since 1584.

Cambridge University Press
Cambridge
New York   Port Chester
Melbourne   Sydney

Editions de la Maison des Sciences de l'Homme
Paris

CAMBRIDGE UNIVERSITY PRESS
Cambridge, New York, Melbourne, Madrid, Cape Town, Singapore,
São Paulo, Delhi, Dubai, Tokyo, Mexico City

Cambridge University Press
The Edinburgh Building, Cambridge CB2 8RU, UK

Published in the United States of America by Cambridge University Press, New York

www.cambridge.org
Information on this title: www.cambridge.org/9780521154987

First published 1990
First paperback edition 2010

A catalogue record for this publication is available from the British Library

Library of Congress Cataloguing in Publication Data
Krahé, Barbara.
Situation cognition and coherence in personality: an individual–centred
approach/Barbara Krahé
     p.   cm. – (European monographs in social psychology)
Includes bibliographical references.
ISBN 0 521 35295 9
1. Personality and cognition.   2. Personality and situation.
I. Title. II. Title: Coherence in personality. III. Series.
BF698. S.C63K72   1991
155.2–dc20   90-31386   CIP

ISBN 978-0-521-35295-6 Hardback
ISBN 978-0-521-15498-7 Paperback

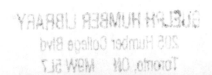

For Peter and Charlotte

Contents

List of figures   *page* ix
List of tables   x
Preface   xi
Acknowledgements   xiii

Part 1: Theoretical foundations

1 **Cross-situational consistency: an issue at the interface
   between personality and social psychology**   3

2 **The history of the consistency debate**   15
   Problems with the situationist model   17
   Problems with the trait approach   21
   The 'cognitive turn' in personality psychology   28

3 **P × S: the promise of modern interactionism**   38
   Basic concepts and propositions   39
   Methodological strategies   45
   An application: the study of stress and anxiety   57
   Current appraisals of the interactionist model   66

4 **The cognitive representation of situations**   71
   The situation as a variable in personality research   71
   The perception of social episodes   81
   Situations as cognitive prototypes   84
   Cognitive scripts for situations   87
   Implications for the present research   90

5 **Individual-centred strategies in the search for consistency**   92
   The act frequency approach   93
   The template matching approach   97
   The idiothetic approach   101
   Comparing idiographic and nomothetic measures of   105
   consistency

6 **Reconceptualising consistency: the coherence of situation
   cognition and behaviour**   111

Part 2: Empirical investigations

7   An individual-centred approach to the study of cross-
    situational coherence in anxiety-provoking situations   117
    An outline of the research programme   117
    Sampling anxiety-provoking situations: the 'situation grid'   122
    Overview of the studies   124

8   Study 1: Developing an individual-centred methodology   125
    Sample and overview   126
    Eliciting anxiety-provoking situations   127
    A preliminary test of the coherence model   131

9   Study 2: Coherence of situation cognition and behavioural
    ratings   142
    Sample and overview   143
    The situation grid   143
    Situation cognition measures   146
    Behavioural measures   149
    Results   151
    Discussion   157

10 Study 3: Coherence of situation cognition and behavioural
    self-reports   160
    Sample and overview   160
    Measures of situation cognition and behaviour   161
    Results   166
    Discussion   172

11 Beyond the 'nomothetic vs. idiographic' controversy in the
    search for cross-situational consistency   176

    References   183
    Author index   200   *Subject index*   204

Figures

7.1 Features of the individual-centred methodology   *page* 121
8.1 Situation experience questionnaire   128
8.2 Example of the behavioural measure   132
8.3 Format for eliciting global ratings of perceived similarity   133
8.4 Example of the prototype measure   135
8.5 Example of the social episode measure   135
8.6 Example of the script measure   135
9.1 Format of the situation grid   145
9.2 Situation grid data (Respondent A, male)   146
9.3 Situation grid data (Respondent B, female)   147
9.4 Example of the situation cognition data (Respondent C, male)   149
9.5 Example of the situation cognition data (Respondent D, female, a trained nurse)   150
10.1 Example of the behavioural self-report measure (Respondent E, male)   164
10.2 Example of the behavioural self-report measure (Respondent F, female)   164

Tables

8.1 Means and standard deviations of the number of situations
listed per category (N = 25)   *page* 129
8.2 Anxiety-provoking situations with five or more nominations   130
8.3 Correlations between situation perception and behaviour:
aggregated findings (N = 23)   138
8.4 Individual correlations betweeen situation perception and
behaviour   139
9.1 Individual correlations between situation cognition and
behaviour   153
9.2 Intercorrelations between the cognitive measures   154
9.3 Intraindividual correlations between the two behavioural
measures   154
9.4 Average correlations between cognitive similarity and
behavioural similarity across twelve anxiety-provoking
situations (N = 28)   155
10.1 Intraindividual correlations between the ratings of behaviour
probability at the second and sixth data points   167
10.2 Individual correlations between situation cognition and
behaviour   167
10.3 Intercorrelations between the cognitive measures   169
10.4 Intraindividual correlations between the behavioural measures 169
10.5 Correlations between cognition–behaviour correlations and
self-rated consistency   171
10.6 Average correlations between the cognitive and behavioural
measures (N = 25)   172

Preface

Not long ago, admitting to a sympathy for idiographic thought was tantamount to heresy in personality psychology. Times have changed and today, if anything, such a confession is more likely to provoke suspicions that one is jumping onto a fashionable bandwagon along with progressive critics in the field. At the same time, personality researchers have found another bone of contention in the issue of how to define the relationship of their discipline with social psychology. While some leading figures unreservedly welcome and recommend the closer convergence of the two fields, others adopt a more critical stance, arguing in favour of defending the autonomy and distinctness of personality research as a psychological discipline.

This is the sensitive terrain on which the present volume has to define its place.

The research reported in this volume aims to make both a theoretical and a methodological contribution to the consistency controversy in personality theory which, despite numerous research efforts in recent years, is still far from being settled satisfactorily. The basic proposition underlying this endeavour is that previous attempts at resolving the consistency controversy have failed to give sufficient consideration to two essential tasks: (1) to offer an adequate theoretical treatment of the 'psychological situation', i.e. the situation *as perceived* by the person, which is widely proclaimed as a major determinant of regularity and change in individual behaviour; (2) to develop methodological strategies appropriate to the conceptual understanding of consistency as pertaining to regularities in *individual* behaviour, i.e. methods which would facilitate the discovery of cross-situational consistency at the level of the individual person.

The volume is divided into two parts: Part 1 consists of an analysis of the consistency problem and a critical discussion of the available approaches to its solution, both conceptually and methodically. The modern interactionist perspective on personality is undoubtedly the most prominent of recent developments and will be reviewed in greatest detail. What will become clear from this discussion is that modern interactionism has as yet failed to present a convincing and comprehensive treatment of situational variables despite its emphasis on the psychological meaning of situations for the person in the process of person–situation interaction. As a consequence, recent work in cognitive social psychology will be consulted for a better understanding of the cognitive representation of situations. As far as the methodological side of the consistency controversy is concerned, a number of approaches have recently been suggested. Their impact will be discussed against the background of the newly revived controversy over the adequacy of nomothetic vs. idiographic strategies in personality measurement. On the basis of the evidence reviewed thus far, the first part ends with the presentation of a revised conceptualisation of the consistency issue, defining consistency in terms of the covariation between situation cognition and individual behaviour across situations. In Part 2, the suggested reconceptualisation of consistency is examined empirically in the domain of anxiety which has been a paradigmatic field of application for interactionist thinking. Support for the model is sought (and found) in three related investigations which examine the correspondence between perceived situational similarity and behavioural similarity across a range of anxiety-provoking situations. In line with the understanding of consistency in terms of intraindividual regularities, an individual-centred methodology is developed, aiming to combine the principles of idiographic inquiry with the search for nomothetic generalisations. This methodological framework facilitates the sampling of individually valid situations, perceptions, and behaviours without precluding the examination of general hypotheses about the proposed structural relationships between situation cognition and behaviour. The volume concludes with a discussion of the advantages of an individual-centred approach to cross-situational coherence and its implications for bridging the gap between nomothetic and idiographic orientations in personality research.

Acknowledgements

The main part of the research reported in this volume was conducted when I was a Visiting Fellow at the University of Sussex, Brighton. My thanks are due to the Alexander von Humboldt-Foundation (FRG) for facilitating this stay with a Feodor-Lynen Fellowship and to the School of Social Sciences at the University of Sussex for its hospitality. I would also like to thank the Economic and Social Research Council of Great Britain for the grant (G 00232235) that contributed to the present research. The completion of the manuscript was facilitated by a Heisenberg Fellowship awarded by the Deutsche Forschungsgemeinschaft.

On an 'interpersonal' level, I am most grateful for the encouragement and help I received from colleagues in Germany and Britain. Throughout the project, Bernd Six provided vital advice and moral support which helped to keep me going vis-à-vis the inevitable pitfalls and vagaries of empirical research. At Sussex, Gün R. Semin was always ready for critical and constructive discussions of the issues at the core of this research. Helga Dittmar and Alan Blair offered their reliable assistance in preparing the studies and analysing the data. I am also indebted to the editors of the 'European Monograph' series, in particular Dick Eiser, for encouraging the preparation of this volume.

Finally, I would like to extend a special word of thanks to the participants in the three studies for their stamina and their willingness to share their personal and often intimate experiences with me.

Part 1
Theoretical foundations

1 Cross-situational consistency: an issue at the interface between personality and social psychology

In search of a definition of *personality* that would be sufficiently general and hence uncontroversial to be accepted as a minimal consensus by personality psychologists of different provenance and theoretical orientation, two basic features soon crystallise out:

1 *Personality* refers to stable characteristics of the individual which are reflected in his or her behaviour in a consistent and predictable way. This defining feature implies that evidence of behavioural regularity over time as well as situations is required as an expression of an individual's personality.

2 *Personality* encompasses those psychological qualities which are 'characteristic' for the individual, i.e. which account for ways he or she is different from other persons. This defining feature implies that observed differences between individuals must be interpretable unambiguously as a result of intrapersonal as opposed to situational factors.

This understanding of personality, which emerges as a kind of common denominator from the various theoretical orientations in the field, can also be found pervasively in the current literature of neighbouring psychological disciplines. It is prominently represented, for example, in the *Handbook of Social Psychology* in a chapter by Snyder & Ickes (1985, 883) who further underscore its timeless validity by a reference to Allport (1937). Another case in point is the overview of different definitions presented by Forgus & Shulman (1979) in their 'cognitive view' of personality.

Each of the two defining features highlights the central importance assigned to the concept of *consistency* in personality research: Whether the field of personality is accepted and established as a legitimate and independent domain of psychological research depends, to a large extent, on the success of its representatives in providing empirical evidence for consistency, both *intraindividually* in terms of temporal and cross-situational regularities of behavioural profiles and *interindividually* in terms of the stability of individual differences across time and situations. Accordingly, any challenge of the concept of personality consistency is almost tantamount to attacking the very basis and *raison d'être* of the field as a whole. As Loevinger & Knoll (1983, 196) poignantly put it: 'If there is no consistency in behavior [. . .] then the field of personality should disappear [. . .].' It is not surprising, therefore, that such challenges have typically provoked intense and persistent reactions ranging from critical self-reflection to determined self-defence (e.g. Mischel & Peake, 1982a, and the responses to their paper by Bem, 1983b; Conley, 1984b; Epstein, 1983a; Funder, 1983; and Jackson & Paunonen, 1985).

A prime example illustrating the sensitivity of personality research to criticism of the consistency concept is provided by Mischel's (1968) devastating assessment of the empirical evidence for consistency and the effect it had on the field of personality. After reviewing the empirical evidence for the consistent manifestation of traits in behaviour, he concluded: 'With the possible exception of intelligence, highly generalized behavior consistencies have not been demonstrated, and the concept of personality traits as broad response dispositions is thus untenable' (Mischel, 1968, 146). Pressed by this criticism, the currently prevailing paradigm of 'modern interactionism' emerged. Modern interactionism offered not only a new theoretical approach to personality which finally introduced the analysis of *situations* into the agenda of personality research; it also stirred up a renewed concern for methodological developments which would be appropriate for the proposed dynamic nature of person–situation interactions.

At the same time, Mischel's critique acted as trigger or at least catalyst of a profound crisis of confidence in the field of personality which is discernible in the regular 'state-of-the-art' reviews in the *Annual Review of Psychology* (e.g. Carson, 1989; Pervin, 1985a, Phares & Lamiell, 1977; Rorer & Widiger, 1983; Sechrest, 1976; also Feshbach, 1984; Mischel, 1984a) and gave rise to questions like: 'What shall we do to revitalize the study of personality?' (Tomkins, 1981, 448). As early as 1971, Carlson examined the question 'Where is the person in personality research?' and arrived at a sobering answer: 'That the person is not really studied in current personality research is clearly shown in the survey of the literature' (Carlson, 1971, 217). Thirteen years later, the same author came to a similarly disappointing conclusion in addressing the extended question of 'What's social about social psychology? Where's the person in personality research?' This time, her verdict was that 'currently, the two fields appear to be linked mainly by their deficiencies and appear to have little content worth sharing' (Carlson, 1984, 1304).

Even though such fundamental criticism has not gone unchallenged (e.g. Kenrick, 1986), it is indicative of the widespread recognition among personality psychologists that their field is under pressure to arrive at a new and convincing self-image in both theoretical and methodological respects.

In this process, the task of defining its identity with regard to related disciplines, most notably social psychology, plays a crucial role, whether prompted by the desire to uncover similar difficulties and stake territorial claims or guided by the search for solutions which might turn out to be applicable to the problems in one's own field (e.g. Ajzen, 1987; Baron & Boudreau, 1987; Blass, 1984; Buss, 1987; Heilizer, 1980; Kenrick & Dantchik, 1983; Rosenberg & Gara, 1983; Sherman & Fazio, 1983; see also R. B. Taylor, 1983; S. E. Taylor, 1981).

The present research is committed to this latter, integrative view in its attempt to present a social psychological perspective on the issue of cross-situational consistency which is subjected to empirical test *in the domain of anxiety-provoking situations*. In particular, this perspective involves a closer examination of the ways in which the features of situations – the units across which behaviour is supposed to be consistent – are perceived and cognitively represented by the person. Drawing upon recent work in social cognition research, different models of *situation cognition* are examined as to their suitability for providing a clearer understanding of the concept of the *psychological situation*. This concept, which refers to the subjective interpretation of situational cues as opposed to the definition of situations in objective, physical terms, is suggested as a key notion in the modern interactionist model of personality (Magnusson & Endler, 1977b, 4) and, more specifically, the interactionist explanation of individual behaviour in anxiety-provoking situations (Endler, 1983).

However, the interactionist approach to personality is as yet lacking a proper theoretical treatment of the 'psychological situation'. Such a treatment would have to contain specific propositions about the nature of the cognitive representation of situational features and the principles whereby situations are cognitively construed as being similar or different. It is with regard to these issues that Argyle, Furnham & Graham (1981, 15) concluded: 'In an important sense, interactional psychology has not practised what it preached.'

The aim to furnish a theoretical basis for the notion of the psychological situation from a social psychological perspective is linked with a second, equally central objective. This objective involves a reformulation of the consistency concept in terms of *cross-situational coherence* and the development of an individual-centred methodology to provide empirical evidence of coherent, i.e. individually lawful patterns of behaviour. In the traditional understanding of *absolute* consistency, any form of behavioural variation across situations is typically interpreted as evidence against personality consistency or, conversely, in favour of the overriding impact of situational influences. The less rigorous concept of *relative* consistency, while allowing for variation in individual behaviour, still requires the rank order of individual differences to be stable across situations. To put it differently, the concept of relative consistency implies that situational factors affect the individuals involved in very much the same way (cf. Argyle & Little, 1972; Magnusson & Endler, 1977b).

In contrast, the more recent concept of *coherence*, proposed as part of the interactionist model of personality, incorporates both the importance of personal dispositions and the differential sensitivity of individual behaviour to situational influences (for a more detailed discussion of the different meanings of consistency cf. Krahé, in press, ch. 2). A concise definition of coherence is offered by Magnusson:

> A third meaning of behavioral consistency is that an individual's
> behavior is consistent in the sense that it is coherent and predictable,
> without being stable in either absolute or relative terms [. . .] The
> consistency of an individual's behavior is expressed in lawful, reliable
> *patterns* of stable and changing behaviors, which can be described on the
> data-level, in cross-situational profiles for a number of relevant variables.
> (Magnusson, 1976, 257)

However, despite the claim that 'the meaning of consistency in terms of coherence is advocated by the interactional model of behavior' (Magnusson, 1976, 257), the model suffers from an undeniable shortage of methodological strategies designed to deal empirically with the proposed intraindividual regularities of behaviour in different situations. Therefore, the present research advances a more specific understanding of cross-situational coherence which lends itself immediately to empirical analysis: Coherence is operationally defined in terms of the *systematic covariation of perceived situational similarity and behavioural similarity over a range of situations*, whereby it is argued that the study of such covariations requires an *intraindividual* as opposed to an *interindividual* level of analysis. At the core of the work reported in this volume, therefore, is the proposition of a functional relationship between situation cognition and behaviour which opens the way for accommodating the stability *as well as* change of behavioural profiles within the concept of consistency. To the extent that behavioural variability in different situations is matched by corresponding differences in the perception and interpretation of the situations involved, patterns of change are as indicative of cross-situational coherence as patterns of stability.

Given the two objectives briefly outlined above, the present research faces the following essential tasks in its attempt to provide a conceptual as well as empirical contribution to the consistency debate from a social psychological perspective:

At a theoretical level, to advance a clearer understanding of the 'psychological situation' with a view to creating a conceptual link between the cognitive representation of situational meaning and the issue of cross-situational coherence of behaviour. To achieve this aim, recent models of situation cognition developed in cognitive social psychology are regarded as potential building blocks of a theoretical framework for explicating the interactionist concept of the 'psychological meaning of situations' as well as reconceptualising the contentious role of the situation concept in the consistency controversy.

At a methodological level, to develop an empirical strategy which would facilitate the assessment of the proposed intraindividual coherence of situation cognition and behaviour. At the same time, this strategy should lend itself to the examination of generalized hypotheses about the structural relationship between perceived similarity and behavioural similarity across situations. As will be argued in more detail later on, these methodological requirements can only be met by an individual-centred approach which ensures that both the situations involved and the perception of their characteristic properties are representative samples of each person's individual experience.

From what has been said so far, it is obvious that the present research is located at the interface between personality research and social psychology. In this respect, it is potentially subject to the accusation of further abetting the 'social psychological invasion of personality research' diagnosed by Kenrick & Dantchik (1983). Thus, before the theoretical background of the research is outlined in the next chapters, a brief look at a more general question is in order: Is the current relationship between social and personality psychology appropriately described in the language of military metaphors or can any profit be expected for personality research from a more extensive reference to social psychological thinking?

In recent years, the issue of whether personality and social psychology *do* as well as *should* share a common identity has received increasing attention (cf. Kenrick & Funder, 1988, as well as the Special Issue devoted to this theme by the *Journal of Personality and Social Psychology*, 1987) and has led to controversial exchanges between the representatives of both camps. Leaving aside those aspects of the controversy related to professional politicking (e.g. the control of journal space) and involving a good deal of in-group favouritism or 'professional ethnocentrism' (Kenrick, 1986, 839), there is a growing number of substantive contributions aiming to identify parallel developments, research strategies and, not least, shortcomings in the two disciplines.

This latter aspect is at the centre of the critical appraisal by Carlson (1984), briefly mentioned above, who addresses the following question: To what extent does current research in social psychology actually contribute to the understanding of 'social behaviour', and to what extent can current personality research be said to facilitate a comprehensive analysis of the individual? In order to provide an answer to this double question, she specifies a list of essential methodological requirements for each of the two fields:

For social psychology	*For personality psychology*
the study of meaningfully defined groups	the use of non-student samples
the inclusion of social structural variables	the inclusion of biographical information
the observation of genuine social interactions	the choice of experimental treatments relevant to subject characteristics
the observation of social influence processes	the temporal extension over at least two months
the study of attitudes relevant to the subjects	the retainment of the individual as unit of analysis

Applying this list to a sample of empirical studies published in two volumes of the *Journal of Personality and Social Psychology*, she found that almost half of the social psychological (47%) and personality psychology studies (44%) failed to meet any of the criteria while not a single study was found to meet more than three criteria. This result led Carlson (1984, 1308) to the provocative conclusion that 'the attempt to forge a shared identity of personality and social psychology was done in such a way as to draw upon the worst qualities of both fields'. Obviously, the yardstick on which this verdict is based is open to question (e.g. Kenrick, 1986), and a different set of criteria would have yielded a somewhat different picture. What would be hard to repudiate, however, is the general point that both social psychology and personality psychology are characterised on a large scale by a lack of correspondence between the definitions of their subject matter and the prevailing strategies for exploring that subject matter in empirical analyses.

While Carlson's critique is directed first and foremost at the level of methodological strategies, other writers adopt a more conceptually oriented perspective. They examine theoretical development and change in both fields by tracing the history of individual concepts with a view to discovering parallel and convergent trends.[1] In this attempt, the concepts of *traits* and *attitudes*, each referring to the dispositional basis of individual behaviour, suggest themselves most readily for closer analysis. As Ajzen (1987, 1) states:

> The historical and largely artificial boundaries between personality and social psychology have resulted in divergent research traditions that have tended to obscure the conceptual similarities and common vicissitudes of the two concepts.

Like Blass (1984), he draws attention to the fact that the concepts of traits and attitudes twice came under attack at similar points in their history

---

[1] A third type of approach, illustrated by Rosenberg & Gara (1983), explores the theoretical as well as methodological structure of both fields via their most prominent representatives, past and present.

(Hartshorne & May, 1928, and LaPiere, 1934, and subsequently Mischel, 1968, and Wicker, 1969), resulting in profound crises of confidence in their respective disciplines as a whole. These historical parallels, however, are of little interest in themselves. They gain importance only in connection with the kinds of changes and developments that emerged in the two fields as a consequence. As far as the more recent critiques by Mischel (1968) of the trait concept and Wicker (1969) of the attitude concept are concerned, Blass (1984) and Sherman & Fazio (1983) identify a number of consequences.

The critical appraisals of Mischel and Wicker referred to the same basic problem, namely the lack of empirical evidence for the proposed consistency between a latent disposition (attitude or trait) and overt behaviour. In response to this challenge, researchers in both fields embarked on the search for feasible ways to enhance the strength of the relationship between dispositions and behaviour. In the process, the initially intra-disciplinary endeavours frequently turned out to be applicable also to the respective other field. Thus, it has been shown, for example, that the concepts of *self-monitoring* and *objective self-awareness* are not only effective moderators of the attitude–behaviour relationship but also facilitate the differential predictability of trait–behaviour consistency (e.g. Ajzen, 1988; Snyder & Ickes, 1985; cf. also Baron & Kenny, 1986). The conceptual analogies between traits and attitudes are also stressed by Baumeister & Tice (1988) with regard to their concept of 'metatraits', presented as part of a strategy for identifying those persons for whom consistency in a given trait may be expected. In the same way, the aggregation of behavioural data, either across time or in the form of multiple-act criteria, was shown to be a successful strategy for increasing the consistency of both traits and attitudes with overt behaviour (eg Blass, 1984; Rushton, Brainerd & Pressley, 1983).

In their extensive discussion of the parallels between attitudes and traits as predictors of behaviour, Sherman & Fazio (1983) arrive at a similar conclusion: Notwithstanding some differences between the two concepts, they show a substantial overlap both in terms of pertinent research questions and current theoretical perspectives, speaking in favour of a more intensive exchange between the domains of social and personality psychology.

Possible forms that this intensified exchange might take are illustrated by recent attempts to include situational variables in dispositional models of behaviour prediction. In the field of attitude–behaviour research, models of 'contingent consistency' have been proposed, suggesting that situational constraints critically affect the extent to which individual attitudes are manifested in overt behaviour (e.g. Acock & Scott, 1980; Andrews & Kandel, 1979). In a parallel fashion, personality research has offered modern interactionism as a comprehensive model of the interdependence of personal and situational determinants of behaviour. The applicability of this model to issues of attitude–behaviour consistency has recently been illustrated by Kahle (1984). Furthermore, Blass (1984) makes the point that a number of variables that were originally conceived of as situation-dependent and operationalised as experimental manipulations have subsequently been reformulated or extended in terms of dispositional constructs and vice versa. This is true, for instance, for the concepts of *self-consciousness* (Fenigstein, Scheier & Buss, 1975) and *belief in a just world* (Lerner, 1980) which were shown to be strongly affected by situational manipulations while displaying, at the same time, stable differences between individuals. In the same vein, Buss (1987) points out that self-esteem has been studied by personality researchers as an enduring disposition and by social psychologists as a psychological state susceptible to specific situational manipulations. Finally, Singer & Kolligian (1987, 534–5) note that the strong interest in social cognition, and cognitive schemas in particular, has implied 'that what was once thought to be a fuzzy area of personality has become increasingly central to the understanding of interpersonal and group behavior as well as to the organization of personality'.

In sum, these authors converge on the judgement that the current relationship between personality and social psychology is marked by cross-fertilisation rather than antagonism, and there is general agreement that modern interactionism is the paradigm of choice at the interface between the two fields. In this vein, Blass (1984) notes an increasing interdisciplinary consensus about the adequacy of an interactionist view on explaining and predicting individual behaviour, leading him to describe interactionism as 'a natural bridge between personality and social psychology' (p. 1018). The very negative verdict reached by Carlson is thus contrasted with an unreservedly positive appraisal of the emergence of a shared identity of personality and social psychology, hailed as the beginning of 'an era of cordiality between the two disciplines' (Blass, 1984, 1023). Which of these radically different viewpoints is more appropriate cannot be decided conclusively since both perspectives rely on different criteria and support for one side or the other is ultimately a matter of how these criteria are evaluated. Both perspectives, however, gain special relevance from the fact that they represent facets of the current self-definitions of personality and social psychology from which directions of future development may be inferred.

This is also the respect in which the paper by Kenrick & Dantchick (1983) is best understood. The title itself, which claims the already cited 'social psychological invasion of personality', reveals that unlike the previous examples, this critical appraisal of the current relationship between personality and social psychology does not aim to identify common foci of interest from an 'impartial' position. Instead, the argument is presented from a personality 'in-group' perspective. To start with, attention is drawn to social psychologists' growing presence in and control of the publication outlets originally designed for personality psychologists. Kenrick & Dantchik then explore the different ways in which social psychologists have infused their preferred theoretical and empirical paradigms into personality research and provide an assessment of these new ingredients of the current picture of the field. Here, they argue that the current unpopularity of the trait concept is a direct consequence of the social psychological bias in favour of situationist accounts of social behaviour which, in turn, is regarded as being largely due to the preference for experimental methods and the influence of sociological thinking. This view is also shared by other authors such as Feshbach (1984, 448) who sees the negative implications of the general disinterest of social psychologists in individual differences, noting that 'when an issue is defined solely in social psychological terms, such that personality psychologists accept the social psychological approach or simply abandon the problem, then the consequence is, indeed, a negative one for the field'.

Furthermore, Kenrick & Dantchick discern a distinct 'cognitive bias' in current social psychology which – despite its relevance to certain issues of person perception – has led to a general overemphasis on the social construction of personality, regarding traits as cognitive categories used by the perceiver rather than psychological properties of the person observed (cf. Baron & Boudreau, 1987, and Sears, 1986, for a related point). Modern interactionism is equally accused of placing excessive weight on the cognitive mediation of person–situation links while being overly individualistic in its emphasis on the idiosyncratic nature of situation perception and behaviour. Finally, it is argued that the social psychological predilection for minitheories designed specifically for single phenomena and more or less incoherent 'laundry lists' of variables at the expense of more general conceptual frameworks is conducive to impoverishing the theoretical basis of personality research.

Kenrick & Dantchik (1983) thus arrive at a fundamentally negative assessment of social psychological contributions to personality research.[2] However, one could argue that their reasoning is impaired by their pervasive strategy of narrowing down broad research programs as well as theoretical perspectives to very specific negative effects, thus barring the way to a recognition the potentially fruitful implications of those developments. With this objection in mind, the aims and assumptions of the present research can be described as direct challenges to Kenrick & Dantchik's judgements in virtually every respect: the research reported in this volume is guided by the aim of demonstrating the cross-situational consistency of behaviour within a conceptual framework

---

[2] Even though they end on a more conciliatory note, this is not actually in accord with the serious challenges raised in the remainder of their paper.

– which is committed to an interactionist understanding of personality in the sense of a reciprocal relationship between personal characteristics and situational features,
– in which the controversial notion of cross-situational consistency is rephrased in terms of the coherence, i.e. cross-situational covariation of situation perception and behaviour,
– where the focus is on the issue of how situations are perceived and cognitively represented by the indvidual,
– which draws upon social psychological models of situation cognition in order to arrive at theoretical conceptualisations of the 'psychological situation' as yet lacking in personality research, and finally
– which involves the development of an individual-centred strategy for studying the proposed covariation of situation perception and behaviour, accessing both the content and structure of the subjective meaning that persons assign to the situations they encounter in their daily lives.

In addressing these aims, the present research is based on a broad understanding of the concept of cognition. It does not deny in any way that emotional and motivational states play an important part in explaining how impressions about situations are formed. However, the person's appraisal and processing of these states on the one hand, and of the objective features of a given situation on the other, are conceived of primarily as a cognitive task. Accordingly, situation cognition is broadly conceptualised as reflecting the individual's attempt to establish the meaning of situations in a subjectively accurate way.

The purpose of this introductory chapter has been to present a general outline of the research reported in the remainder of this volume, sketching its place on the current agenda of personality research. Briefly, it was argued that a new perspective on the perennial problem of cross-situational consistency can be opened up by relocating it at the interface between personality and social psychology, stating the case for a closer convergence of the two fields at the expense of theoretical and methodological particularism. This perspective now has to be elaborated in the following chapters.

In chapter 2, the history of the consistency debate is traced from the work of Hartshorne & May and G. Allport up to the mid-1970s which saw the emergence of the modern interactionist approach to personality. Different varieties of both the situationist and the trait positions are discussed along with the increasing prominence of cognitive variables in personality theory and research since the work of Kelly and other authors some thirty years ago.

This discussion provides the background against which the aims and achievements of the modern person-by-situation perspective on personality are reviewed in chapter 3. Following a summary of the central theoretical postulates and preferred methodological strategies of modern interactionism, the type of research generated in this paradigm is exemplified in the field of stress and anxiety. Finally, current appraisals of the modern interactionist model are presented along with a critical analysis of the issues which have as yet to be addressed convincingly. Among the latter, the theoretical treatment of the 'psychological situation', introduced as a key concept, features most prominently.

Chapter 4, therefore, looks at recent developments in social psychology which offer theoretical models of the cognitive representation of social situations. In particular, the work of Cantor & Mischel on *cognitive prototypes* of situations, Forgas' model of *social episodes*, and Schank & Abelson's work on the representation of situations in the form of *cognitive scripts* are discussed as potentially fruitful contributions to a more elaborate theoretical account of the psychological situation and its impact on individual behaviour. Particular emphasis is placed on the adaptation of the three models to the study of cross-situational consistency within an idiographic mode of analysis.

Different methodological remedies developed by personality researchers in response to the challenge of the consistency concept are discussed in chapter 5. A broad distinction is made between strategies that are based on the search for general or nomothetic principles of personality functioning and those which are directed towards a comprehensive, idiographic analysis of the individual person. It will be argued that the basic incompatiblity of the two strategies claimed by the proponents of a strictly nomothetic understanding has increasingly been questioned in recent years, and new approaches have emerged that lend themselves to both types of inquiry.

Chapter 6 presents a revised formulation of the consistency concept where consistency is defined in terms of the intraindividual regularity or coherence of behaviour across situations. It is argued that in order to understand the psychological processes by which the subjective interpretation of situations affects behaviour, theoretical models are required explaining how impressions are formed about situations. The current theoretical and methodological state of research on cross-situational consistency is summarised to clarify the point of departure for the present empirical studies.

In the second part of the volume, the theoretical approach developed in the previous chapters is subjected to empirical test in three successive studies. The proposed reformulation of consistency in terms of coherence poses a number of crucial demands on the methodological framework required for its empirical validation. These demands are outlined in chapter 7 along with the reasons for choosing the domain of anxiety-provoking situations as the content area for the present research. It is pointed out that coherence can only be expected if the situations involved are psychologically meaningful for the individual and if respondents are allowed to apply their own criteria of situational similarity or difference. Moreover, a measure of coherence must be employed which can be interpreted as an index of intraindividual coherence independent of the standing of other members of the sample. These requirements call for the development of an individual-centred methodology. An important aspect of such an approach refers to the sampling of relevant situations from each individual, and a method derived from Kelly's (1955) Repertory Grid Technique is introduced to meet this objective. The chapter ends with a preview of the three empirical studies reported in the next chapters.

The first of these investigations, described in chapter 8, is designed as a pilot study for testing the various newly developed measures of situation cognition and behaviour and providing a first tentative examination of the proposed intraindividual covariation of perceived similarity and behavioural similarity across different anxiety-provoking situations.

This study forms the basis for a more comprehensive examination, reported in chapter 9, of the link between situation cognition and behaviour, requiring each participant to attend five experimental sessions in the course of six months. The results from this study provide convincing support for the coherence model, permitting further refinement and standardisation of the materials.

These revised instruments are subsequently applied to a further test of the coherence model in the third study, presented in chapter 10. This study, which also extended over several months and involved six data points, broadens the scope of the previous studies by including a more complex measure of individual behaviour and assessing its stability over time.

The concluding chapter 11 discusses the findings from the three studies with reference to the theoretical and methodological issues raised in the first part of the volume. This involves a critical appraisal of the progress achieved by drawing upon theoretical models of situation cognition in conceptualising the interaction between the person and the situation. At the same time, the advantages, but also limitations of the newly developed methodology for discovering intraindividual regularities in behaviour are examined along with the implications of the findings for further investigations into the concept of cross-situational coherence. Finally, a plea is made for overcoming the antagonism between nomothetic and idiographic approaches to the study of personality in favour of an integrative perspective which combines the search for nomothetic principles of personality functioning with an explicit recognition of the uniqueness of individual experience.

2 The history of the consistency debate

The beginnings of the controversy between trait theorists and S–R-theorists over the validity of dispositional concepts in explaining and predicting individual behaviour date back as far as the 1920s and 1930s. In the early stages, the positions in the debate were epitomised by the now classic work of Hartshorne & May (1928) and Allport's (1937) critical response to their conclusions. They set the tone for the course of the debate up to the present day which has focused on the issue of whether behaviour is situation-specific and can only be explained with reference to the characteristics of the respective situation or whether there is evidence for broad, cross-situational behavioural tendencies which can be systematically linked with corresponding dispositions.

In their well-known study, Hartshorne & May examined the cross-situational consistency vs. specificity of dishonest behaviours. More than 10,000 school-children were unobtrusively provided with the opportunity to perform three types of deceptive behaviour: cheating, stealing, and lying. Each of the three types was represented by several behavioural indicators (e.g. stealing money in a party situation, a play situation, or a classroom situation). In order to assess the extent to which the children were consistent in their honest or deceptive responses, average correlations were computed between the different measures of dishonest behaviour. The obtained correlations ranged from $r = -.003$ to $r = .312$, thus accounting, at best, for just 9% of the variance (cf. Hartshorne & May, 1928, 383).

This pattern of results led the authors to reject the idea that the manifestation of a variety of dishonest behaviours may be attributed to a temporally stable, intrinsic disposition towards dishonesty. Instead, they argued that predictions of whether or not a person will resist the temptation to act in a dishonest way are more adequately based on the characteristic features of the situation as either encouraging or counteracting the performance of deceptive behaviour.

Throughout the subsequent course of the debate, the Hartshorne & May study has been quoted as prime empirical evidence against the validity of the trait approach, despite concurrent criticisms of their statistical analyses and interpretations (e.g. Burton, 1963; Epstein & O'Brien, 1985; Maller, 1934).

At least as important as these criticisms, relating to the empirical procedures employed by Hartshorne & May, is the conceptual critique advanced by Allport (1937), which highlights some of the fundamental problems with approaching the consistency issue in this way.

Allport identified various implicit and questionable stipulations of this study which are also inherent in many subsequent investigations in support of the situationist position. In the present context, two aspects of his analysis are particularly pertinent.

The first refers to the fact that the lack of cross-situational consistency was inferred from low intercorrelations between the observed behaviours purportedly belonging to one and the same behavioural category, i.e. the category of deceptive behaviour. As Allport argued, this inference would have been justified only if the meaning of the selected behavioural indicators had been unequivocally established as referring to the concept, or for that matter, to the *trait* of 'dishonesty'. Since one may reasonably assume – and no evidence to the contrary is presented – that the various behavioural indicators chosen by Hartshorne & May could have represented different behavioural categories, cross-situational differences in behaviour cannot be interpreted conclusively as a reflection of inconsistency. The following example illustrates this point. Although Hartshorne & May regarded lying and stealing as conceptually equivalent behavioural criteria for dishonesty, it is conceivable that for the children in their sample the two behaviours had different functional meanings, and could therefore be regarded as belonging to two different trait categories. A child may have lied to protect her- or himself against an anticipated punishment, but had no reason for stealing money from a classmate because she or he received ample pocket money. As long as such differential responses follow a systematic, temporally stable pattern, the meaning of the consistency concept would be distorted if one were to describe a child as inconsistent only because she or he told a lie in one situation without also stealing in another.

Allport's reasoning on this point has apparently failed to make a deep impression on subsequent researchers so that many decades later the same point had to be made again in unusual unison by Bem (1983c) and Mischel (1979). Bem reminded the parties in the debate of the fact that the 'traditional inference of inconsistency is not an inference about individuals but a statement about the disagreement between a group of individuals and an investigator over which behaviors and which situations may properly be classified into common equivalence classes' (1983c, 568). Similarly, Mischel pointed out 'that individuals organize and pattern their behavioral consistencies and discriminations in terms of their subjectively perceived equivalencies and their personal meanings, not those of the trait psychologist who categorizes them' (1979, 742).

In his second objection to Hartshorne & May's conclusions, Allport transfers the above reasoning to the methodological level. He argues that since their unit of analysis was the entire sample of children, the observed patterns of behaviour could only speak to interindividual, but not intra-individual, consistencies. Therefore, their low correlations revealed no more than the fact that the behavioural patterns of the children did not vary in the same way across the recorded situations. Consequently, he claimed that the proper examination of the postulated intraindividual consistency of behaviour would have required an idiographic methodology where the subjective definition of equivalence classes of behaviours and situations had been given central importance (cf. Allport, 1937, 280). Again, subsequent investigators did not take Allport's point very seriously. It is only recently that his argument has been echoed in the work of various authors, such as Epstein (1980), Lamiell (1982) and Valsiner (1986). As Epstein put it: 'Too often, the highly questionable assumption is made that correlations derived from nomothetic studies of groups of individuals are applicable to processes within individuals' (1980, 803).

Following this brief discussion of some of the core issues raised very early in the debate and never addressed quite satisfactorily in its later stages, the next two sections will examine in somewhat greater detail the thrust of the arguments advanced by the situationist and trait positions, respectively. In so doing, we shall not attempt to provide comprehensive descriptions of the two approaches, since these are easily available in a variety of recent personality textbooks (e.g. Brody, 1988; Bandura, 1986; Loevinger, 1987; Mischel, 1986). Instead, the emphasis will be on examining the problems associated with each of two competing positions, both conceptually and methodologi-cally, which eventually gave rise to the modern interactionist perspective on personality.

Problems with the situationist model

Rather than denoting a unified theoretical orientation, 'situationism' is a summary term (cf. Edwards & Endler, 1983). It comprises such diverse viewpoints as radical behaviourism, which explains behaviour exclusively in terms of reinforcing factors present in the environment (e.g. Skinner, 1963), and social learning theories which acknowledge the importance of intraper-sonal, and in particular cognitive variables to varying degrees (e.g. Bandura, 1969; Mischel, 1973). Nevertheless, it is possible to extract some common theoretical and methodological assumptions shared by the different varieties of situationism (Bowers, 1973):

1 Behaviour is highly situation-specific rather than cross-situationally consistent.

2 Individual differences within a situation are largely due to measurement error rather than reflecting broad internal dispositions.

3 Observed response patterns can be *causally* linked to the stimuli present in the situation.

4 The experiment is the most appropriate method for discovering such stimulus–response links.

For a critical appraisal of the strengths and weaknesses of the situationist position as a conceptual alternative to the trait model, a closer look is required at each of these four assertions.

1 The major postulate of situationism as far as the person–situation debate is concerned is that there is little consistency in behaviour. Thus, theorising and research have concentrated on the relationship between situational properties and individual behaviour, a link which has been typically conceptualised in terms of reinforcement contingencies. Accordingly, the focus is on those features of the situation which regulate the probability of occurrence of specific behaviours and are therefore considered effective determinants of the individual's behavioural performance. The emphasis on reinforcement principles implies a rather narrow understanding of the concept of situation, concentrating on just one out of a great variety of potentially relevant defining features.

Since situational factors are seen as the most powerful determinants of behaviour, different situations should produce different behaviours. Temporal stability of behavioural patterns is expected only to the extent that the central reinforcing stimuli recur or remain constant: 'Whether social behavior is invariant or changes over time depends, partly, on the degree of continuity of social conditions over the time span' (Bandura, 1986, 12). It should be noted, however, that behavioural variation across different situations is not only interpreted as negative evidence in terms of a lack of consistency. It is also positively recognised as reflecting discriminativeness which is highly adaptive in allowing the person to respond flexibly to situational changes, whereas extreme levels of cross-situational consistency, i.e. indiscriminate patterns of behaviour, are often indicative of the individual's inability to cope with environmental demands (e.g. Mischel, 1984a, cf. Phares & Lamiell, 1977, for a similar argument).

2 If behaviour is determined by situational variables, then it follows that individual differences within any one situation should not occur and if they do, should be treated as error variance. This postulate takes a somewhat different form in social learning theories which acknowledge the role of person variables, like cognitive competencies and attention processes, as mediating variables between situation and behaviour (Bandura, 1986). Situational stimuli are regarded as affecting behaviour through the mediation of internal variables which regulate both the interpretation of objective

stimuli and the ensuing behavioural response. Thus, social learning theories allow some room for individual differences due to internal mediators between stimulus and response, even though, as Mischel (1973) points out, they are likely to manifest themselves only if the situational stimuli are weak and ambiguous. What remains, however, is the rejection of the view, entailed in the concept of relative consistency, that individual differences within a situation are the result of differences in broad personality traits actualised in that situation.

3 According to the situationist position, the principles governing individual behaviour can only be properly understood if causal relationships are established unambiguously or 'objectively' between overt behaviour and its antecedent conditions in the form of stimulus–response (S–R) links. This argument implies that situational stimuli (which can be defined and operationalised in a consensually accepted way) are regarded as a superior type of data compared to more 'subjective' measures, such as trait ratings by self and others.

However, as Bowers (1973) points out in a persuasive argument, establishing evidence for a systematic link between stimuli as independent variables and responses as dependent variables is a far cry from providing a *causal* explanation of why certain stimuli bring about certain responses. In his view, it is one of the metaphysical assumptions underlying the situationist position to mistake the observation that antecedents cause consequences for an explanation of the principles accounting for the observed relationship. Drawing upon an analogy from the natural sciences, Bowers argues that scientific explanation requires theoretical perspectives to be imposed on observed regularities: To say that 'letting go' of an apple 'causes' it to fall to the ground is not an adequate causal explanation unless the principle of gravitation is brought in. In the same way, explanation in psychology must go beyond the mere identification of observed regularities and advance theoretical models in which the conditions producing those regularities are spelt out. If this is the ultimate target of psychological research, then there is no reason why situational stimuli should be credited with greater scientific value as building blocks for a theory of psychological functioning than any other type of explanatory concepts, including traits, goals or cognitive variables.

4 The fourth general assumption is that in order to establish stimulus–response links as required by the situationist model, a methodology is needed which examines the effect of one independent variable on another dependent variable. This is best achieved by experimental manipulations, and thus the experiment is generally accepted as the method of choice for situationism.

The reliance of situationists on the experiment for challenging the trait model and providing support for the situation-dependency of behaviour is encumbered with another metaphysical assumption, related to the first one discussed above. Bowers (1973) argues that situationism has tended to misidentify its preferred theoretical perspective, i.e. the S–R model, with a particular methodological strategy, i.e. the experiment. The problem involved in this misidentification is that an essentially 'neutral' method, which can be employed in principle by a diversity of theoretical orientations interested in the relationship between independent and dependent variables, is imbued with specific theoretical stipulations. This has led situationists to interpret the failure to find behavioural consistency in experimental studies as prima facie evidence for the validity of their theoretical position.

Yet, it is obvious that the very nature of experimental designs is systematically biased in favour of the situationist model (e.g. Bowers, 1973; Kenrick & Dantchick, 1983). Two aspects of the experiment are of particular importance here:

Firstly, it is an explicit aim of experimental procedures to minimise differences between subjects due to personal qualities. Randomisation both in sampling participants and in allocating them to the different experimental treatments is generally employed as a strategy to ensure that interindividual differences are cancelled out.

Secondly, the aim of experimentation is to discover the covariation of a dependent variable with an independent variable. Thus, the focus is on the effect of different treatments on subjects' behaviour, which implies a general orientation towards uncovering change rather than stability. Successful manipulations are those that produce noticeable differences between experimental conditions, i.e. change across situations. Conversely, failure to observe significant behavioural differences across situations is usually attributed to inadequacies in the experimental treatment rather than the operation of some generalized personal disposition.

The connection of situationism as a theoretical perspective with experimentation as the corresponding methodological approach has been used as a basis for declaring this perspective superior to the trait approach with its predominance of correlational studies. As the above analysis suggests, along with empirical refutations from the areas of language acquisition and children's sex-role identity quoted by Bowers (1973), this claim turns out not to stand up on closer scrutiny.

The confrontation between situationism and the trait approach is thus linked inseparably with the opposition between correlational and experimental research methods (cf. also Funder & Ozer, 1983). This questionable link may provide a clue as to why it took so long before the parties involved in the consistency debate realised that their prevalent strategy of refuting one approach with the methods of the other had contributed to the longevity of the controversy rather than facilitating a proper evaluation of the *conceptual validity* of the two perspectives.

Problems with the trait approach

There are at least three general features associated with the use of traits as theoretical constructs in personality research (cf. also Levy, 1983, and Brody, 1988 for recent critical discussions of trait conceptions):

1 Traits are invoked as differential constructs accounting for the fact that individuals differ in the behaviours they show in identical or similar situations.

2 A person's behaviour is assumed to show relative temporal stability and consistency across situations due to the operation of some latent internal disposition.

3 Research based on the trait concept generally employs personality testing in the form of trait ratings and other self-reports as preferred methods of investigation, and relies on correlational methods in the analysis of data.

These common characteristics should not, however, distract from the fact that the concept of 'trait' is used in personality psychology with different meanings. Among these, the distinction between traits as summary labels for stable and consistent *behaviour patterns* and traits as *latent dispositions* is of particular importance. Hirschberg (1978) describes the first perspective as the 'summary view' and contrasts it with the 'dispositional view' of the trait concept.

According to the *summary view*, traits are descriptive constructs that link together and impose meaning on observed patterns of behaviour without providing *causal explanations* for it (cf. Mischel, 1973). By definition, this meaning of traits can be employed only from a post hoc perspective, since it presupposes that trait-specific behaviours have actually been observed. Consequently, the ascription of a trait is justified only if a sufficient number of behavioural instances can be grouped together and interpreted as expressions of one common trait category. Due to its reliance on the face validity of behavioural evidence, there is no need for the summary view to concern itself with situational properties that might facilitate or inhibit the manifestation of behavioural instances: if someone shows no evidence of friendly behaviour in a given period of observation, then there is no reason to ascribe friendliness as a trait to that person.

This straightforward approach to assessing the strength of personality traits, however, rests on a problematic premise: it assumes that the person is free to choose between performing or not performing actions that are expressive of the trait in question, as it is only then that observed behaviours constitute an unambiguous basis for or against the ascription of that trait.

This premise has largely remained implicit, with researchers failing to recognise that a trait can only be ascribed to a person if he or she has the opportunity to exhibit trait-relevant behaviours in a sufficient number of situations. The problem becomes particularly salient in interpreting non-occurrences of trait-relevant behaviours, often invoked as evidence against the validity of the trait concept. Thus, for example, it may be a mistake *not* to ascribe traits such as 'generous' or 'brave' to a person on the grounds of insufficient evidence of corresponding behaviours. Individuals may not have the opportunity to act bravely simply because they rarely find themselves in situations where bravery is called for or are unable to behave generously because they lack the necessary resources.

A related argument, quoted by Hirschberg (1978), refers to the fact that such individual characteristics are excluded a priori by the summary view whose translation into observable behaviour is suppressed because of normative restrictions inherent in the situation. This would apply, for instance, to traits like jealousy or avarice, which a person might not choose to express in behavioural terms for fear of negative evaluation or other unwanted repercussions. Allport's (1966) reminder that the non-occurrence of trait-consistent behaviour as well as the occurrence of trait-inconsistent behaviour do not constitute evidence against the ascription of a trait has to be understood in precisely this sense.

Thus, the summary view of traits fails to recognise both low frequency of occurrence of trait-relevant situations and trait-irrelevant constraints on behaviour as alternative causes for what may at first sight appear as a lack of behavioural evidence for a particular trait. A recent line of research which is less susceptible to this criticism and aims to rehabilitate the summary view of traits is the 'act frequency approach' suggested by Buss & Craik (e.g. 1980, 1983a, 1984) which will be discussed in connection with recent method-ological developments in chapter 5. The main improvement is that behavioural indicators of a given trait are sampled empirically and assessed in terms of their average frequency as well as their typicality as referents for the trait in question. A further advantage is that each trait domain is represented by multiple acts. This implies that the ascription of a trait to a person does *not* require the person to show one particular act with high frequency. All that is demanded is that high act frequencies, i.e. strong act trends, should be observed across the full range of acts within the category. With earlier versions of the summary view, however, this new approach shares the problem that the informational significance of the non-occurrence of trait-typical behaviours is not discussed. Furthermore, it is not specified how the model would deal with a person performing acts which are incompatible or inconsistent with an otherwise strong act trend.

A second conceptualisation of traits, which has been more widely endorsed by personality theorists and has played the dominant role in the consistency debate, is the *dispositional view* of traits. This perspective, which underlies the factor analytical models of personality developed by Cattell (1950), Eysenck (1952) and Guilford (1959), avoids some of the problems of the 'summary view' by emphasising the potential instead of the actual manifestaton of traits in behaviour. According to the dispositional view, traits are not directly observable but have the status of latent tendencies which dispose the person to behave in a particular way *if he or she meets with trait-relevant situational conditions*. Traits are assigned a causal role in eliciting specific patterns of individual behaviour as well as being responsible for behavioural differences between individuals. In this sense, traits are theoretical constructs that should facilitate both the explanation and the prediction of overt behaviour.

Traits as latent dispositions are assumed to find their expression in overt behaviour in a positive monotone function: the greater the strength of the underlying trait, the more pervasive and/or intense the corresponding behavioural manifestations, whereby the relationship between traits and behaviour is a probabilistic one. This means, as Epstein (1979) points out, that a trait refers to a generalised tendency of a person to behave in a certain way over a sufficient sample of situations, but does not imply that the person will show trait-relevant behaviour in all situations or even in all instances of one and the same situation.

Accordingly, it becomes necessary for this perspective on traits to specify the situational properties that elicit the behavioural expression of a particular trait. For example, what are the situational features that facilitate the manifestation of conscientious or dominant behaviours one would expect from a person with a strong trait of conscientiousness or dominance? In order to answer questions like this, a functional link between traits and situational conditions has to be established so that the probability of occurrence of trait-specific behaviour can be determined more precisely. The dispositional perspective suggests a conceptualisation of consistency in terms of 'relative consistency'. If concrete behaviour is the product of personal dispositions actualised in particular trait-relevant situations, then the manifestation of trait-specific behaviour may well vary depending on the situation, but differences between persons across situational conditions should remain constant. However, as Brody (1988, 8) notes: 'The circumstances that result in the actualization of trait dispositions are not specified in the development of a descriptive system based on the factor-analysis of self-descriptions or of descriptions derived from ratings.'

The controversy surrounding the dispositional view of traits throughout the consistency debate has not so much centred on the theoretical status of traits as constructs to explain and predict human behaviour. The main question has been whether there is convincing empirical evidence to demonstrate their explanatory and predictive power as well as to support the validity of the consistency concept intimately linked to the notion of traits. In his already-cited review of the literature, Mischel (1968) came to conclude that there was little evidence for consistency in the vast majority of personality domains, with certain areas of intellectual functioning being the only exceptions. While some recent authors have been critical of Mischel's analysis (e.g. Levy, 1983), advocates of the trait concept have generally found it hard to fight off this powerful attack on the very foundations of their field. As Epstein (1979, 1103) notes: 'The arguments in defense of traits are, for the most part, speculations that if things had been done differently, stability in personality might have been demonstrated.'

Given this state of affairs, one might wonder just why personality theorists have spent so much effort on defending the notions of traits and consistency. One answer to this question lies in what has become known as the 'consistency paradox'. The paradox consists in the opposition between intuitive beliefs that our own as well as other persons' behaviour shows considerable consistency in different situations and the failure to support these beliefs through systematic empirical research. Intuitive beliefs in consistency, held not only by laypersons but also professional psychologists who have retained a sense of intuition, often prove successful in making sense of a person's behaviour in everyday life. Therefore, they tend to be quite robust, with even scholars like Bem confessing to the belief that his intuitions are right and the research wrong (Bem, 1983a). How pressing, then, is the evidence challenging the conviction that there is consistency in personality?

Attempting to provide an overall evaluation of the empirical findings bearing on the issues of stability and consistency as a function of personal dispositions is not an easy task. As mentioned earlier on, problems are largely due to the fact that evidence in favour of the trait concept is usually based on different methodological strategies and different types of data than the evidence quoted against it. This means that one has to look very carefully at the ways in which support for both the trait and the situationist positions is sought in empirical research. Building upon a distinction first made by Cattell (1957), Block (1977) adopts such a fine-grained perspective by reviewing evidence for consistency based on three different data sources:

1 The first type of data, termed *R-data*, represent information obtained through observer ratings of an individual's personality. These include ratings by peers and other knowledgeable informants who are in a position to form an impression about the person in his or her everyday life. As Block himself as well as subsequent authors (e.g. Deluty, 1985; Koretzky, Kohn & Jeger 1978; McCrae, 1982; Woodruffe, 1984, 1985) were able to show, studies relying on R-data provide convincing evidence for the stability and consistency of

personality traits and their corresponding behaviours in a variety of personality domains.

The impact of this evidence for the consistency issue is questioned, however, by the increasingly popular view that traits should not be conceived of as categories applying to qualities of the person observed. Instead, the argument is that traits are more adequately conceptualised as categories employed by the observer to organise and structure his or her cognitive activities and to 'construct' observed behaviour patterns as being (in)consistent (e.g. Hampson, 1982; Mischel & Peake, 1983a; Shweder, 1975). If one accepts this view, then observer ratings lose their validity as sources of information about an individual's personality. However, Kenrick & Funder (1988) challenge this position by quoting a substantial body of recent evidence which cannot be explained conclusively on the basis of observer biases or the semantic similarity of trait terms.

2 A second widely used type of data, *S-data*, contain self-reports about an individual's behaviour, feelings as well as broad personality dispositions. S-data are often used to relate latent trait measures to specific state measures, and the correspondence between traits and states is interpreted as an index of consistency. In the domain of anxiety-provoking situations, for example, self-report measures of trait anxiety have been shown to be significantly related to measures of state anxiety obtained in actual anxiety-provoking situations (e.g. Spielberger, 1972). Moreover, S-data have been used successfully in the validation of trait concepts by showing their links with other relevant variables.

Nevertheless, it should be noted that even among those personality theorists defending the trait concept, reliance on S-data is regarded as problematic. They acknowledge that it is hard to rule out the possibility of S-data telling us little more about consistency than that individuals are consistent in their beliefs about themselves which is 'a far cry from demonstrating that the behaviour itself is consistent' (Epstein, 1979, 1100). The force of this argument is somewhat weakened, however, by studies demonstrating significant relationships between self-ratings and observer ratings of different personality variables (e.g. Block, 1977; Cheek, 1982; Edwards & Klockars, 1981).

3 A third category of data is composed of *T-data* based on objective behavioural information obtained in standardised test or laboratory situations. According to Block (1977, 45) evidence for consistency based on T-data is 'extremely erratic, sometimes positive but often not'. By implication, this means that the relationship between T-data and the two other data categories is also far from systematic. The fact that it is empirical strategies leading to T-data which are favoured by the situationist model of personality

may help to explain why the failure to obtain evidence for consistency on the basis of T-data has had such a profound impact on the controversy.

As the review of the different data sources has shown, evidence for as well as against the dispositional view of traits remains ambiguous. An obvious response to this state of affairs is to embark on the search for improved methodologies which would allow us to translate the theoretical foundations of the dispositional view into more adequate empirical strategies and should ultimately lead to more conclusive evidence for consistency in personality. While there have been numerous efforts in recent years (cf. chapter 5), the problems confronting the trait concept at this stage are not solely of a methodological nature. The present section discusses some of the conceptual problems associated with both the summary and the dispositional view, arguing that a solution to these problems is at least as pressing as the search for improved empirical strategies.

A general problem is the essentially a-theoretical nature of both perspectives as pointed out by Hirschberg (1978), Levy (1983) and Snyder & Ickes (1985), among others. What these critics argue is that so far traits have been largely treated as isolated constructs and little effort has been made to study the relationship between different traits. Moreover, traits are often treated as handy constructs to invoke whenever regularities are observed in individual behaviour and in interindividual differences, without recognition that little is gained in terms of (causal) explanation until the traits themselves are subjected to further theorising. A case in point is the well-known study by Bem & Allen (1974). They found that individuals differ substantially in the extent to which they show consistent behaviours across situations, with those individuals who rate themselves as generally consistent displaying greater consistency in specific personality domains. From these findings, a new 'trait' of general cross-situational consistency was readily extrapolated which, although serving in at least some of the subsequent studies to distinguish the consistent from the inconsistent, did not help in any way to explain just why some people are more consistent than others.

There is another, more specific conceptual problem which has immediate implications for drawing upon traits to describe an individual's personality and on marshalling empirical evidence for or against the trait concept. Both conceptualisations of traits are faced with the task of establishing specific behavioural criteria which are then either combined into a common trait term (summary view) or used as a basis for inferring the strength of an underlying disposition (dispositional view). The issue here is, how many confirming behavioural instances are required in order to warrant the ascription of a trait to a person and how many disconfirming instances are permitted before a trait is rejected and/or its opposite invoked as a psychological description of the person. There are two aspects involved in this issue: firstly, the explicit recognition of normative behavioural base-rates indicating how common and widespread the different behavioural criteria are, and secondly, the diagnostic value of these criteria with respect to the generalised trait, specifying how much impact the presence, or absence, of particular behaviours has on ascribing a trait to a person.

The implications of these two aspects for the description of personality in terms of traits are outlined in a persuasive argument by Rorer & Widiger (1983). They make it clear that traits differ in terms of their base-rates as well as the 'ascription rules' associated with them. This means, for example, that only very few positive instances are required to ascribe the trait 'violent' to a person, whereas negative evidence, i.e. the failure to observe violent behaviours, would not be sufficient to characterise the person as non-violent or even peaceable. In contrast, for other traits, such as 'friendly' or 'honest', few negative behavioural instances, e.g. not returning a polite greeting or not taking a found wallet to the police, are sufficient to deny the respective attribute to the person. These examples illustrate that the outcome of such ascription processes is not determined solely by behaviour which actually occurs but to a large extent by the very nature of the ascription rules used to link behavioural evidence to trait interpretations. Similarly, Brody (1988, 8) argues that the rules for aggregating behavioural indicators of a given trait across different contexts so as to make an overall trait ascription remain, for the most part, 'unspecified and difficult to derive from our ordinary understanding of the words that form the foundation for the trait concept'. Rothbart & Park (1986) provided empirical support to this line of reasoning. They demonstrated that trait terms vary in the number of instances required for their confirmation or disconfirmation, and that this variation is systematically linked to the favourability of the trait terms. Using a large sample of trait-descriptive adjectives, it was shown that favourable traits, like honest, intelligent or kind, require a larger number of instances to be confirmed and a smaller number of instances to be disconfirmed than unfavourable traits, like cruel, malicious or sly, which are 'easy to acquire but hard to lose' (Rothbart & Park, 1986, 137).

Thus, personality researchers need to become aware that both the understanding of traits as abstractions from observed behaviour patterns and the view of traits as dispositions reflected in overt behaviour lead to valid conclusions about personality functioning only
– if the situational features eliciting the overt expression of dispositional tendencies are included in the search for trait-related regularities in behaviour,
– if the rationale behind the selection as well as aggregation of specific behavioural manifestations as indicators of a given trait is made explicit, and, finally

–if it is recognised that linguistic conventions provide ascription rules which are conceptually independent of and yet exert a powerful influence on the psychological meaning of trait descriptions.[1]

The preceding discussion of problems associated with both the situationist and the trait model has highlighted the limitations of either approach in providing a comprehensive explanation of social behaviour and personality. In addition to the criticisms raised above, there is a further problematic point which the two models shared in common in the past: the widespread neglect of cognitive variables as affecting the relationship between the person and the situation. In recent years, however, the social learning approach to personality (e.g. Bandura, 1986), emphasising the role of cognitive processes as mediators between reinforcing properties of the situation and the person's acquisition of new behaviours, has become more and more prominent in the 'situationist' tradition. At the same time, the scope of the trait approach has been expanded to include the conceptualisation of 'traits as cognitive categories' (e.g. Cantor & Mischel, 1979a; Hampson, 1982). These developments may be regarded as a revival of interest in a development that started in the 1950s with the work of Kelly, Witkin and other cognitive personality theorists. The implications of this 'cognitive turn' in personality psychology for the consistency controversy will be examined in the next section.

The 'cognitive turn' in personality psychology

In the 1950s, a paradigm shift took place in psychology bringing the predominance of behaviourist thinking to an end. Theorising and research now ventured to explore what was, until then, regarded as the 'black box' between stimulus input and output that eluded scientific inquiry. Based on the recognition that 'human beings bring meaning and organization into almost every new encounter in the physical or social environment, the study of latent, cognitive processes now acquired central importance' (Singer & Kolligian, 1987, 354). This development also made a lasting impact on the field of personality. The proposition and empirical analysis of 'cognitive styles', such as *field dependence* (Witkin et al., 1962), *cognitive control* (Klein, 1954) or *repression-sensitization* (Byrne, 1964), as well as the development of constructivist theories of personality, such as Kelly's (1955) theory of *personal constructs*, may be seen as direct implications of the new analytical

---

[1] This claim is not to be equated with the view of traits as 'linguistic artifacts' suggested, most notably, by Shweder in his 'systematic distortion hypothesis' (e.g. Shweder, 1982). He entirely rejects the view that judgements of personality, and in particular consistency, in trait terms have anything to do with 'real' behavioural evidence. Instead, he argues that observer ratings of others' behaviour are determined by linguistic categories which have no immediate reference to actual behavioural co-occurrences – a position that denies the trait approach any relevance for exploring personality (cf. Kenrick & Funder, 1988, for a critical appraisal).

perspective. Since then, the concept of cognition has become so universally accepted in psychological thinking that its meaning is mostly taken for granted and is rarely defined in explicit terms. However, a broad definition of cognitive processes which applies to those earlier developments as well as the understanding of situation cognition advanced in the present research is offered by Kreitler & Kreitler (1982, 103):

> Cognition is defined as the meaning processing subsystem within the organism, that is the subsystem that grasps, elaborates, assigns, and manipulates meaning. It is the cognitive system, mainly meaning and operations with meanings, that decides the course of action.

Cognitive styles are hypothetical constructs referring to a person's consistent mode of organising incoming information from his or her environment. They are typically conceived of as mediating variables between situational stimuli and the individual's response to these stimuli, whereby the focus of interest is on the structural organisation rather than the content of the relevant perceptual and cognitive operations (cf. Goldstein & Blackman, 1981). Cognitive styles denote a variety of principles by which objective stimuli are translated into subjective representations and thus acquire psychological significance. For the person–situation debate this implies that situation variables may not be conceptualised independently from the person, as Golding (1977, 406) has pointed out: 'Situational forces reside primarily within the individual.'

Cognitive styles also refer to individual differences in responding to social stimuli, and in this respect they are similar to traits. However, the fact that they are focused specifically on processes of perception and meaning construction renders them distinctly different from the trait concept, casting doubts on the utility of equating cognitive styles with traits (e.g. Hampson, 1982).

A synthesis of differential and individual-centred objectives in personality research is provided by Kelly (1955) in his 'theory of personal constructs'. Kelly postulates that individuals differ, as a function of their 'cognitive complexity', in their ability to interpret and predict social events in a sufficiently sophisticated way. At the same time, at least as much emphasis is placed by the theory on the analysis of individual construct systems, considered as holding the key to the individual's personality. According to Kelly, the scientist's strategy to predict and explain events on the basis of hypothetical constructs is also characteristic of individual information processing, which leads him to apostrophise the 'person as scientist'.

Personal constructs are conceived of as enabling the individual to organise and, most notably, reduce the host of environmental stimuli impinging upon him or her, thus facilitating the anticipatory understanding of social events. Accordingly, the 'Fundamental Postulate' of the theory of personal constructs states: 'A person's processes are psychologically channelized by the ways in which he anticipates events' (Kelly, 1955, 46). This fundamental postulate is elaborated further into eleven corollaries, of which two are particularly important in the present context. The first is the 'Individuality Corollary', postulating that individuals differ in their construction of events. The second is the 'Organisation Corollary', according to which each person develops a construct system that is typically characteristic of him or her and in which the different constructs are arranged in a hierarchical structure. Kelly's (1955, 105) definition of a construct as '[. . .] a way in which some things are construed as being alike and yet different from others' already highlights the central importance attached to the subjective definition of similarities between events. In this sense, the covariation of perceived situational similarity and behavioural similarity as proposed in the present research is directly compatible with personal construct theory.

Since personality is expressed in the very individuality of a person's construct system, an idiographic or individual-centred methodology is required in order to gain empirical access to those systems. Of the different methodological strategies ranging from direct interviewing to role-playing (cf. Kelly, 1955, chapters 7 and 8), the 'Repertory Grid Technique' represents the most elaborate and widespread instrument for the analysis of personal constructs (Slater, 1977). Starting from a sample of significant others (e.g. friends, teachers, family members), this technique involves the elicitation of constructs for describing similarities and differences between the persons named. The constructs thus elicited are then interpreted as representative examples of the individual's construct system. The decisive advantage of the Grid Technique is that very few constraints are imposed on the respondent by the investigator, since both the objects, i.e. persons, to be judged and the criteria for those judgements are chosen by the respondents themselves. It is this feature of the Repertory Grid Technique which makes it particularly suitable for studying the perceived similarity of individually sampled situations as part of the individual-centred methodology proposed in the present research. Therefore, it was applied to the task of eliciting personally relevant samples of situations as well as constructs differentiating between them in two of the empirical studies reported in the second part of this volume (cf. chapter 7).

The theory of personal constructs, whose lasting popularity is underlined in several recent readers (e.g. Adams-Webber & Mancuso, 1983; Beail, 1985; Epting & Landfield, 1985), has also had a stimulating effect on the second line of development in an emerging 'cognitive personality psychology'. This line originated in Bandura's (1969) social learning theory and has been further expanded in his more recent writings (Bandura, 1986) as well as in the work of other authors such as Mischel (1973) and Pervin (1981).

Starting from his own critical analysis of research based on the trait model, Mischel (e.g. 1968, 1973, 1976) has presented an alternative perspective in which the interaction of person and situation variables is conceptualised on the basis of social learning processes.[2] As far as the issue of consistency is concerned, his approach suggests that behaviour will be consistent across situations to the extent that similar behavioural consequences are anticipated in the situations involved. The similarity of anticipated outcomes, in turn, is seen as being determined largely by the person's previous learning experiences. It is because of this emphasis on individual learning biographies that Mischel – who occasionally still has to put up with being quoted as a strict advocate of a situationist or 'generalist' point of view – claims that his approach is particularly committed to the idiographic study of the single case: 'To the degree that idiosyncratic social learning histories characterize each person's life, idiosyncratic (rather than culturally shared) stimulus equivalences and hence idiosyncratic behavior patterns may be expected' (Mischel, 1973, 259).

Mischel also suggests giving up the term 'inconsistency' in favour of 'discriminativeness' to underline the functional significance of behavioural variability in the sense of adapting one's behaviour to the changing demands of the environment. What is particularly important about this suggestion is that it is designed to help personality research move away from an understanding of consistency in terms of absolute or relative constancy of behavioural patterns to an understanding which recognises the dynamic, although coherent flow of behaviour in response to situational requirements.

The cognitive social learning model of personality suggested by Mischel is not a fully specified theoretical network but rather a combination and integration of promising concepts developed as part of cognitive psychology as well as social learning theory. On the person side, five relevant types of variables are distinguished:

1 *Individual construction competencies*, referring to the ability to generate specific cognitions and behaviours, which is the prerequisite for showing situationally appropriate behaviour;
2 *Encoding processes and personal constructs*, which guide the selection and appraisal of information and thus determine the cognitive representation of actions and events;

[2] There is no shortage of contributions dealing with the social cognitive learning approach. Yet they are not entirely free from the problem of redundancy (cf. Mischel, 1973, 1976, 1977, 1978, 1979, 1984a; as well as Mischel & Peake, 1982a, 1983a and Mischel, 1984b).

3 *Subjective expectancies* referring to the consequences associated with certain stimuli and behaviours, which are formed essentially on the basis of previous experiences with comparable situations;

4 *Subjective evaluations* of stimuli in terms of their functional significance for achieving certain consequences which interact with subjective expectancies in determining the person's choice between specific behavioural alternatives.

5 Finally, *self-regulatory systems* are required, facilitating the intrapersonal control of perceptual and behavioural processes independent of external reinforcers and control mechanisms. Self-regulatory systems are composed of sets of subjectively valid rules indicating which behaviour is appropriate for the attainment of certain goals under certain circumstances and also which consequences are entailed in reaching (or missing) different goals.

While the model does not provide a clear indication of the relationship between the five classes of variables, they have been shown individually to be effective determinants of children's delay of gratification behaviour in a series of studies reported by Mischel (1984a). In the cognitive social learning model, personality-specific behaviour is regarded as a function of the interaction between situational stimuli and the way in which the meaning of those stimuli is construed by the individual. In this respect, there are obvious similarities with Kelly's thinking (cf. Mischel & Peake, 1983a) as well as the modern interactionist understanding of personality suggested by Magnusson and Endler (cf. chapter 3). Parallels to the latter approach also extend to the role of situational stimuli, where both models agree that objective situational stimuli come to affect behaviour only via their cognitive representation and subjective interpretation. However, notable differences remain between Mischel's cognitive social learning theory and the modern interactionist framework as delineated by Magnusson & Endler (1977b; Magnusson, 1981b; inter alia).

First of all, there is no place in the cognitive social learning model for any form of trait concepts, either in terms of broad response dispositions or specific personality dimensions. Instead, the anticipated consequences of behavioural decisions as well as their subjective evaluations are allocated central importance. As Mischel (1976, 506) points out, his 'person variables' refer to processes of information processing and behaviour generation which are imbued with specific contents depending on the nature of the respective situation. Furthermore, due to the emphasis placed by the cognitive social learning model on individual learning histories the temporal dimension becomes an integral part in this understanding of 'personality'.

Building upon Mischel's reasoning, Athay & Darley (1981) argue in their 'interaction-centred theory of personality' that for social encounters to satisfy the aims and needs of the interactants, the actions of both partners have to be calculable, while at the same time allowing flexible adaptation to the specific requirements of a particular encounter. The ability to strike a balance between routinisation, i.e. acting consistently in similar situations, and contextualisation, i.e. adapting one's thought and action to the peculiarities of a given interaction context, is regarded as a fundamental prerequisite of competent interaction. According to Athay & Darley, personality dispositions should therefore be conceptualised as 'interaction competencies' with a clear emphasis on the cognitive handling of social encounters: 'Cognitions of the shared social situation are the basic "handles" by which people attempt to manipulate each other into providing strategically useful responses' (Athay & Darley, 1981, 285).

A typical example of the type of research generated by the cognitive social learning model is provided by the 'Carlton Behavior Study' (Mischel & Peake, 1982a). A large pool of information was gathered from a sample of students concerning their behaviour in the two domains of friendliness and conscientiousness, whereby the different criteria of friendly and conscientious behaviour were named by the respondents themselves. Self-ratings on the different behaviours were combined with ratings from peers and relatives as well as direct observation over several days. In the domain of conscientiousness, for example, nineteen behavioural referents were observed on between two and twelve occasions. To obtain indices of temporal stability, observations of any one referent were correlated across occasions, yielding both single (i.e. based on pairwise correlations) and aggregate indices of stability. To establish cross-situational consistency, correlations were computed between the nineteen referents, again both pairwise and for the total number. The findings revealed that mean coefficients of stability increased from $r = .29$ to $r = .65$ from single to aggregated scores, while the consistency measure increased only from $r = .08$ to $r = .13$ for single as compared to aggregated scores.

The conclusion derived from these findings by Mischel & Peake (1982a) is to reject the idea that a solution to the consistency problem may be found on methodological grounds through the strategy of aggregation advocated by Epstein (1979). Instead, they argue, the idea of cross-situational consistency should be abandoned altogether in favour of accepting the view that persons respond flexibly, i.e. variably to the changing conditions of their environment (for the controversy triggered by their conclusions cf. Bem, 1983b; Conley, 1984b; Epstein, 1983a, Funder, 1983 inter alia). However, a weakness of the Carlton Behavior Study, as far as the cognitive social learning model is concerned, lies in the fact that the data were aggregated not only cross observations and behavioural referents, but also across respondents, thus failing to acknowledge the unique impact of idiosyncratic learning histories stressed by the model.

In contrast, Champagne & Pervin (1987) conducted an idiographic study to demonstrate the impact of expected behavioural consequences on the relationship between situation cognition and behaviour. They showed that people rated their behaviour as similar across situations to the extent that the situations were similar with respect to the reinforcers present in them. In addition, it was shown that behaviours which were different in form yet associated with similar reinforcers were assigned similar probabilities of occurrence. Including the subjective evaluation of reinforcers did not, however, increase the strength of the relationship between situation perception and behaviour.

This individual-centred analysis of the interaction of situational stimuli, cognitive processes, and previous learning experiences as determinants of behaviour underlines two essential implications of the cognitive social learning model for the consistency debate. Firstly, it suggests an understanding of consistency which recognises – like the concept of coherence – that the systematic *variability* of behaviour is an important source of information about individual personality over and above the relevance of *stability* (cf. Mischel, 1983, 598). Secondly, it confirms once more the necessity, already claimed by Allport, to take the subjective definition of situational similarity into account when making behavioural predictions (cf. Mischel, 1979, 742; Pervin, 1981, 355).

Another recent extension of Mischel's work at the interface of cognition and personality has involved the reconceptualisation of traits as 'cognitive categories'. Unlike traditional trait conceptions, this view states that in order to understand the nature of trait ascriptions one has to look at both the person described *and* the person making the description. This approach acknowledges the reality and stability of individual differences, but it also suggests that the observation of coherent patterns of behaviour requires some sort of pre-existing structure to be imposed on the continuous flow of behavioural activity. Coherence is 'constructed' by the observer in the sense that it involves a decision about which behaviours go together as indicators of a certain personality domain as well as which situations should be grouped together as pertaining to the domain in question.

To address these issues, Cantor & Mischel (1979a) have proposed a cognitive prototype approach to the categorisation of persons and situations (cf. chapter 4 for a more detailed discussion of situation prototypes). This approach holds that impression formation is based on consensual knowledge about the typical features of trait categories, such as 'introversion' or 'neuroticism'. More specifically, the model suggests that the great variety of person and situation information is cognitively organised in terms of fuzzy, i.e. partly overlapping categories and that judgements about personality are formed by assessing the extent to which the person involved fits any of the available prototypes. By permitting the construction of orderly taxonomies in the personality domain, the prototype approach is not limited to the level of person perception but also provides an organising framework for classifying the situations in which behaviour actually takes place. As Mischel & Peake (1983a, 244) summarise: 'A thorough account of the construction of behavioral consistency, then, must both describe the relations that objectively exist in behavior and clarify the process by which those relations are linked to perceptions of coherence in personality.'

To conclude our review of theoretical developments recognising the role of cognitive processes for the understanding of personality, a less well-known but interesting approach will be introduced briefly: the 'theory of cognitive orientation' presented by Kreitler & Kreitler (1982; 1983). In contrast to the cognitive social learning approach, their theory is concerned first and foremost with the *contents of* situational stimuli and the processes through which their meaning is established by the individual. Accordingly, the basic postulate of the theory states that behaviour is guided by cognitions, i.e. meanings, which perform an orientative function for behaviour by promoting or repressing certain behavioural decisions (Kreitler & Kreitler, 1983, 207).

The transformation of situational stimuli into behaviourally relevant cognitions is conceived of as involving five steps:

1 In the first phase, called *meaning action*, incoming stimuli are compared with immediately preceding stimuli stored in short-term memory. This comparison is based on a 'match vs. mismatch' strategy. If a new stimulus 'matches' the preceding one, this indicates that no change has taken place in the environment and present information processing can continue without adaptation. In case of a 'mismatch', the new stimulus is subjected to a first search for meaning guided by four potential interpretations (cf. Kreitler & Kreitler, 1982, 109):

(a) The stimulus is a signal for a defensive or an adaptive reflex, or for a conditioned response;

(b) It is a signal for molar action and requires a more elaborate clarification of its meaning before a behavioural decision can be made;

(c) It is known to be irrelevant for the present situation;

(d) The stimulus cannot be interpreted conclusively in terms of the first three options because it is entirely new for the person. This means that another exploratory reaction is triggered so as to collect further information until a meaning in terms of options (a) to (c) can be assigned.

2 If, after the first stage, the meaning of a stimulus still requires further clarification, as in option (b), the second phase, *meaning generation*, is activated. In this phase, a complicated system of meaning dimensions and types of relations between those dimensions facilitates the ascription of more specific meanings. Kreitler & Kreitler (1982, 195) suggest a total of twenty-

two meaning dimensions, including the spatial and temporal parameters of a stimulus as well as its causal antecedents. The smallest units of which the dimensions are composed are termed 'meaning values'. In this phase of the cognitive orientation process, individual preferences for certain meaning dimensions could be demonstrated empirically, leading Kreitler & Kreitler (1983, 217) to suggest a redefinition of traits in terms of 'patterns of preferred meaning assignment tendencies'.

3 If the person has assigned a meaning to the stimulus that involves the requirement to respond behaviourally to it, then the cognitive orientation process enters into the third stage, called *belief evocation*. 'Beliefs' are defined as cognitive units consisting of at least two meaning values plus a rule relating the two (e.g. conjunction or disjunction). The main characteristic of a belief is that it predisposes the person to develop certain behavioural intents. Apart from 'general beliefs' and 'beliefs about norms and rules' referring to issues not immediately related to the self, two more specific types of self-related beliefs are distinguished: beliefs about goals aspired to by the person and beliefs about the self. Taken together, the four types of beliefs form a 'belief cluster' associated with a particular behavioural response.

4 A person is expected to develop a *behavioural intent* to perform a particular response option if at least three out of the four belief categories are favourable towards that option. The behavioural intent regulates the selection as well as the actualisation of behaviour programmes containing detailed instructions about how to perform the response in question. Behaviour programmes may be innate, learned or formed ad hoc or may be composed of a combination of innate and learned elements.

5 The final phase consists of *programme execution*, i.e. the realisation of the behavioural intent. Cognitive orientation plays a crucial role even in this final phase inasmuch as it provides feedback about relevant stimuli as well as discrepancies between desired and actual behavioural effects which may eventually require a revision of the original behaviour programme.

Empirical applications of the theory to the issue of behaviour prediction have so far concentrated on the interaction between the four belief categories in determining behavioural intentions. Subjects are typically assigned a total score of cognitive orientation towards different behaviours based on questionnaire measures of the four belief categories. These measures are such that the stronger the beliefs are in favour of performing a given response option, the higher the cognitive orientation score. In support of the theory, the frequency as well as intensity of behavioural performance has repeatedly been shown to be a linear function of the strength of the corresponding cognitive orientation (cf. Kreitler & Kreitler, 1982; Lobel, 1982).

As far as the consistency debate is concerned, the theory of cognitive orientation joins other research discussed in this section speaking against the search for absolute or relative constancy in individual behaviour. As Kreitler & Kreitler point out: 'Consistency of behavior is neither a substitute for lawfulness of behavior nor a reliable criterion for it. If at all definable in measurable terms, it is a special case that has to be dealt with in the broader context of behavior prediction' (1983, 202). Instead, personality is seen as being reflected in the extent to which similarities and differences at the level of behavioural performance are systematically linked with similarities and differences in cognitive orientation, i.e. in the generation of meaning, the evocation of beliefs, and the formation of behavioural intentions.

The different theoretical perspectives that were discussed in this section share in common a dynamic understanding of 'personality' emphasising the person's constructive activity in interpreting situational stimuli and forming decisions about appropriate behaviours. According to this view, neither situational stimuli nor personal disposition can affect behaviour unless they are subjected to a process of cognitive construction in which their relevance with regard to given behavioural alternatives is established by the person.

Such an understanding of personality also involves a new perspective on the role of subjects in psychological research which recognises their intimate knowledge about themselves as an asset – rather than a bias-producing liability – and assigns them a much more active part in the empirical assessment of personality theories. As Mischel (1984b, 273) suggests, subjects should be enrolled 'at least sometimes, as active colleagues who are the best experts on themselves and who are eminently qualified to participate in the development of descriptions and predictions about themselves and about the principles of our field'. As will become clear in the second part of this volume, the individual-centred approach advocated by the present research involves just that in making the search for coherence in individual behaviour a cooperative effort between participants and investigator.

The present chapter has looked in some detail at the history of the consistency debate and the competing positions which have kept it alive for such a long time. With the emergence of a cognitive perspective on personality, new paths have been opened up for overcoming the antagonism between trait and situationist models in favour of a view which stresses the mediation of cognitive processes between environmental stimuli and intra-personal qualities. In the next chapter, we will examine another powerful line of development in recent personality psychology aimed to resolve the consistency controversy: the modern interactionist or $P \times S$ approach. This approach started off with the attempt to apportion the relative contributions of situations and traits in accounting for behavioural variance but soon recognised, at least in theory, that it is the dynamic, continuous interaction of person and situation variables which holds the key to understanding individual behaviour.

3 P × S: the promise of modern interactionism

The discrepancy between empirical evidence failing to find cross-situational consistencies in behaviour and intuitive beliefs, grounded in everyday observations, that such consistencies do, in fact, exist is commonly referred to as the 'consistency paradox'. It is perhaps in recognition of this paradoxical state of affairs that Block (1968) referred to the 'apparent inconsistencies' in personality, implicitly questioning the validity of the psychological evidence. His analysis of the reasons for such an *apparent inconsistency* as well as the strategies required for demonstrating *real consistency* may serve as a starting point for delineating the tasks to be resolved by the modern interactionist approach to personality. Block identified the following fundamental problems, conceptual as well as methodological, which he regarded as preventing personality psychologists from discovering consistent and stable patterns of individual behaviour:

1 The failure to take into account the personal significance of the situations and behavioural indicators selected for empirical study by the investigator. For different behavioural criteria to be correlated and interpreted with regard to consistency in a given personality domain, it has to be ascertained that they are at a comparable level of salience or involvement for the individual.

2 The failure to acknowledge the context in which behaviour takes place. Whether personal characteristics are manifested in overt behaviour is largely dependent upon the situational context which may invite, suppress or simply be irrelevant for the performance of certain behaviours. This implies that the features of the situational context pertaining to the manifestation of personality-specific behaviours are to be recognised as important constituents of behaviour predictions.

3 The failure to consider the possibility that identical behaviours may express different psychological constructs in different individuals. Phenotypically similar behaviours may reflect entirely different dispositions and, accordingly, can vary in different ways across situations without indicating inconsistency. This point is related to Allport's (1937) example, quoted earlier on, that lying and stealing may both be indicators of dishonesty for some people, while for others they may represent two different trait categories due to differences in their functional significance for the person.

From Block's analysis of the consistency problem, which coincided with Mischel's attack on the trait concept, three major tasks can be derived as confronting the 'modern interactionist' approach to personality:

1 The conceptualisation of individual behaviour as a joint product of personal characteristics and situational determinants;

2 The inclusion of an *intraindividual* level of analysis in the search for behavioural regularities; and finally

3 The consideration of cognitive as well as motivational processes as mediators between personal dispositions and behaviour.

After referring briefly to the so-called classical interactionism (Ekehammar, 1974), the following review of the modern interactionist approach to personality looks first at its theoretical assumptions before turning to a discussion of the prevailing methodological strategies as well as the type of evidence generated by them. The study of stress and anxiety is then presented as an exemplary field of interactionist research which is also selected as the content domain for the present research. Against the background of other current appraisals of the interactionist perspective, the chapter concludes with a critical assessment of the contribution this approach has made so far towards resolving the consistency issue.

The most prominent precursor to the current interactionist understanding of personality was undoubtedly Kurt Lewin (1936) who, in his equation of $B = f(P, E)$, presented a terse formula for the idea that personal and environmental forces act together in determining behaviour. Jointly, person and environment constitute the 'total situation' (S), suggesting a conceptualisation of the situation in which the person is included as an integral element. Thus, the situation is seen as a psychological force which cannot be reduced to its objective physical properties but becomes a reality only by virtue of being mentally represented by the person. The differentiation involved in this reasoning between physical and psychological features of the situation was shared by other contemporary authors such as Koffka (1935), Murray (1938) and Tolman (1935) without necessarily implying unanimity about the relative contributions of person and situation factors as determinants of behaviour (cf. Ekehammar, 1974, for a more detailed discussion of these positions). Nevertheless, there appears to have been agreement, at least at a theoretical level, that the clue for understanding the impact of situations on behaviour lies in the subjective meanings assigned to them by the person and that special attention has to be devoted to the exploration of these meanings in the study of personality.

Basic concepts and propositions

The failure to translate the early interactionist conceptions into empirical paradigms for personality research may serve to explain why they did not have sufficient impact to prevent the field's ensuing polarisation on the issue of the generality vs. specificity of behaviour and had to be rediscovered in the late 1960s amidst the growing sense of crisis entailed in the consistency controversy. Both situationists, most notably Mischel (1973), and trait theorists (cf. Epstein, 1977) revised their positions in favour of a converging search for models and methodologies to explain as well as predict individual behaviour as part of a new, more complex unit of analysis: 'behaviour-in-the-situation'.

Among the most prolific representatives of this 'synthesis of personologism and situationism' (Ekehammar, 1974) are Magnusson and Endler. They deserve credit ont only for demonstrating the utility of the P × S approach in the area of stress and anxiety but also for editing two comprehensive volumes which provided a critical documentation of the progress in interactionist thinking and research at a relatively early stage (Endler & Magnusson, 1976a; Magnusson & Endler, 1977a).

The term 'interactionism' is perhaps best understood as an umbrella term covering a variety of conceptual approaches which share the general idea that behaviour is a joint function of personal and situational characteristics, yet differ over how exactly these two components as well as their interaction should be defined. Magnusson & Endler (1977b, 4) summarise the core assumptions underlying the interactionist perspective:[1]

1 Actual behavior is a function of a continuous process of multidirectional interaction or feedback between the individual and the situations he or she encounters.
2 The individual is an intentional, active agent in this interaction process.
3 On the person side of the interaction, cognitive and motivational factors are essential determinants of behavior.
4 On the situation side, the psychological meaning of situations for the individual is the important determining factor.

These general postulates, however, offer no more than a broad framework for theoretical and empirical research which requires more precise elaboration in at least two important respects (cf. Endler, 1983):

1 The first is to clarify exactly how person and situation variables interact in evoking behaviour. This involves demonstrating that a substantial proportion of variance in behaviour is attributable to the interactive effect of personal and situational characteristics.

It also involves specifying the relevant units of analysis as far as the person and his or her behaviour is concerned as well as defining more specifically what is meant by the concept of interaction.

[1] The main features of the interactionist approach have been described in a large variety of papers. The following discussion refers primarily to Magnusson & Endler (1977b) as one of the earlier sources. Very similar information is presented in Endler (1981, 1982, 1985); Endler & Magnusson (1976 a, b) and Magnusson (1976, 1980), inter alia.

2 The second requirement is to provide a description, classification, and systematic analysis of stimuli, situations, and environments. In accordance with the fourth postulate quoted above, the emphasis here is on understanding the process whereby objective situational cues are transformed by the individual into subjectively meaningful representations of his or her social world. In addition, this task includes the search for a comprehensive taxonomy or 'differential psychology' of situations which is regarded as an urgently required complement to the differential psychology of persons.

In order to differentiate between behavioural variables and their antecedents on the person side, Magnusson & Endler (1977b) introduce the distinction between *reaction variables* and *mediating variables*. Reaction variables refer to different types of responses which the individual displays as a result of the interaction between situational stimuli and their internal processing. *Reaction variables* fall into four main categories: (a) overt observable behaviour, e.g. helping another person; (b) physiological responses, e.g. heart rate; (c) covert reactions, e.g. emotional responses; and (d) artificial behaviour, e.g. responding to experimental instructions. In looking for behavioural coherence, therefore, it is important to consider the regularity of behaviour patterns both within and across different types of reaction variables.

Whether or not the individual shows a certain response in a given situation is determined to a large extent by the operation of a latent mediating process in which situational information is selected and interpreted in relation to the individual's cognitive and affective predispositions. Three types of *mediating variables* are assumed to be involved in this process. They are not directly accessible but have to be inferred from the person's responses (e.g. Edwards & Endler, 1983): (a) the *content* of the mediating process, i.e. the meaning which is attached to the selected situational information on the basis of either stored social knowledge or information inherent in the specific situation; (b) the cognitive *structure* into which that content is integrated, i.e. the person's intellectual capacity and cognitive schemata which link a particular content with other already existing contents in a meaningful way; and (c) *motivational variables* which explain why the process of selecting and interpreting certain situational cues is instigated and sustained; e.g. the person's momentary needs. This set of variables bears a close resemblance to the person variables proposed as part of Mischel's cognitive social learning theory discussed in the previous chapter.

The modern interactionist view, like the trait approach, assumes the operation of latent variables within the person which have a significant effect on overt behaviour and explain why people respond differently to the same situational cues. However, unlike the trait approach, these latent variables are not conceived of as stable dispositions but as interdependent facets of a flexible inner system for matching incoming situational information with an individually characteristic form of response.

The introduction of reaction and mediating variables as referring to an overt and a latent level of analysis, respectively, requires a review of the consistency concept in the light of this distinction. At the level of mediating variables, consistency is postulated only for the category of structural variables, while the actualisation of content and motivational variables is seen as being determined largely by the specific nature of the situation. At the level of reaction variables, cross-situational coherence is defined in terms of systematic, though not necessarily constant, patterns of behaviour which vary across situations in an idiographically predictable way (Magnusson, 1976, 257). Coherent behavioural patterns are regarded as the result of the individual's characteristic mode of selecting and processing situational stimuli guided by his or her motivational states.

According to the concept of coherence, behaviour is to be identified as inconsistent or incoherent if it is at odds with behavioural expectations formed on the basis of valid and reliable information about the person and his or her previous behaviour. Mischel (1977, 250) makes a similar point in his thoughts on the future of personality measurement: '"Consistency" in personality need not imply sameness, but it does imply a degree of predictability based on the individual's qualities.'

For such an understanding of consistency to be translated into empirical research strategies, it is essential to identify the determinants which would make the person's behaviour idiographically predictable. This requirement is particularly pertinent with respect to the new parameter introduced into the consistency controversy by the modern interactionist approach: the 'psychological situation'. In contrast to the 'objective situation', which is definable in terms of its physical or consensually perceived features, the analysis of the psychological situation involves exploring in detail the intrapersonal determinants of translating objective situational features into subjectively meaningful interpretations. The explanation and prediction of individual behaviour thus requires the description and classification of situations in terms of their perceived meaning. This 'stimulus-analytical' approach to the study of situational meaning is complemented by the 'response-analytical approach' (Magnusson & Stattin, 1982) in which situations are described and classified in terms of the reactions typically elicited in them. The empirical findings generated by these two perspectives are presented in the next section where the methodological strategies of modern interactionism will be discussed.

In the present context, however, it has to be noted that the advocates of modern interactionism, despite their long-standing call for a comprehensive theory of situation cognition to facilitate the search for cross-situational coherence, have as yet failed to address this task seriously, as Magnusson (1981b) admits. Those contributions which do analyse the relationship between situation cognition and behaviour seldom go beyond the descriptive study of situation interpretations and global similarity judgements (Endler, 1983; Magnusson, 1974; cf. Dworkin & Goldfinger, 1985, for a critical voice). The only exceptions here are a few dimensional studies such as Ekehammar, Schalling & Magnusson (1975) and Magnusson (1971) which are limited, however, by their reliance on small samples as well as the strategy of presenting an identical set of (fictitious) situations at all respondents.

Thus, it may be concluded that interactionism is as yet lacking a conceptualisation of situation cognition which (a) lays down the criteria on which impression formation about situations is based and (b) specifies the principles whereby these criteria are transformed into behaviourally relevant perceptions. This shortcoming is all the more serious as the analysis of the relationship between situation perception and behaviour is at the core of the interactionist understanding of coherence. However, two postulates of the interactionist model advanced by Magnusson (1980, 30) may be regarded as starting points for a conceptual elaboration of the process of situation perception:

1 The behaviour of the person in a given situation is determined by the meaning assigned to that situation by the person.
2 There are individual differences in interpreting situational stimuli so that one and the same situation may be interpreted differently by different persons.

For the empirical analysis of behavioural coherences, these two postulates cogently suggest methodological requirements which have so far largely been ignored within the interactionist mainstream (cf. Wakenhut, 1978, 84, for a critical appraisal) and therefore present the major objectives of the present research:

1 The development and application of theoretical models of situation cognition, including the individual construction of situational meaning and situational similarities;
2 The elaboration of a methodological framework which allows one to capture individuals' characteristic and possibly unique ways of interpreting situational stimuli.

Both tasks highlight the fact that the cognitive representation of situations is the variable representing the interface of personal and situational influences of behaviour. An adequate conceptualisation of the personal significance of situations therefore requires a precise definition of the meaning of 'interaction'.

From the start, the term 'interaction' has been used in the modern interactionist approach with different, though not always well-defined meanings. This has led to a variety of views on person–situation interactions, each involving different methodological and data analytical approaches. At a most basic level, the meaning of the term interaction varies as a function of whether it is employed as part of a psychological theory or as part of a measurement model (cf. Magnusson, 1976).

At the level of personality theory, the psychological meaning of 'interaction' refers to the joint impact of personal and situational qualities on social behaviour. This psychological meaning has been represented by at least two different understandings of 'interaction' at the level of measurement models. Each of them has specific methodological implications and consequences (cf. Buss, 1977 and Howard, 1979, for controversial assessments of this issue).

The first type of interaction is called *mechanistic* or *statistical* interaction, assuming a unidirectional influence of person and situation variables on behaviour.[2] Inherent in this view is a clear distinction between independent and dependent variables and the assumption of a linear combination of person and situation variables in their effect on behaviour.

The second meaning by which the psychological concept of interaction is represented at the methodological level is called *dynamic* or *reciprocal* interaction. This meaning of the term 'interaction', which some authors refer to as 'transaction' (e.g. Pervin, 1968), designates the continuous and reciprocal interaction between behaviour and both person and situation variables. By emphasising the reciprocity of the link between persons, situations, and behaviour, the distinction between independent and dependent variables becomes inapplicable. Instead, the concept of dynamic interaction recognises that by their behaviour persons may affect and modify the situations in which they act and also their internal cognitive and emotional states – both of which have been instrumental in prompting the behaviour in the first place.

Although the dynamic concept of interaction is generally regarded as more appropriate to the theoretical framework of interactionism, the great majority of empirical research available today has relied on the analysis of unidirectional statistical interactions of person and situation variables on behaviour. The main reason for this discrepancy between theoretical claims and empirical practice is generally seen in the lack of appropriate measurement models and designs which would allow one to capture the complex process of the continuous interplay between internal qualities, situational properties, and overt behaviour (Endler, 1983). For a critical assessment of

---

[2] Distinguishing between 'person' and 'behaviour' may at first sight seem unreasonable since it is, of course, the person who shows the behaviour. However, 'person', in this context, refers to (latent) personal characteristics which have the status of hypothetical constructs in the interactionist model. (cf. Krauskopf, 1978; Hyland, 1984).

the interactionist approach to personality, this state of affairs raises the question of whether empirical research based on the mechanistic meaning of interaction has, indeed, made a significant contribution towards understanding the interdependence of person, situation, and behaviour. To answer this question, the next section will examine the prevalent strategies of empirical research as well as the type of evidence they can provide in support of the interactionist model.

Methodological strategies

Three types of methodological and data analytical strategies have dominated the investigation of person–situation interactions as determinants of behaviour. In line with the traditional formulation of the consistency issue, the first relies on correlational analyses in order to explore the extent to which individual differences in trait-related behaviours remain constant across situations. In a second group of studies, dimensional and cluster analytical procedures are employed to identify a limited number of categories or dimensions for the classification of person and situation variables. By far the most common strategy, however, is the analysis of variance design which corresponds directly to the concept of mechanistic interaction and allows one to quantify the relative contributions of person variables, situation variables and their interaction to the explanation of behavioural patterns. It is not surprising, therefore, that the 'variance components strategy' has also received the most critical attention.

These 'conventional' empirical strategies which are intricately linked with the theoretical postulates of the interactionist approach to personality are discussed in the present section. In addition, there are several more recent methodological developments aiming to improve the search for behavioural coherence which are not explicitly committed or just loosely tied to the interactionist mainstream. These approaches will be examined in chapter 5.

As far as the evidence based on *correlational analyses* is concerned, most studies have concentrated on examining the correlations between different behavioural indicators measured at one point in time. The study of temporal stabilities of behaviours in identical or similar situations, while being an equally central task, has been addressed much less frequently, not least due to the practical difficulties involved in this kind of longitudinal research. However, there is some recent evidence suggesting that trait-related behaviour does, indeed, show considerable stability in similar situations over periods ranging from a few weeks to several years (e.g. Backteman & Magnusson, 1981; Block, Buss, Block & Gjerde, 1981; Costa & McCrae, 1988; Diener & Larsen, 1984; Mischel & Peake, 1982a; Olweus, 1980, cf. Conley, 1984a, for a review).

Magnusson (1976) examined a sample of correlational studies in which behaviour was assessed across several hypothetical or real situations through self reports, observations of overt behaviour or objective behavioural indicators. He concluded that evidence for consistency was typically found only with respect to similar situations, failing to emerge when dissimilar situations were considered. The failure to obtain high correlations between behavioural indicators in dissimilar situations is interpreted by Magnusson (1976, 263) as casting doubt on the concept of relative consistency as a general hypothesis about behaviour. Instead, he argues, the low correlations indicate that individual behaviour follows coherent and idiographically predictable patterns. This latter point, however, is more difficult to accept, mainly because the classification of situations as similar or different was typically made ad hoc by the investigator, not the respondents, without resting on a systematic analysis, let alone variation, of situational similarities. Low intercorrelations between behaviours across different situations, therefore, do not in themselves provide any positive information as to their underlying pattern. Furthermore, in the evidence reviewed by Magnusson, the criterion for identifying coherence as well as temporal stability was always the relationship between two or more behavioural measures, which means that coherence was sought only on the behavioural side. This, however, is clearly at odds with the interactionist model inasmuch as no attempt was made to take the perception of situational meaning into account.

For a more adequate correlational analysis of person–situation interaction acknowledging the proposed importance of perceived situational meaning one would have to investigate the covariation of situation cognition and behaviour both over time and situations. If, as claimed in the concept of coherence, individual behaviour is a function of the processing of situational stimuli guided by cognitive and motivational mediators, then significant correlations should emerge between situation cognition and behaviour. What is essential, however, is that such correlations are obtained at the level of the individual person so that they are not affected by the covariation patterns of other people. As Ozer (1986, 40) points out: 'Why the assessment of consistency in personality should be based on the comparative standing of persons in a distribution has never been justified. The consistency of any given individual's personality should not depend on the consistency of someone else [. . .].' Far from being self-evident, the point that correlations based on group data are inappropriate indices of *individual* consistency needed to be stressed repeatedly in different theoretical contexts (e.g. Epstein, 1980; Lamiell, 1981; Valsiner, 1986). It is only in the rare event of a perfect correspondence $(r = 1)$ that correlations based on aggregated data permit conclusive inferences about the single case.

There are just a few studies currently available which have looked at the cross-situational covariation of situation perception and behaviour in individual data, as proposed in the coherence concept. Magnusson & Ekehammar (1978) examined the congruence between how individuals perceive situations and how they actually react in the same situations. To this end, their subjects were presented with descriptions of twelve anxiety-provoking situations covering four types of stressful situations: 'threat of punishment', 'ego threat', 'threat of pain', and 'inanimate threat'. The subjects' task consisted in (a) providing ratings of perceived similarity between each pair of situations and (b) rating each situation in terms of the experienced intensity of twelve reactions, whereby these reaction ratings were subsequently converted into similarity matrices using four different indices of profile similarity (cf. Magnusson & Ekehammer, 1978, 44, for details). The correspondence between perceived and behavioural similarity was assessed by computing *individual* correlations between the two data sets for each of the thirty-nine participants. Magnusson & Ekehammar found that, depending on the index of profile similarity applied to the reaction data, between 67% and 85% of the intrasubject correlations were in the expected direction, between 33% and 44% respectively were statistically significant. The average correlations between situation perception and situation reaction ranged from $r = .11$ to $r = .17$. Despite these fairly low correlations, Magnusson & Ekehammar (1978) conclude that their findings corroborate the interactionist emphasis on the subjective meaning of situations as determinants of behavioural regularities.

Using a wider range of situations as well as a different method of data analysis, namely multidimensional scaling, Klirs & Revelle (1986) present further evidence in support of the proposed correspondence between perceived similarity and response consistency across situations. Yet they only provide partial support for the idea that an idiographic mode of analysis is superior to a nomothetic or combined idiographic/nomothetic approach in predicting behavioural variability from perceived situational similarity.

It may be argued, however, that both Magnusson & Ekehammar (1978) and Klirs & Revelle (1986) missed an important point in their purportedly idiographic analyses by presenting an identical, i.e. nomothetically defined, set of situations to each of their subjects. When perceived similarity and behavioural similarity were studied by Champagne & Pervin (1987) with respect to situations from each subject's personal experience, the average intraindividual correlation was $r = .36$, representing a substantial increase over the Magnusson & Ekehammar (1978) findings. The importance of studying consistency with respect to individually sampled situations is further underscored by Dolan & White (1988). In two related studies, they explored coping strategies in response to daily hassles encountered by their participants over several weeks. They found that the consistency of coping responses was substantially higher when examined at the level of the individual subject as opposed to the sample as a whole. Furthermore, their findings support the interactionist view in so far as consistency was found to be higher for hassles associated with particular contexts, such as work, health or finances, than for the total range of hassles across different contexts.

These last examples illustrate that a total rejection of correlations as indices of coherence may not be appropriate. Rather, a critical assessment would appear to be in order of the shortcomings associated with the predominant way in which the correlational strategy has been utilised in the search for consistency. In particular, these shortcomings refer to

1 the derivation of statements about individual persons from correlations based on group data;

2 the limitation of correlational analyses to the behavioural level;

3 the typically ad hoc selection of (hypothetical) situations by the investigator; and finally,

4 the tacit assumption, implied in the previous point, that the selected situations are perceived and interpreted in the same way by the respondents involved.

The second characteristic strategy of modern interactionism is represented by *factor analytical and cluster analytical methods* aimed at reducing specific information about persons, situations, and responses to a limited number of factors or categories. A typical example of this strategy with respect to analysing perceived situational meaning is presented by Magnusson (1974). To begin with, subjects were asked to judge the similarity of pairs of situations and these global similarity ratings were subsequently subjected to either dimensional or cluster analytical procedures. For a set of various situations from the everyday lives of a student sample, Magnusson (1974) obtained five factors which were labelled 'positivity', 'negativity', 'passivity', 'social interaction' and 'individual activity' and showed a high degree of overlap with corresponding categories yielded by a cluster analysis of the same situations. Such a procedure facilitates the development of taxonomies of situations which form the basis for a systematic variation of situation variables and a more precise assessment of the relative contributions of person and situation variables as determinants of behaviour.

Factor analytical procedures serve an equally important purpose in the development of 'situation–response (S–R) inventories' (e.g. Endler, Hunt & Rosenstein, 1962; Endler & Okada, 1975). Situation–response inventories are composed of two integral parts: a set of situation categories and a set of response scales, with subjects being required to describe their responses separately for each situation category. Thus, S–R inventories differ from traditional personality inventories inasmuch as they measure people's responses conditional upon the specific features of the situation category. In this context, factor analysis provides a strategy for exploring the extent to which a priori classifications of persons, situations and behaviours are confirmed by empirical data (cf. also Briggs & Cheek, 1986). A prominent field of application for this type of analysis is the interactionist conceptualisation of stress and anxiety, of which a study by Ekehammar, Magnusson & Ricklander (1974) provides a typical example. They started off with a heuristically derived sample of anxiety-provoking situations for which similarity ratings and factor loadings had been established in a pretest. On this basis, seventeen situations were retained which loaded on four factors labelled 'ego threat', 'threat of pain', 'inanimate threat' and 'threat of punishment'. At the same time, a sample of eighteen responses was selected and assigned to three factors found in an earlier investigation: 'autonomic arousal', 'muscle tension', and 'feelings of fear'. The two sets of situations and responses were combined into an S–R-inventory where subjects were asked to imagine being in each of the seventeen situations and indicate the extent to which they typically show each of the eighteen reactions in that situation.

On the basis of correlating the responses across subjects as well as situations, three factors were identified, one of which was labelled 'psychic anxiety' and the second 'somatic anxiety'. The third factor was classified as 'uninteresting' since it referred only to those responses characterised by low intensity. Factor analysis of the situations collapsed across subjects and responses yielded three factors which were interpreted as 'threat of punishment', 'anticipation fear' and 'inanimate threat'. Despite the fact that these findings fail to replicate exactly the initial classification of situations and responses, the relatively high degree of overlap between the a priori and empirical classifications suggests that the search for a limited number of relevant situations and responses in the domain of anxiety may ultimately prove successful. Further evidence along these lines is provided by a study by Ekehammar, Schalling & Magnusson (1975) in which perceived similarity of and behavioural similarity in anxiety-provoking situations were measured in two independent samples. The factor analyses of the perceptual and behavioural similarities showed a high degree of correspondence in the resulting factor structures and, moreover, largely confirmed the initial classification of the situations involved.

For a critical appraisal of the studies discussed so far, it has to be borne in mind, however, that all of them were guided by the aim of establishing an interindividually valid range of situations and responses. This implies that the factor analytical strategy for studying person–situation interactions is equally unsuitable as the correlational analysis of group data for uncovering behavioural coherence at the level of the individual person (cf. Wakenhut, 1978, 101, for a similar point).

An alternative mode of applying factor analytical techniques to the search for individually relevant taxonomies of situations has been demonstrated by Pervin (1976). He asked four subjects to generate a list of situations from their everyday lives which they subsequently described in terms of (a) the general characteristics of, (b) the feelings elicited by and (c) the behaviours displayed in each of the situations. When these data were factor-analysed separately for each participant, clear individual differences emerged in the resulting situation profiles with regard to the number of extracted factors despite a relatively high degree of correspondence in the contents of the situations named (e.g. family vs. school/work). Looking at the feelings and behaviours generated by each respondent as pertaining to the different situations, systematic patterns emerged both within and across the two types of data, suggesting that personality may be 'defined as one's pattern of stability and change in relation to defined situational characteristics' (Pervin, 1976, 471). If defined in this way, it is obvious that personality can only be properly understood within the framework of an individual-centred methodology.

Beyond the correlational strategy and the use of factor as well as cluster analysis, the third methodological approach that has been widely popular in interactionist research is *the analysis of variance or ANOVA design*. In contrast to the type of idiographically oriented analysis described in the last paragraph, this approach is concerned, once again, with the exploration of consensually valid classes of situations and responses that was already shown to be the major objective of S–R inventories. The ANOVA design is the method of choice for capturing the 'mechanistic' understanding of interaction described in the previous section. It allows one to quantify – though not to explain – the proportion of the total behavioural variance accounted for by the interactive effect of person and situation variables and compare it with the proportion of variance due to the person and situation main effects. The strategy of apportioning behavioural variance to the relative contributions of person and environment factors has remained in constant use despite numerous criticisms (e.g. Golding, 1975; Olweus, 1977). Recently, it has received further attention in the context of suggestions to apply behaviour-genetic methods to the study of personality (e.g. Plomin, 1986; Rowe, 1987). Here, the aim is to determine the genetic vs. environmental origins of individual differences by studying twins and adopted children as well as family pedigrees.

Bearing in mind that the modern interactionist perspective emerged as a product of the controversy over the generality vs. specificity of behaviour, it is not surprising that the variance components strategy has served an important purpose in corroborating the claims of this new approach. By allowing one to quantify the interactive effect of person and situation variables, it enables advocates of an interactionist reconceptualisation of personality to provide 'hard' evidence in support of their position. This is how

Bowers (1973), for example, underlined his plea for an interactionist revision revision of the consistency issue when he quoted eleven empirical studies showing that the proportion of variance accounted for by the interaction of person and situation variables was substantially higher than the proportion of variance accounted for by the respective person and situation main effects.

The input required by the variance components strategy consists of three types of data:

– a sample of persons and a sample of situations as independent variables, and

– a behavioural measure as dependent variable.

If the dependent variable is operationalised by different behavioural criteria, it is possible to include the behaviour as a third factor in the analysis (cf. Endler & Hunt, 1966, for an early example). Beyond establishing the significance of main and interaction effects, their magnitude may be expressed in terms of the percentage of variance accounted for by each effect. In the early days of modern interactionism, variance percentages were typically computed as Omega² measures. In their review of empirical evidence based on the variance components strategy, Sarason, Smith & Diener (1975) computed Omega² scores for a sample of 102 studies. They concluded that person and situation variables accounted for about an equal, though generally small percentage of variance, with person–situation interactions accounting for even less variance than the two main effects. The authors note, however, that the studies considered in their analysis varied widely in terms of their conceptual backgrounds as well as the theoretical meaningfulness of the selected person and situation variables with regard to the behaviour under study.

The inadequacy of the Omega² index for capturing the psychological significance of interactions as opposed to person and situation main effects was pointed out by authors like Golding (1975) and Olweus (1977). As an alternative approach, generalisability theory has repeatedly been advocated (Golding, 1975; Lantermann, 1980; Malloy & Kenny, 1986, Ozer, 1986) as providing a statistical instrument for generalising from empirical samples of persons, situations and responses to their respective populations. Looking, for example, at the impact of person variables, generalisability studies would allow inferences from empirically observed responses in a limited sample of situations to individual behaviour in the corresponding population of situations, i.e. they would allow to assess the stability of behavioural patterns and/or intensities with respect to different classes or types of situations. However, despite these obvious advantages, even the advocates of this approach remain doubtful that generalisability theory can provide a tool for discriminating conclusively between situationism, interactionism, and the trait model (cf. Olweus, 1977; Fiske, 1978).

A fundamental criticism of the variance components strategy for analysing person–situation interactions refers to the problem that person and situation variables are usually defined independently of each other (Alker, 1977). In a typical P × S study, subjects characterised by certain trait scores are exposed to certain (experimental) situations, and it is only in the subsequent statistical analysis that the two sources of behavioural variation are considered in combination. This problem is avoided by those studies which rely on S–R inventories for the collection of data (cf. Furnham & Jaspers, 1983). These instruments are designed so that respondents are required to describe their behaviour (e.g. in anxiety-provoking situations) with respect to different situational contexts. This means that the interdependence of person and situation variables is already created by the respondent in the process of data collection rather than being established by the investigator in the process of statistical analysis. This distinctive quality renders the findings from S–R inventories especially relevant for the evaluation of the interactionist model.

On the basis of the information provided by S–R inventories, one can assess the influence of differences between individuals, situations and response modes (i.e. the main effects due to persons, situations and responses) and, more importantly, the following statistical interactions: (a) the interaction between individuals and response modes, (b) the interaction between individuals and situations, (c) the interaction between situations and response modes, and (d) the three-way interaction of individuals, response modes, and situations. Interactionists usually interpret evidence from S–R inventories as supportive of their theoretical claims if the proportion of variance accounted for by the interactions exceeds the proportion of variance accounted for by the main effects (e.g. Dworkin & Kihlstrom, 1978).

A critical analysis of research based on S–R inventories is presented by Furnham & Jaspers (1983; cf. also Golding, 1977). Looking separately at two-factorial (P × S) and three-factorial (P × S × R) designs, they identify a number of serious problems with these instruments. Despite the fact that many of the P × S studies considered in their review relied on observational data, observers were rarely included as factors in the analysis, leaving their impact on the total variance unexplained. Furthermore, interaction variance was typically confounded with error variance in this design, leading to an overestimation of the true magnitude of the interaction effect (cf. also Argyle & Little, 1972). On the other hand, most P × S × R studies employed self-reports of reaction profiles across different situations; yet researchers have paid little attention, either theoretically or empirically, to the response factor, either alone or in interaction with person and situation variables.

In addition, a basic problem with S–R inventories identified by Furnham & Jaspers (1983) refers to the issue of sampling persons, situations and response modes as constituents for any particular S–R study. Here, Furnham & Jaspers argue that the strength of the various variance components can be easily predetermined by selecting either very homogeneous or very heterogeneous samples of persons, situations, and responses which are bound to result in correspondingly low or high variance components. Accordingly, it is concluded that 'the implicit or explicit theories of the experimenters, as regards P × S interaction, may have been confirmed by a non-random unrepresentative sampling of Ss and questionnaire items' (Furnham & Jaspers, 1983, 640).

Further criticisms which are not limited to S–R inventories but apply to the variance components strategy in general are advanced by Endler (1983). He points out that S–R inventories can only demonstrate the relative contribution of person and situation variables and their interactions, they do not provide any clue towards a psychological explanation of the processes involved. Finally, S–R inventories, and the variance components strategy in general, are based on the mechanistic understanding of 'interaction' which is considered of limited value in the study of dynamic person–situation interactions.

Altogether, these shortcomings undermine the suitability of this approach as an empirical strategy for investigating the dynamic interaction process (Endler, 1983, 178). On the other hand, it cannot be denied that modern interactionism has as yet failed to develop a methodological framework capable of capturing the proposed complex process of reciprocal interaction of personal qualities, situational characteristics and behavioural responses. Of the few attempts that have been made in this direction, three examples will be presented briefly to conclude this section.

The first example of research based on the dynamic meaning of interaction is provided by Peterson's (1979) work in the domain of interpersonal relationships. In this domain, the 'situation' is constituted by the presence and behaviour of one or more other persons. Peterson asked married couples to decide at the end of each day of the testing period on the single most important interaction they had had in the course of the day. Each partner then provided an independent account of that interaction guided by three questions; What were the conditions under which the interaction took place? How did it start? What happened then? These free-response interaction records were subjected to a complex coding process in which they were judged in terms of their main acts as well as the message (meaning) and the dominant affect associated with each act. On this basis, a detailed inspection of 'interaction cycles', each consisting of an action by one partner and a reaction by the other, became possible.

The second recent line of research aimed at investigating the reciprocal influence of person, situation and behaviour is part of the 'Social Relations Model' by Malloy & Kenny (1986; Kenny & La Voie, 1984). This model, too, rests on the assumption that individuals not only respond in their character-istic ways to situational conditions but also function as social stimuli for the behaviour of others. Accordingly, social interaction is regarded as a para-digmatic case of dynamic person–environment interactions. Depending on the analytical perspective, the actor may either be looked at as the 'person' influenced by the partner's behaviour representing the 'situation' or vice versa, with the specific relationship between actor and partner being conceived of as the 'interaction' term. Thus, the social relations model deals with dyadic interactions as its basic units of analysis whereby the behaviour of one member is influenced by and, at the same time, influences the behaviour of the other member. This results in interrelated, i.e. non-independent patterns of behavioural data for each of the two partners. By combining observations obtained for different dyads, the model can be extended to multiple member interactions.

The non-independence of behavioural observations would present a serious methodological problem for traditional analysis of variance proce-dures aiming to separate the effects due to the person and the situation (represented here by the interaction partner). In the social relations model, it is treated as a significant source of information with regard to the reciprocal nature of person–situation interactions. To exploit this source, the model offers a formal mathematical rationale for the analysis of non-independent data patterns resulting from multiple interactions. The formal model, which is rooted in the logic of the general analyis of variance design (cf. Malloy & Kenny, 1986, 208ff. for details), allows one to identify the relative strength of the following components in accounting for the variance in individual behaviour:

1 The *actor* component, representing the person's behavioural tendencies averaged across multiple interaction partners;

2 The *partner* component, referring to the extent to which an individual elicits similar responses from a variety of social interaction partners;

3 The *relationship* component, expressing the uniqueness of the interaction between two partners on any one occasion which is purged of the influence of both actor and partner effects.

In a study pertinent to the social relations model, Miller, Berg & Archer (1983) investigated the determinants of subjects' readiness for self-disclosure on a variety of topics classified as involving either high or low intimacy. When the proportions of variance accounted for by each of the three components were computed, an interesting pattern of results emerged: only a minimal proportion of the variance, i.e. 1%, was due to the generalised partner effect for both high and low intimacy topics, suggesting that at least in their sample there were no individuals who particularly and pervasively encouraged self-disclosure from others. The amounts of variance accounted for by the actor and relationship components were substantially higher although affected significantly by the intimacy of the topic. For the highly intimate topics, 14% of the variance was attributable to the person's general tendency towards self-disclosure, while 86% was due to the relationship component (confounded, however, by error variance). For the low intimacy topics, the actor component became more important with 39% of the variance, while the relationship component was reduced to 60%. This suggests that a person's general openness towards self-disclosure is an important predictor of actual self-disclosure particularly when the topic is less intimate or ego-involving. In contrast, the willingness to discuss intimate topics is determined almost exclusively by the specific nature of the relationship between the two partners.

A third innovative approach to the issue of person–situation has been presented by Diener and his colleagues (Diener, Larsen & Emmons, 1984; Emmons, Diener & Larsen, 1985; 1986). At the centre of their work is the hypothesis that an individual's personality influences his or her choice of situations as well as co-determines the extent to which positive affect is experienced as a consequence of the 'goodness of fit' between personal dispositions and situational characteristics. Two complementary models are advanced to conceptualise the proposed link between person and situation characteristics (Diener, Larsen & Emmons, 1984): The first is the 'situation choice model', suggesting that people spend more time in situations that correspond to their personal dispositions. The second is the 'congruence response model', stating that individuals experience more positive and less negative affect in situations that are congruent with their personality characteristics.

Emmons, Diener & Larsen (1985) examined the relationship between, on the one hand, different personality measures (e.g. extraversion, sociability, impulsivity) and, on the other hand, the frequency with which the individual engaged in various recreational activities as well as the intensity of positive or negative affect experienced in those activities. The overall pattern of their findings supports the situation choice model, suggesting that individuals tend to prefer those activities which are congruent with their personal dispositions. High scores on extraversion, for example, correlated significantly with high frequencies of activities involving arousal seeking and social contact and also with positive affect experienced in these types of activities. However, support for the congruence response model was generally less conclusive, leading the authors to examine more specific emotions, rather than global positive or negative affect, experienced by individuals as a function of the person–situation fit.

This task was addressed in a study by Emmons & Diener (1986) which also illustrates the distinctive differences between a methodological approach aimed at discovering reciprocal interactions and research strategies based on the statistical meaning of interaction. They asked their subjects to name twenty typical situations from their current life and classify each situation into one of four categories: 'social', 'alone', 'work' and 'recreation'. Over a period of one month, subjects were then asked to keep daily records in which they rated the intensity of different emotions (e.g. happy, depressed, angry) experienced in those of the listed situations they had encountered in the course of the day. In addition, each situation was rated in terms of whether the person had chosen to be in that situation or whether it had been imposed on him or her. Finally, all subjects completed two standard personality inventories tapping a variety of personality dimensions, such as extraversion, aggression and need for achievement. Average levels of intensity of the different emotions as well as correlations between intensity of emotions and personality scores were established separately for chosen and imposed situations in each of the four categories of social, alone, work, and recreation situations.

For the dynamic understanding of person–situation interactions, one aspect of their results is particularly relevant. It was shown that the fit between personality measures and corresponding emotions in situations pertaining to or congruent with those personality dimensions is generally better for chosen than for imposed situations. Feeling joyful, for example, was found to correlate substantially higher with extraversion in social situations chosen by the individual than in social situations that were imposed on him or her.

Altogether, the findings of Emmons & Diener (1986) underline that the fit between personality variables and situational features is a significant factor in accounting for emotional states experienced in a particular situation. Furthermore, the fact that the correspondence between stable personality traits and more short-term, transient emotional states is generally closer in chosen than in imposed situations highlights the role of the person as an active and intentional agent in the interaction process.

These three examples illustrate different possibilities of implementing the dynamic meaning of 'interaction' into specific research strategies. Yet, they are only a first step in the search for a comprehensive methodological framework to replace the analysis of unidirectional statistical interactions of person and situation variables on behaviour. As far as the consistency debate is concerned, the present discussion has shown that the prevalent methodological strategies of modern interactionism are largely inappropriate for the analysis of the proposed coherence of individual behaviour across situations. Two shortcomings in particular are responsible for this state of affairs:

1 The neglect of the *psychological* meaning of situations as perceived by the person, which is reflected in the pervasive practice of studying behaviour

with respect to a nomothetic sets of situations preselected by the investigator.
2 The lack of correspondence between the theoretical and empirical levels of analysis. This is reflected, first and foremost, in the attempt to corroborate the concept of coherence, defined in terms of *intraindividual* regularities, on the basis of data aggregated across individuals.

The methodological problems highlighted in this section are as yet largely unresolved. There has been an increasing number of critical contributions in recent years (cf., for example, the two special issues of the *Journal of Personality*, 1983; 1986) but the programmatic claims for a more adequate analysis of person–situation interactions (Bem, 1983c; Endler, 1983; Mischel, 1983) are slow in being converted into strategies for empirical investigation. It is with these reservations in mind that the next section reviews an exemplary body of evidence from the most prolific domain of modern interactionist research: the study of stress and anxiety.

An application: the study of stress and anxiety

In its relatively short history, the modern interactionist model of personality has been applied to a wide variety of domains and issues: aggression and hostility (e.g. Olweus, 1980; Pervin, 1984c), emotions (e.g. Emmons & Diener, 1986; Staats & Burns, 1982), prosocial behaviour (Romer, Gruder & Lizzardo, 1986; Wilson & Petruska, 1984), leisure activities (Bishop & Witt, 1970), machiavellianism (Vleeming, 1981), person perception (Zuroff, 1982), self-disclosure (Miller, Berg & Archer, 1983) and jealousy (Bringle, Renner, Terry & Davis, 1983) are but a few examples. The earlier outcomes of that research are documented comprehensively in three edited volumes by Endler & Magnusson (1976a), Magnusson & Endler (1977a) and Pervin & Lewis (1978). More recently, different approaches towards the study of situational variables from an interactionist point of view have been brought together by Magnusson (1981a), while interactional perspectives on issues of personality development and change are collected in a volume by Magnusson & Allen (1983).

This section presents a closer examination of one line of empirical research which is located explicitly within the modern interactionist model of personality and explores the interactive effect of person and situation variables in the domain of *anxiety*. This work represents the most extensive single effort of putting the interactionist model into practice so that the domain of anxiety-provoking situations can almost be regarded as the paradigmatic field of application for modern interactionism. Due to its prominent role in substantiating the claims of the modern interactionist model, this domain was also chosen as the exemplary field of application for the coherence model advanced in the present research (cf. Part 2).

One of the main precursors to the interactionist view of anxiety was Spielberger's (1966; 1972) cognitive theory of anxiety which is based on the distinction between trait anxiety (A-trait) and state anxiety (A-state). State anxiety is defined as a transient emotional condition which is accompanied by physiological arousal. Its actualisation is a function of the cognitive appraisal of external stimulus conditions which, in turn, depends on the individual's enduring dispositions towards anxiety. The relationship between A-trait and A-state is conceptualised in probabilistic terms:

> The stronger a particular personality trait, the more probable it is that an individual will experience the emotional state that corresponds to this trait, and the greater the probability that behaviors associated with the trait will be manifested in a variety of situations.
> (Spielberger, 1972, 31)

In order to examine the correspondence between trait and state anxiety, Spielberger, Gorsuch & Lushene (1970) developed the 'State–Trait–Anxiety Inventory' (STAI). The STAI consists of two partly overlapping sets of response scales comprising both physiological symptoms (e.g. feel jittery) and affective responses (e.g. feel upset) to anxiety-provoking situations. In completing the STAI subjects are requested to indicate, on the first set of scales, the extent to which they experience each response at that particular moment in time (state measure). On the second set, they indicate the extent to which each of the responses is typically characteristic for them in reacting to anxiety-provoking situations in general (trait measure).

The Spielberger model emphasises that cognitive processes mediate between anxiety-provoking stimuli and individual responses. Nevertheless, it is clear from both the theoretical formulation of the relationship between trait and state anxiety and the format of the STAI that this approach remains committed to the traditional trait model. The focus is on explaining individual differences in responding to anxiety-provoking stimuli as a function of individual differences in the strength of a broad underlying disposition, namely A-trait. This view implies that trait anxiety is treated as a unidimensional construct and no allowance is made for the differential effect of the particular nature of the anxiety-provoking situation on the link between A-trait and A-state.

It was precisely this assumption of a unidimensional A-trait which prompted the interactionist critique of Spielberger's model and the subsequent development of a multidimensional interaction model of anxiety (Endler, 1975; 1980; 1983). The empirical basis for criticising the state-trait theory was furnished by a number of studies showing that individual differences in A-trait predicted corresponding differences in A-state only for certain types of anxiety-provoking situations. Primarily, these were situations involving threats to self-esteem and interpersonal threats. For other types of situations, in particular those involving physical danger, A-trait levels failed to predict the intensity of A-state reactions.

What this evidence suggested, then, was to think of A-trait not as a global disposition but as a multidimensional concept, with different dimensions of A-trait pertaining to different types or classes of stressful situations. Accordingly, four dimensions or facets of trait anxiety are distinguished in Endler's model of anxiety which have emerged from factor analyses of different samples of anxiety-provoking situations in a series of studies (cf. Endler, 1975). The four facets are labelled

> – *Interpersonal* A-trait, referring to situations which involve interactions with other people that are perceived as anxiety-provoking;
> – *Physical danger* A-trait, activated by situations in which the person faces the probability of physical injury;
> – *Ambiguous* A-trait, referring to threats posed by situations in which the person does not know what is going to happen to him or her;
> – *Daily routines* A-trait referring to anxiety-provoking circumstances encountered in everyday and routine situations.[3]

These four facets are addressed in the 'S–R Inventory of General Trait Anxiousness' (S–R GTA) by Endler & Okada (1975) which is the most widely used instrument for measuring multidimensional trait-anxiety. In a subsequent revision of the model, Endler (1980) has added a fifth facet, namely

> – *Social evaluation* A-trait, activated in situations which involve threats to the person's self-esteem as a result of being evaluated by other people.

By distinguishing between different facets of A-trait as pertaining to different classes of anxiety-provoking situations, it becomes feasible to predict specific interactions between A-trait and the situation in producing individual differences. In general terms, the model holds that individual differences with respect to one facet of A-trait are predictive of corresponding differences in A-state *only in those situations* which are congruent with the respective A-trait facet. For example, persons differing in 'social evaluation' A-trait would be expected to respond with different levels of A-state to situations involving evaluation by others but not necessarily differ in their responses to situations involving physical danger or ambiguity. In the same vein, intraindividual changes in A-state may be predicted. Increases in A-state as a result of changing from a non-stressful situation to a stressful one are no longer assumed to be a function of the person's overall level of trait anxiety. Instead, predictions are based on the person's standing on that facet of A-trait which is congruent with the type of anxiety-provoking stimuli involved in the respective situation.

---

[3] The exact meaning of this facet, however, remains somewhat obscure, since it is not made clear by Endler in what sense everyday or routine situations are regarded here as being anxiety-provoking.

As far as the dimensionality of A-state is concerned, a study by Endler, Magnusson, Ekehammar & Okada (1976) suggests that state anxiety should not be understood as a unidimensional construct either. According to their findings, at least two dimensions can be distinguished which are interpreted as 'psychic' and 'physiological' state anxiety. This distinction is reflected in more recent measures of A-state as, for example, in the 'Present Affect Reactions Questionnaire' (PARQ; Endler, 1980) which consists of ten 'autonomic arousal' items (e.g. perspire, hands feel unsteady) and ten 'cognitive worry' items (e.g. feel self-conscious, unable to concentrate). However, no specific hypotheses have as yet been formulated about the interaction between the two dimensions of A-state and particular types of anxiety-provoking situations.

In numerous studies, support was obtained for the interactionist model of anxiety and its major propositions, namely (a) that instead of being characterised by a general trait of anxiety, individuals may show high levels on certain facets of A-trait while scoring low on other facets; and (b) that only those facets of A-trait which are congruent with the specific nature of the threats inherent in particular situations are predictive of A-state responses in those situations. Endler (1983, 184ff.) presents a summary of the research conducted by himself and his co-workers. There is, however, a general problem with this type of evidence that should be mentioned before turning to the results from individual studies. This problem refers to the pervasive failure to compare trait and state measures with respect to their temporal stability vs. variability. In order to justify the distinction between traits and states, evidence is required that while state measures vary substantially from non-stressful situations to stressful situations, corresponding trait measures remain unaffected by changes in the anxiety-provoking nature of situations. The predominant design of empirical studies seeking support for the interaction model of anxiety does not, however, provide this evidence. Generally, what these studies do is to elicit base rates of A-state in non-stressful situations and compare these with the level of A-state in stressful situations. A-trait, on the other hand, is only measured at one point in time, namely in the non-stressful situation. Thus, no information is available as to whether A-trait levels do, in fact, remain stable across situations which differ in terms of their anxiety-provoking nature. Therefore, little can be said on the basis of this evidence to conclusively counter the claim of Allen & Potkay (1981, 1983) that the distinction between state and trait measures is essentially an arbitrary one (cf., however, Fridhandler, 1986, for a conceptual defence of this distinction).

With this reservation in mind, we can now turn to a more detailed examination of the findings presented in support of the interaction model of anxiety. Kendall (1978) conducted one of the few investigations that allow an immediate comparison between unidimensional and multidimensional conceptualisations of A-trait. His study, addressing physical danger and social evaluation situations, offers clear support in favour of the proposed multidimensional nature of dispositional anxiousness. Participants were sampled on the basis of their scores on three measures of A-trait administered some time prior to the actual study; the A-trait scale of Spielberger's STAI as a global measure of A-trait and the 'Physical Danger' and 'Social evaluation' subscales of the revised S–R GTA (cf. Endler, 1980, 262). Subjects were included in the sample when they scored either high (upper 40%) or low (lower 40%) on the trait measures. In order to allow for a conclusive test between the two models, an additional requirement was introduced: subjects scoring high (or low) on 'Physical danger' A-trait should not score high (or low) on the STAI and 'Social evaluation' A-trait measures and vice versa.

In the actual experiment, subjects were exposed to two types of anxiety-provoking situations: in the 'physical danger' situation, they were shown a film depicting vivid scenes of car crash tests. In the 'social evaluation' situation, they were asked to complete a word decoding task which was construed in such a way that no subject would be able to complete the task successfully within the available time. A-state was measured three times: first after the subjects had arrived for the experiment to obtain a base rate level of A-state and then again immediately after the film and after the word coding task. The increase in A-state from the base rate scores to the two post-treatment levels constituted the dependent variable in this study. Two competing hypotheses about the relationship between A-trait and A-state as well as the proposed increase in A-state after the experimental treatments follow from the unidimensional and multidimensional models of anxiety, respectively:

1 According to the unidimensional model, subjects scoring high on general A-trait as measured by the STAI should show higher increases in A-state than their low scoring counterparts in both the physical danger and the social evaluation situation.

2 According to the multidimensional model, an interaction between dimensional A-trait and type of situation is expected to account for the increase in A-state. More specifically, it is predicted that subjects scoring high on the physical danger A-trait measure show higher increases than low scoring subjects only after being exposed to the physical danger situation. Subjects scoring high on social evaluation A-trait are expected to respond with higher increases in A-state than their low anxiety counterparts only after failing in the social evaluation situation.

Kendall's findings strongly support the second set of hypotheses derived from the interactionist model. Subjects with high A-trait levels on the physical danger facet showed a significantly higher rise in A-state levels than low scorers following the crash film, while no difference emerged between the two groups in response to the social evaluation situation. Conversely, subjects with high scores on the social evaluation A-trait showed a significantly higher A-state increase than subjects scoring low on this anxiety facet after failing to complete the word coding task, while no such pattern was found following the crash film. Thus, the results of Kendall's study speak in favour of the superiority of a multidimensional conceptualisation of A-trait over the assumption of a general trait of anxiety.

In a similar investigation, Donat (1983) identified four groups of subjects on the basis of their responses to the 'social evaluation' and 'physical danger' scales of the S–R GTA. One group (I) of subjects with high general trait anxiety (i.e. high scores on both scales), a second group (II) with low general trait anxiety (i.e. low scores on both scales), a third group (III) scoring high on the 'social evaluation' scale only and, finally, a fourth group (IV) consisting of high scorers on the 'physical danger' scale only. All participants were required to solve two experimental tasks involving either physical danger or social evaluation during which measures of A-state were taken. Base rates of A-state were obtained in a non-stressful situation. The findings from this study reveal a complex interaction of specific and general measures of A-trait. In support of the multidimensional conceptualisation of A-trait, groups III and IV showed higher level of A-state for the task that was congruent with their A-trait level (i.e. the 'social evaluation' task for group III and the 'physical danger' task for group IV) than for the respective incongruent task. In addition, however, a significant interaction emerged between specific and general A-trait: A-state levels in each of the two situations were significantly higher for those subjects who scored high on A-trait on both dimensions (group I) than for those subjects scoring high only on the corresponding facet of A-trait (groups III and IV). What Donat's (1983) analysis suggests therefore, is that in predicting state anxiety, global levels of A-trait should be considered along with more specific A-trait scores referring to certain types of anxiety-provoking situations. Findings obtained by Lazzarini, Cox & Mackay (1979), who factor analysed individual response profiles to twelve different anxiety-provoking situations, point in the same direction. While their analysis yielded four specific factors similar to those postulated in the interaction model, the authors also report a powerful factor of general trait anxiousness which speaks against a straightforward multidimensional conceptualisation of trait anxiety.

The interaction model of anxiety received further support in a field study by Flood & Endler (1980) where the relationship between the interpersonal and social evaluation facets of A-trait and A-state levels was explored in an athletic competition situation. They asked participants in a running contest to complete a measure of A-state, the Behavioral Reactions Questionnaire (BRQ; Hoy & Endler, 1969), shortly before the start of the competition.

Immediately after the race, subjects completed another measure tapping their subjective interpretation of the situation. In this so-called 'Perception of Competitive Events Questionnaire', which was included on the basis of the interactionist stipulation that the meaning of a situation is a crucial factor in explaining individual behaviour, subjects were asked to indicate the extent to which they perceived the contest as being an 'interpersonal situation', a 'physical danger situation', 'an ambiguous situation' and a 'social evaluation situation'. Base rates of A-state in a non-competitive situation as well as measures of A-trait using the S–R GTA had been collected as part of a training session two weeks prior to the race. This information was used to examine the following hypotheses:

1 Participants characterised by high levels of interpersonal A-trait and social evaluation A-trait will show a higher increase in state anxiety from the neutral situation to the contest situation than those who score low on the two A-trait facets.

2 No corresponding interaction between A-trait and situation will emerge with respect to the remaining facets of A-trait, namely physical danger, ambiguous, and daily routines.

The analyis of the situation perception questionnaire confirms, first of all, that the situation was perceived predominantly as a 'social evaluation situation'. The category of 'interpersonal situations' received the second highest ratings and was not significantly different from the social evaluation category, the two, however, differing significantly from the remaining situation categories. An interaction of dimensional A-trait and situation could be demonstrated for the social evaluation A-trait but not for the interpersonal facet of A-trait. Thus, the hypotheses were only confirmed for one of the two A-trait facets thought to be involved in an athletic contest situation; yet it was that facet which corresponded most closely to the subjective interpretation of the situation by the participants.

A similar study by Phillips & Endler (1982), carried out in an authentic exam situation, also confirms the proposed interaction between the situation and the congruent dimension of A-trait for the social evaluation facet but not for the interpersonal facet. In this study, the subjective interpretation of the situation was incorporated as a separate factor in the analysis. When subjects were classified on the basis of whether or not they perceived the exam situation primarily as a social evaluation situation, significant differences between A-state levels in the stress and non-stress situations emerged only for one group of subjects: those who scored high on social evaluation A-trait and, at the same time, interpreted the exam situation primarily as involving social evaluation. Additional analyses revealed that the extent to which the situation was perceived as being a social evaluation, interpersonal, ambiguous or physical danger type of situation was not significantly related to the level of A-trait on the corresponding facets. This suggests that the subjective interpretation of anxiety-provoking situations is an additional, independent factor determining an individual's anxiety responses.

Yet, what exactly is the impact of situation interpretation on the level of A-state experienced in a given situation as well as on the link between dimensional A-trait and A-state? At present, research within the framework of the interaction model of anxiety does not provide a conclusive answer to this question. This is illustrated, for example, by two studies reported by Endler, King, Edwards, Kuczynski & Diveky (1983). They chose two situations, namely an academic examination and a demanding occupational situation, as pertaining to the social evaluation facet of A-trait. Accordingly, they tested – and supported – the hypothesis that changes in A-state levels from stress to non-stress situations should be significantly higher for subjects scoring high as opposed to low on the social evaluation facet of A-trait. High vs. low scorers on the remaining facets of A-trait showed no corresponding differences in their patterns of A-state change. While their findings thus conformed to the experimental hypotheses, disturbing evidence came to light when the subjects' interpretations of the two situations were taken into account. These revealed that, in general, the participants had failed to share the experimenters' a priori interpretation and had not considered the situations as being significantly more of a social evaluation than an interpersonal, ambiguous, physical danger or daily routine nature. Similar ambiguities were recently reported by King & Endler (1989) in a test of a more elaborate measure of situation perception.

Equally problematic patterns of results were found with regard to the 'ambiguous' A-trait facet by Ackerman & Endler (1985) as well as King & Endler (1982) who studied patients undergoing medical intervention. In each of these studies, the interaction model was confirmed *in spite of the fact* that the stipulated correspondence between the perceived nature of the situational threat and the activation of a particular facet of A-trait had obviously failed to materialise. By way of a post hoc explanation, King & Endler speculate that A-trait dimensions may differ with regard to the strength of situational features or 'prompts' they require to be activated. They argue that few situational cues or low levels of situational threat may be sufficient to arouse the social evaluation or physical danger facets of A-trait, while comparatively stronger cues indicating ambiguity or interpersonal threat may be required before the corresponding A-trait facets are activated. However, this explanation does not appear to be entirely convincing, since one would assume that the proposed differences in the anxiety-provoking potential of different types of situations would not only affect the arousal of A-trait but would influence the subjective interpretation of the situation in the same way. If a situation is not perceived as being particularly ambiguous by the person, then why – and, more importantly, how – should the ambiguous facet of A-trait be activated at all?

It appears, therefore, that a more complex conceptualisation is needed of the process whereby the subjective interpretation of the situation affects the state-trait relationship. An illustrative example of how this task may be approached was offered by Dobson (1983). He examined the relationship between A-trait and A-state for the two facets of physical danger and interpersonal threat. In his analysis, he drew on the cognitive theory of emotion by Lazarus & Launier (1978) where two types of cognitive appraisal are distinguished as influencing an individual's response to stressful situations. The first type, 'primary appraisal' refers to the person's subjective evaluation of the situational cues in terms of whether they have any negative significance for his or her well-being. As an operational definition, the perceived difficulty of different situations involving physical danger and interpersonal threat was measured in Dobson's study. The second type, 'secondary appraisal', refers to the perceived ability of the individual to cope with the situation, i.e. to handle the difficulties inherent in that situation.

Both types of cognitive appraisals are regarded by Dobson as mediating between the situation-congruent facets of A-trait and the amount of anxiety experienced in the situation in such a way that 'in the context of a given situation, the situationally specific traits of the person would predispose certain appraisals of the situation. The situational appraisals would, in turn, predict a rating of stress in that situation' (Dobson, 1983, 165). After completing the S–R GTA as a measure of A-trait, participants in his study were instructed to imagine themselves being in four different anxiety-provoking situations, two involving physical danger and two involving interpersonal threat. They were then asked to make ratings of the perceived difficulty of each situation, the ease of coping with the situation and the extent to which they would find the situation stressful.

Results from this study support the proposed role of cognitive appraisals as mediators between situation-specific A-trait and A-state. It was found that the only significant predictors of both situation difficulty and ease of coping were the respective situation-congruent facets of A-trait. When A-state was considered as the dependent variable, situation difficulty turned out to be a highly significant predictor of the stress ratings for each of the four situations, while ease of coping failed to produce any significant effects. An unexpected finding was obtained in the form of a significant direct influence of physical danger A-trait on stress levels in the two situations pertaining to this facet.

From the studies discussed in this section, it can be concluded that increases in the level of A-state as a function of encountering anxiety-provoking situations are predicted more accurately on the basis of situation-specific measures of A-trait than on the basis of a global, unidimensional measure of dispositional anxiousness. In addition to the clear-cut effects obtained for physical danger situations, the social evaluation dimension appears to be a particularly powerful component of A-trait. Support for the interpersonal and ambiguous facets of A-trait has been far less conclusive, suggesting that the present version of the interaction model of anxiety may have to be revised in the light of these recent findings (cf. also Mothersill, Dobson & Neufeld, 1986).

Taken together, the studies considered in this section illustrate how the theoretical assumptions concerning the interaction of personal and situational determinants of behaviour may be translated into empirical research strategies. They demonstrate how specific hypotheses may be derived from the general postulate of person–situation interactions, calling for a methodological approach which facilitates the measurement of personality variables contingent upon particular types of situational characteristics. Additional credit derives from the fact that the majority of research presently available has been carried out in natural settings where individual responses to anxiety-provoking situations could be studied in an ecologically valid way.

However, what remains problematic from the point of view of the present research, is the prevalence of an individual difference approach in studying the interactive effect of traits and situations of behaviour. The close association between the interaction model of anxiety and the trait concept highlights its limitations with respect to the issue of cross-situational consistency. The strategy of investigating individual differences in A-state as a function of corresponding differences in dimensional A-trait continues to operate on the basis of the concept of 'relative consistency', a platform which has been refuted as inadequate by the advocates of modern interactionism for a long time. In its current form, the model fails to make a contribution towards the understanding of *intraindividual* patterns of regularity and change across different types of anxiety-provoking situations. Yet, this would be urgently required to establish the concept of coherence as a conceptual alternative for addressing the consistency problem.

Current appraisals of the interactionist model

In the preceding sections, the theoretical and methodological foundations of the modern interactionist approach to personality have been discussed along with a selective review of empirical research generated within this framework. It is now time for a more general appraisal of the contribution made by this approach to the development of personality psychology over the last fifteen years or so.

In 1982, Endler confidently claimed in the title of a paper that 'interactionism comes of age'. A year later, he qualified this view, admitting that at present modern interactionism is a model but not yet a fully fledged theory of personality (Endler, 1983). There are two problems in particular which prevent interactionism in its present form from being already a comprehensive theory:

1 Most empirical work has been limited to the study of mechanistic interactions of two independent variables, i.e. a personal characteristic and a situational manipulation, on individual behaviour as the dependent variable. What has been largely neglected is the study of sequences of behaviour which reflect the proposed dynamic and bidirectional exchange between person and situation.

However, this should not be taken as suggesting that no further studies are needed to investigate the statistical interaction of personal dispositions and environment. Indeed, the renewed interest in recent years in identifying the genetic bases of personality differences and separating them from environmental sources (e.g. Buss, 1983; Dworkin, 1979; Kenrick, Montello & MacFarlane, 1985; Rowe, 1987) speaks to the contrary. This work indicates that the issue of how much personality is a function of stable hereditary characteristics and how much is due to the social environment with which the person interacts in the course of development is still high on the agenda of personality research. Here, specific methods are adapted from the field of behaviour genetics – in particular the study of adopted children and hereditary patterns within families as well as the comparison of monozygotic and dizygotic twins raised together or apart (cf. Carson, 1989; Plomin, 1986) – to establish the relative impact of environmental influences on individual behaviour.

2 While modern interactionism deserves to be credited for introducing the concept of the situation to the study of personality, little has been achieved so far in terms of illuminating the process whereby persons select and influence the situations in which they act. Nor do we know very much about the properties of situations which are most influential in shaping the person's affective and behavioural responses. Here, Endler suggests that taxonomies of situations are needed. These should be geared not so much towards describing the content of different situations as towards emphasising the respective rules and norms inherent in different situations that provide a kind of structural framework within which actual behaviour takes place (cf. Argyle, Furnham & Graham, 1981). In this way, the ground could be prepared for the development of comprehensive theoretical treatment of the 'psychological situation' which would go beyond the basically ad hoc way of dealing with situational variables that is characteristic of most of the interactionist work carried out so far. The present unsatisfactory state of theoretical development is reflected not least in the fact that one generally looks in vain for an explicit definition of what is meant by the term 'situation' in any specific research context.

Taken together, these two desiderata highlight the need to advance a more elaborate version of interactionism extending to the explanation of the *process* of interaction. An essential requirement for achieving this aim lies in the development of a methodology which would allow one to investigate the dynamic, continuous interplay between situational properties, their cognitive representation as well as their relationship to overt behaviour (cf. also Aronoff & Wilson, 1985). Promising attempts to address this task emerging from the work of Peterson (1979), Malloy & Kenny (1986), and Diener, Larsen & Emmons (1984) have been discussed in the second section of this chapter. But modern interactionism is still a far cry from providing a comprehensive theoretical account of how the process of person–environment interaction is properly understood.

As Lantermann (1980; 1982) argues, such an account would have to recognise that situation cognitions must not be understood as decontextualised elements of person–situation interactions whose impact on behaviour can be determined independently of the specific action context in which they occur. He presents an action theoretical model of person–situation interaction which claims that depending on the person's goals in a particular situation, different aspects of the perceived situation – defined as 'subjective field of action' – become relevant in guiding behaviour (Lantermann, 1982, 46). As far as the coherence of situation cognition and behaviour is concerned, the model predicts that two situational elements perceived as being equivalent by the person will elicit identical responses, whereby the criterion for defining perceived situational equivalence is supposed to be the significance of situational elements with respect to the attainment of specific goals.

Hyland (1984) also presents a critical assessment of modern interactionism as a theoretical alternative to the situationist and trait positions. In his view, the impact of the modern interactionist approach is limited largely to the level of methodological developments and fails to advance a new theoretical model for understanding personality. At the same time, he rejects the view that situationism and trait approach have ever been presented as strict theoretical alternatives arguing that in fact they differed primarily in their preference for particular strategies to measure individual behaviour. Whereas one can go along with much of Hyland's criticism, especially as far as the lack of a comprehensive theoretical network is concerned, his comments on the way in which modern interactionism deals with the concept of the 'psychological situation' cannot be accepted without qualification. When he states that 'certainly from a methodological point of view there has never been any suggestion that the situation which appears in the ANOVA paradigm is anything other than an objective reality' (Hyland, 1984, 319), then this is certainly not true for the large number of studies which are based on S–R inventories. When the interactionist model of anxiety and its empirical validations were discussed earlier on in this chapter, it became clear that S–R inventories, such as the S–R GTA, relied exclusively on the person's subjective interpretations of different anxiety-provoking situations and their relationship to individual behaviour. But in spite of his criticism, Hyland credits modern interactionism with one significant contribution, namely that it has drawn attention to the fact that for the prediction of behaviour to become more successful, one would need to define explicitly those classes of situations and behaviours for which predictions are supposed to hold true. (cf. also Peake,1984, 336). This view is shared by Pervin, who also regards the emphasis of modern interactionism in the systematic *variability* and discriminativeness of behaviour instead of consistency as its major achievement: 'Rather, the real significance of the person–situation debate may be in calling attention to the critical issue of understanding patterns of stability and change' (Pervin, 1984b, 344).

A much more radical criticism of modern interactionism is advanced by Gadlin & Rubin (1979). They alredy make it clear in the title of their paper that they consider the interactionist approach to be a 'non-resolution of the person–situation controversy'. Their critique is not primarily directed against the theoretical postulates or methodological strategies of the interactionist model but against what they identify as its ideological foundations. Gadlin & Rubin argue that the conflict on which the entire person–situation debate has been based is essentially a conflict between psychological explanations of human behaviour on the one hand and socio-historical realities on the other. The central issue at which their argument is directed is, again, the way in which the concept of 'situation' is treated in the interactionist model. They take particular exception to the conceptualisation of situations in terms of ahistorical and asocial, subjective representations of objective stimulus conditions. The view of adaptive social behaviour as resulting from the perfect integration of person and situation is criticised as an essentially ideological notion, tantamount to abolishing the independence of person and situation as analytical units and rooted in the attempt to salvage 'the continued social cohesion of a failing system' (Gadlin & Rubin, 1979, 235). They argue that more often than not there is disjunction between persons and situations rather than congruence, resulting from the constraints imposed by certain socio-historical conditions upon the person's choice of situations and social settings. Accordingly, Gadlin & Rubin postulate that the only way in which situational factors can become meaningful elements of any psychological theory of human behaviour is by acknowledging explicitly the historical and societal determination of individual action:

> People do not act in situations; they act in specific historical
> circumstances that they interpret in certain ways and that constrain and
> compel them in certain ways; and it is the particular features of those
> circumstances we must understand to understand why they act as they
> do. (Gadlin & Rubin, 1979,225)

However, as legitimate as this challenge to the advocates of modern interactionism to be more aware of the historical premises and implications of their research undoubtedly is, it shifts the person–situation debate to a different level. This level is complementary to the present attempts at solving the conceptual and methodological problems involved in the study of person–situation interactions, but it certainly does not make those attempts irrelevant.

4 The cognitive representation of situations

So long as the consistency controversy was dominated by the disagreement of trait psychologists and situationists over the impact of situational influences on behaviour, there was no room for the situation as an explanatory concept in personality research. After all, acknowledging the importance of situational forces in accounting for behavioural patterns would have inevitably been perceived as surrendering to the opposing camp. Therefore, throughout most of the consistency debate, person and situation variables were treated not as joint, but as competing determinants of individual behaviour, with an empirical decision between the two being regarded as an equally urgent and feasible task. Moreover, the affinity of the situationist position for the experiment as its method of choice was responsible for the fact that the dispute rested on a very limited understanding of situational factors in terms of experimental treatments (cf.also chapter 2). This, in turn, implied that individual differences in interpreting situational cues were largely regarded as sources of error that should be eliminated or controlled as far as possible. In contrast, different lines of thinking were advanced in sociological research stressing the importance of the subjective definition of situations for explaining individual behaviour (Stebbins, 1985), but this work remained largely without impact on mainstream personality psychology.

In the course of the previous chapters, it was emphasised that a central aim of the present research is to contribute to a clearer understanding of the subjective construction of situational meaning which is assigned a crucial role in the suggested reconceptualisation of the consistency issue. Therefore, the focus of this chapter is on discussing recent models of the cognitive representation of situations, advanced in cognitive social psychology, with a view to assessing their applicability to the individual-centred analysis of the 'psychological situation'. To begin with, however, we shall present a brief outline of the current status of situational analysis in the field of personality.

The situation as a variable in personality research

With the emergence of modern interactionism in the course of the 1970s, the inadequacy of an understanding of the situation reduced to the characteristics of experimental treatments became increasingly recognised, instigating the search for more elaborate conceptual models and empirical strategies for the analysis of situational variables. A comprehensive range of this work is presented in the volumes by Argyle, Furnham & Graham (1981), Furnham & Argyle, (1981) and Magnusson (1981a) as well as the chapter by Snyder & Ickes (1985) in the *Handbook of Social Psychology*. One basic aspect for systematising the available contributions towards a 'psychology of situations' refers to the units of analysis for defining and measuring situational variables. Five successive levels of complexity are commonly distinguished, each containing a combination of elements specified at the preceding levels (e.g. Furnham & Argyle, 1981; Magnusson, 1978; Pervin, 1978; cf. Edwards, 1984, for a review).

The most fundamental level at which situations may be studied is that of *situational stimuli*. These are constituted by single objects or acts inherent in a situation which are meaningful in their own right, i.e. do not necessarily have to be linked to other information in order to be understood.

At the next higher level, *situational events* or episodes comprising specific parts of a total situation are the units of analysis. Situational events are characterised by a dynamic quality in the sense of being composed of a set of interrelated actions by one or more persons.

Situational stimuli and events are combined into a more complex unit at the level of the *total, actual situation*. What is characteristic of the total situation is its unique occurrence in time and space.

In contrast, at the level of *situational settings* situations are defined in generalised terms, abstracting from specific occurrences. Accordingly, the study of situational settings is designed to discover typical events and sequences of events that would recur in much the same way under similar circumstances.

Finally, the broadest unit of situational analysis is the *life situation* or environment. This category comprises the totality of social and physical factors which affect the person and are affected by his or her actions at a certain stage of individual development.

An independent and equally important feature by which research on the role of situational factors in personality functioning may be distinguished refers to the definition of situations in *objective* versus *subjective* terms. While a variety of studies are interested in situations as defined in terms of objective properties and/or consensual meaning, a smaller but growing number of contributions aim to explore the subjective, possibly idiosyncratic meaning of situations for the individual. The main difference between the two approaches is brought to the point by Argyle, Furnham & Graham (1981, 37): 'To argue for a subjective definition of situations implies the actor's definition, while the objective definition of situations implies the observer's definition.' It should be added that the observer is typically identical to the investigator when it comes to selecting the situational stimuli and settings to be studied empirically. Whether situations are analysed in terms of their objective features or subjective meaning depends, to a large extent, on the broader research context within which situational factors are invoked as explanations of behaviour. So, for instance, Argyle, Furnham & Graham (1981) stress that in the training of social skills the consensual interpretation of situations is of central importance inasmuch as social skills deficits often involve the person's failure to properly understand the meaning of situations *as perceived by others*. In contrast, the focus of the modern interactionist model is on understanding the individual's unique perception of the situation in relation to his or her behavioural decisions.

Among efforts to explore situations defined in objective or quasi-objective (i.e. consensual) terms, a prominent line of research is directed to reducing the almost infinite complexity of situations to a limited number of situation categories. The availability of empirical taxonomies of situations is an essential prerequisite for specifying predictions of behavioural consistencies with reference to defined classes of situations. In order to arrive at a taxonomic classification of situations, the first task consists in systematising the defining features of situations. Different approaches have been suggested for distinguishing situations by their objective or consensually perceived properties (cf. Jaspers, 1985). Despite Endler's (1983, 171) claim that 'ideally, a taxonomy of situations should be derived within a theoretical context and not be developed mainly on empirical grounds', it is the latter strategy that has been employed in most of the studies conducted so far. Some authors suggest classifying situations according to their tendency to elicit similar behaviours (Fennell, 1975; Frederiksen, 1972) or similar affective reactions (Harrison, 1986). Price (1974) has demonstrated that a classification of situations based on consensual ratings of which behaviours are appropriate in them allows one to identify classes of behaviour that are uniquely appropriate in certain classes of situations (cf. also Schutte, Kenrick & Sadalla, 1985). Yet another strategy involves the classification of situations on the basis of the behavioural rules that are prevalent in them (Argyle, Graham, Campbell & White, 1979). Further attributes by which situations have been distinguished include the complexity and clarity of situations as well as their strength, i.e. the extent to which they override individual differences and elicit uniform patterns of behaviour from the persons involved (cf. Magnusson, 1981b).

A comprehensive strategy for deriving a taxonomy of situational attributes was introduced by Baumeister & Tice (1985). They argued that social psychological experiments are typically designed to assess the impact of situational influences on behaviour; hence the independent variables used in a sufficient number of experiments can be regarded as a representative sample of situational attributes. Based on an analysis of the odd-numbered volumes of the *Journal of Personality and Social Psychology*, they categorised situational attributes used as independent variables in experimental studies into a taxonomy defined by four components of situational structure:[1]

1 Stimulus environment, comprising the enduring physical and social structure of the situation;

2 Cognitive and affective dynamics of the situation, including 'situational demand intensity' and 'subject's goal';

3 Relationship background, referring to the different aspects of the relationship between the persons involved in the situation;

4 Matrix of possibilities, denoting those aspects of the situation that relate to the subject's choice of behavioural responses.

The advantage of this framework for a taxonomy of situations is its reliance on a systematic strategy for sampling the initial body of situational attributes from which it is derived. However, the range of the taxonomy is limited to some extent by restricting the definition of situational attributes to those features that lend themselves to and are typically encountered in social psychological experimentation.

In sum, what the different endeavours to establish taxonomic descriptions of situations share in common is the goal to provide a basis for partitioning a heterogeneous range of situations into more or less coherent categories which may then be matched against corresponding categories of behaviours and/or personality characteristics.

Exploring the correspondence between objective or consensually perceived properties of situations and individual characteristics is at the core of another set of recent contributions to an emerging 'psychology of situations'. Lanning (1988) has introduced the concept of 'scalability' to denote the extent to which behavioural patterns vary, both within and between individuals, as a function of the evocativeness of situations. Evocativeness refers to the (normative) meaning of situations in terms of facilitating or demanding specific behavioural responses. He argues that just as persons may be characterised by their average level of trait-related behaviours across pertinent situations, it is posssible to characterise situations by the average level of behaviours typically exhibited in them. For example, in the same way as persons differ in the extent to which they show affiliative behaviours in a variety of situations, situations differ in the extent to which they typically elicit affiliative behaviours. Lanning suggests that cross-situational consistency should be conceptualised in terms of the correspondence between

---

[1]   A fifth descriptive component, 'characteristics of the subject', emerged, due specifically to their strategy of deriving the taxonomy from independent variables used in experimental research. The authors acknowledge that this aspect does not, strictly speaking, refer to situational properties and suggest dropping it if the taxonomy is used to make a clear-cut differentiation between person and situation factors.

changes in situational evocativeness and changes in behavioural level, thereby advocating an understanding of consistency that allows for behavioural stability as well as variability and is highly similar to the concept of 'coherence' underlying the present research. A person is said to be 'scalable' if his or her behaviour in a given situation or set of situations may be predicted jointly by the person's average behavioural level and the situations' average level of evocativeness. Thus, a person characterised by a generally low level of affiliative behaviour is assumed to be less likely to show affiliative behaviour in a situation which typically does not elicit such responses than in a situation which is characterised by high evocativeness with regard to affiliation.

In an empirical study demonstrating the viability of his approach, a 'Situation Behaviour Inventory' was developed which allowed the simultaneous assessment of behavioural level and situational evocativeness in five trait domains: achievement, conscientiousness, friendliness, irritability, and self-consciousness. Respondents were presented with a list of 102 situations and a set of eighteen behaviours and were asked, for each situation, to select the behaviour that best described how they would respond in the situation. In a pretest, numerical ratings had been obtained for each behaviour of the extent to which it was indicative of the five underlying trait dimensions. Situational evocativeness was established by aggregating behavioural responses across subjects for each of the 102 situations. Behavioural level was established by aggregating each subject's responses across the total range of situations. For each cell of the resulting person–situation matrix, expected values, reflecting scalability, were derived from the combined information about situational evocativeness and individual response profiles. Even though evidence on the relationship between scalability scores and corresponding trait measures in the five domains revealed only moderate increases over straightforward behavioural profiles (not taking situational evocativeness into account), this new approach may be regarded as a promising strategy for including the analysis of situations in the search for consistency in personality. In addition, as 'a high scalability score indicates a correspondence between, on the one hand, a particular normative hierarchy of behaviors and situations, and, on the other, an individual's own subjective rules for interpreting and responding to situations' (p. 147), Lanning's approach is also relevant to the issue of conceptualising the relationship between objective and subjective definitions of situations.

Dworkin & Goldfinger (1985) illustrate another approach for clarifying the interdependence of situational variables and personality. Their research is directed at the analysis of individual differences in the cognition of situations with a view to illuminating the cognitive processes underlying cross-situational consistency and person–situation interactions. However, they argue that this task presupposes a taxonomy of situations, defined in objective terms, to serve as a platform for the manifestation of individual differences in situation cognition. In developing such a taxonomy, they draw on the concept of 'affordances' (Gibson, 1979) to describe situations in terms of their inherent potential for positive or negative actions and experiences. For example, a situation like 'travelling in a plane' affords both positive and negative aspects (e.g. quick arrival at a distant destination *and* risk of falling victim to terrorist attacks). Dworkin & Goldfinger point out that affordances are objective properties of situations inasmuch as they exist even without being perceived by any particular observer. However, affordances can only have an effect on cognitions and behaviour if they are perceived and attended to by the person. Therefore, affordances are at the same time objective and subjective because their physical properties can exert an influence on the person only if he or she possesses the complementary characteristic to make use of or 'tune into' a certain affordance (cf. Baron & Boudreau, 1987).

Typically, situations are characterised by multiple affordances, and individuals differ with regard to the particular affordances towards which they direct their attention. Hence, individual differences in situation cognition are conceptualised by Dworkin & Goldfinger in terms of the selective attention to certain situational affordances at the expense of others, whereby attention is supposed to vary as a function of relevant personality characteristics. Applying this reasoning to the analysis of the social affordances of different situations, they addressed the question of whether persons scoring differently on a trait measure of sociability would show corresponding differences in their processing of the social vs. non-social affordances of situations, i.e. those situational characteristics that afford vs. do not afford social behaviour. Three aspects of the cognitive processing of situational affordances were distinguished and assessed separately in their study: the *anticipation* of encountering social vs. non-social affordances in a given situation, the differential *perception* of these affordances in an ongoing situation, and finally, *memory* for the social vs. non-social characteristics of events from their personal experience.

In line with their predictions, Dworkin & Goldfinger (1985) found that both highly sociable subjects and non-sociable subjects, defined through a traditional trait measure as well as a self-schema measure of sociability, showed a stronger tendency to direct attention to social (as opposed to non-social) situational stimuli than moderately sociable subjects. This pattern underlines the functional significance of situation cognition for individual behaviour. Anticipating, perceiving and recalling the social affordances inherent in a particular situation is important for both sociable and nonsociable persons, since the former would generally seek such situations while the latter would try to avoid them. In contrast, moderately sociable persons who are relatively indifferent about whether to seek or to avoid situations affording social interaction are less motivated to attend selectively to the social affordances of a situation. Thus, the analysis of situation cognition presented by Dworkin & Goldfinger illustrates a way of linking objective properties of situations to enduring personal dispositions, such as traits or schemes, via the cognitive processing of situations in anticipation, perception, and memory.

Unlike descriptions of situations in objective terms which are, by definition, largely independent of the perspective of an individual observer, a proper understanding of the subjective meaning that a person assigns to a situation requires an awareness of the person's particular experiential background and possibly idiosyncratic ways of interpreting situations. A classic example of this type of approach to the analysis of situational meaning can be found in the work of Thomas (1928) who summarised the gist of his argument in what became known as the *Thomas theorem*: 'If men define situations as real, they are real in their consequences' (Thomas, 1928, 572). This means, as Ball (1972) elaborates, that the 'definition of the situation may be conceived of as the *sum of all recognized information, from the point of view of the actor, which is relevant to his locating himself and others, so that he can engage in self-determined lines of action and interaction* (1972, 63; italics in the text). Originating from a sociological research tradition, the concept of the definition of the situation became a key notion in the context of symbolic interactionism and ethnomethodology (cf. Stebbins, 1985, for a recent review). However, it also influenced thinking and research in the modern interactionist approach, reflected most notably in the concept of the 'psychological situation'. As Magnusson (1978, 5) points out, 'understanding an individual's conceptions of the world and understanding his perception and interpretation of the specific situation in which he finds himself makes it possible to understand his actual behaviour in that situation'. Similarly, Zavalloni & Louis-Guerin (1979, 310), in their proposal of an 'interactive epistemology', emphasise the interdependence of the situation and its perceived meaning in the explanation of individual behaviour: 'On the one hand, the environment is something out there, on the other, as internalized content, it constitutes a property of the "processor" through which he responds to a particular external task environment.'

What these authors suggest, then, is to replace the dichotomy of the person and the situation as independent elements in the interaction process by a view which stresses the individual's construction of situational meaning as an integral component of personality (cf. also Geis, 1978).

An essential step towards investigating the role of the psychological meaning of situations for the understanding of person–situation interactions consists in the analysis of the central dimensions which underlie people's perception and interpretation of situations. A number of studies have addressed the task of identifying broad evaluative dimensions typically invoked in the interpretation of diverse situations.

An early study by Magnusson (1971) explored the dimensions underlying the cognitive representation of a heterogeneous set of thirty-six situations in three student subjects. On the basis of similarity ratings provided by the respondents for all situation pairs, he identified five factors, labelled 'positive', 'negative', 'passive', 'social' and 'active'. Wish, Deutsch & Kaplan (1976) confined their analysis to a specific type of situation, namely social encounters involving different types of interpersonal relations (e.g. 'between friends' or 'between interviewer and job applicant'). A total list of forty-five relations were presented to their subjects along with a set of twenty-five bipolar scales on which each situation was rated. Multidimensional scaling analysis yielded four dimensions capturing the cognitive representation of interpersonal relations: 'cooperative and friendly vs. competitive and hostile', 'equal vs. unequal', 'intense vs. superficial', and 'socioemotional and informal vs. task-oriented and formal'.

The range of situations was narrowed down even further by King & Sorrentino (1983) who studied the cognitive dimensionality of interpersonal goal-oriented situations. They used a total of twenty stimulus situations that were rated by respondents both in terms of their pairwise similarities and, one by one, on thirteen bipolar scales. Seven dimensions emerged from the multidimensional scaling analysis as facilitating a comprehensive character-isation of the cognitive representation of interpersonal goal-oriented situations: 'pleasant vs. unpleasant', 'accidentally caused or involved vs. intentionally caused or involved', 'physically vs. socially oriented', 'sensitive vs. insensitive', 'intimate vs. nonintimate', 'involved vs. uninvolved', and finally, 'work-oriented vs. relaxation-oriented'. These dimensions are based on group data, thus yielding a nomothetic picture of the central perceptual dimensions pertaining to this type of situation. However, when King & Sorrentino looked at the individual patterns of situation perception, they found that interpersonal variability was substantially higher than interper-sonal agreement, which suggests that the inspection of results at group level may yield a consensual interpretation of situations at the expense of obliterating significant peculiarities in individuals' perceptions.

A general problem confronting research into the dimensional structure of perceived situational meaning refers to the sampling of stimulus situations and rating scales which constitute the input for the subsequent dimensional analyses. In the studies discussed so far, the choice of situations and bipolar scales was based on their intuitive plausibility, a limitation explicitly recognised by Magnusson (1971). Thus, there are no empirical grounds for evaluating the generality of the obtained dimensional solutions with respect to the issue of whether the situations considered in the analyses are representative samples from the domain in question.

This problem is avoided at least to some extent in the study by Battistich & Thompson (1980) who studied students' perceptions of the college milieu. They adopted an explicit strategy for selecting their stimulus situations by asking subjects to keep a written record of the situations they encountered over a two-day period. From these records, the thirty most frequently mentioned situations were presented to a new group of subjects who were asked to provide both pairwise similarity ratings and ratings on bipolar dimensions which had also been derived from the situation diaries. On the basis of this information, multidimensional scaling analysis showed that a four-dimensional solution provided the best fit with the original data. These dimensions were labelled 'emotional involvement', 'group vs. individual activity', 'social isolation', and 'behavioural conformity'.

Altogether, the four studies reviewed in the preceding paragraphs illustrate the type of information provided by the dimensional analysis of situation cognition (cf. Amato & Saunders, 1985; Magnusson, 1974; Russell & Pratt, 1980; and R.B. Taylor, 1981, for further examples). Not surprisingly, the situational dimensions that emerge from the different studies differ as a function of the specific type of situation investigated. At the same time, however, there appears to be a common core to the perception of apparently very different kinds of situations, which refers to the intensity or involvement with which the person participates in the situation.

It is also interesting to note that few dimensions, such as 'group vs. individual activity', refer to the objective or physical features of situations. The vast majority of dimensions refer to the psychological properties of situational events rather than their physical aspects. This finding is partly due to the fact that the scales on which the situations are rated by the respondents, and which to some extent predetermine the subsequent interpretation of the dimensions, address the subjective meaning rather than the objective properties of situations. However, if these scales are selected on the basis of pilot data from independent subjects who are asked to list the characteristic features of the situations in question (e.g. Battistich & Thompson, 1980), then it is fair to conclude that people do, indeed, tend to interpret situations in subjective/psychological rather than objective/ physical terms.

Despite the outstanding importance assigned to the 'psychological situation' for the conceptualisation of cross-situational coherence, the modern interactionist approach to personality has so far devoted relatively few efforts to the task of developing a theoretical model of situation cognition, just as its empirical strategies are essentially limited to the assessment of global judgements of situational similarity. Even the more recent contributions reviewed in this chapter are, for the most part, directed at providing descriptive information about situation categories and dimensions without being linked to a theoretical framework containing structural hypotheses on the cognitive organisation of situational information. This deficit may be phrased more specifically in terms of two open questions:

1 What are the elements, or classes of elements, in the objective situation, which determine the subjective construction of situational meaning?

2 How do different modes of situation cognition affect the individual's construction of perceived situational similarities?

These unresolved issues imply a further question highlighting the need for a theory-guided approach to identifying subjective equivalence classes of situations which play an important part in the conceptualisation of cross-situational coherence:

3 To what extent do profiles of perceived situational similarity – derived from explicit models of situation cognition – correspond to profiles of behavioural similarity across different situations, whereby it is such intraindividual correspondence that is required as evidence for coherence in personality.

As became clear in the discussion of the modern interactionist approach and its empirical contributions in chapter 3, this currently prevailing paradigm in personality research offers no convincing solutions to these issues. Therefore, the search for theoretical models that might lend themselves to the analysis of situational meaning as a determinant of coherence has to turn to other psychological disciplines. Here, the field of social psychology appears as the most promising candidate, not least because of its many parallels with personality research regarding conceptual as well as empirical problems and attempts at their resolution (cf. chapter 1).

In the remainder of this chapter, three recent models of situation cognition developed in social psychology are discussed in terms of their potential applicability to the task of exploring the intraindividual covariation of situation cognition and behaviour proposed in the concept of coherence. These models, which can be regarded as the most prominent and best-supported theoretical approaches currently available, are based on

1 the concept of *social episodes* referring to the dimensional structure underlying the cognitive representation of everyday situations (Forgas, 1979a, 1982);

2 the concept of *situation prototypes* pertaining to the principles of categorisation of social situations (Cantor, 1981; Cantor, Mischel & Schwartz, 1982); and finally,

3 the concept of *cognitive scripts* referring to the dynamic interaction of situational knowledge and the cognitive processing of specific situations (Abelson, 1981).

The following discussion of the three approaches will be guided by the question of whether theoretical propositions as well as empirical strategies may be derived from each model which can be applied to the individual-centred analysis of the proposed covariation of situation cognition and behaviour.

The perception of social episodes

The concept of *social episodes* was introduced by Forgas (1979a; 1982) as a key concept in his analysis of the cognitive representation of everyday social situations. *Social episodes* are defined as 'cognitive representations of stereotypical interaction sequences which are representative of a given cultural environment' (Forgas, 1979a, 15). Since the terms 'social episodes' and 'social situations' are explicitly treated as interchangeable, one may read the work of Forgas as a theoretical perspective on the psychological situation as demanded by the modern interactionist perspective.

Episode cognition involves the individual's knowledge of the socially accepted rules and norms of appropriate behaviour in different interaction situations and the application of this knowledge to specific interpersonal encounters. The model postulates that a consensus exists within a cultural community on how to distinguish between different episodes as well as on the different norms and behavioural expectations pertaining to them, which are available to the individual members in the form of 'implicit knowledge structures'. It is this link between socio-cultural rules and their recognition as part of the individual's interpretation of the situation which constitutes the dual nature of social episodes: 'Social episodes may thus be on the one hand regarded as the building blocks of social life, and in this respect they exist independently of individuals [. . .] On the other hand, each and every individual has private, idiosyncratic cognitive representations about the stock of episodes practiced within his/her culture' (Forgas, 1982, 67).

The structural features by which the cognitive representation of situations is described also reflects the simultaneous operation of socio-cultural and individual determinants. In particular, seven features are listed by Forgas (1982, 60f.) to describe the properties of social episodes as cognitive structures:

1 *Complexity*, defined in terms of the number of aspects that distinguish an episode from others;

2 *Integration*, referring to the degree of dispersion or clustering of episodes in the episode space;

3 *Consensuality*, denoting the extent to which members of a cultural community agree in their perceptions of an episode;

4 *Level of abstraction*, distinguishing between episodes described in general terms and those referring to specific, concrete events;
5 *Rigidity of behavioural prescriptions*, implying that episodes differ in the extent to which they impose constraints on the person's behavioural options;
6 *Prototypicality*, referring to the representativeness of an episode with respect to the situational category to which it belongs; and, finally,
7 *Validity of definitional cues*, referring to the characterisation of episodes in terms of their salient cues which facilitate easy identification.

The cognitive structure of the proposed implicit situational knowledge is represented in the *episode space*. Therefore, the major empirical objective of the social episode approach lies in the modelling of consensual episode spaces to reveal the perceived patterns of relationship between different kinds of social encounters within a cultural milieu (Forgas, 1979a, 172). Thus, unlike the previous examples aimed at providing essentially ad hoc information about the dimensions of situation perception in various domains, the analysis of perceived dimensions of social episodes is based on an explicit definition of the situation and embedded into a specific theoretical framework. The so-called 'perceptual strategy' which is geared towards the task of modelling individual and consensual episode spaces involves five steps (cf. Forgas, 1979a, 116):[2]
1 The sampling of episodes which are representative of the subjects' daily interaction routines (e.g. by obtaining diary records over a certain period of time).
2 The selection of appropriate measures for tapping the subjects' perception and evaluation of the selected episodes (e.g. by presenting bipolar adjective scales on which each episode is rated and from which psychological distance measures between episodes can be derived).
3 The analysis of episode (dis-)similarities through multidimensional scaling procedures which facilitate the identification of central dimensions underlying the cognitive representation of different episodes and also provide the basis for developing descriptive taxonomies (cf. Forgas, 1979b).
4 The interpretation of the obtained statistical solutions which involves the labelling of the dimensions constituting the episode space. Typically, no more than four or at most five dimensions are found to be sufficient to represent the total range of situations studied.
5 The formulation and testing of hypotheses about differences in episode cognition between individuals and groups, as well as about potential determinants of the perception of social episodes.

The perceptual strategy has been applied in a variety of studies to explore

---

[2] The three other strategies distinguished by Forgas, i.e. the 'ecological', 'structural sequencing', and 'roles–rules' approaches, have generated far less empirical research than the perceptual approach.

the dimensional structure of episode cognition among different *social groups* (e.g. Forgas, 1976; 1978; 1981), with respect to different *types of situations* (e.g. Forgas, Brown & Menyhart, 1980, for aggressive episodes; Amato & Pearce, 1983, and Amato & Saunders, 1985, for helping and help-seeking episodes), as well as to investigate the *link between personal characteristics and episode cognition* (e.g. Forgas, 1983a, b).

The general empirical procedure for uncovering the dimensions of episode cognition is exemplified in the study by Forgas (1976) which compared the episode spaces for members of two cultural milieux, housewives and students. It was found that while the episode space of the housewives was best represented by a two-dimensional solution, a three-dimensional solution was most adequate for the student sample. The first two dimensions were highly similar for both groups and were interpreted as 'perceived intimacy and involvement' and 'subjective competence', respectively. The additional dimension obtained for the student sample was interpreted as a general evaluative, 'pleasant–unpleasant', dimension. A comparison of the dimensional location of select episodes revealed a further interesting result; activities involving socialising and entertainment outside the family context (e.g. 'having a drink with some friends in a pub') were strongly associated with feelings of incompetence for the housewives, while the same situations were closely linked to feelings of competence and self-confidence for the students.

Using a similar procedure, Forgas (1983a, b) found systematic differences in the cognitive representation of episode spaces due to individual differences on different personality and social skills measures. For example, subjects scoring high on personality measures of introversion and/or low on measures of assertiveness and social competence were shown by Forgas (1983a) to organise situational information predominantly in terms of the 'self-confidence' dimension. A different perceptual style emerged for subjects characterised as extraverted and 'high self-monitors' (Snyder, 1974) who tended to interpret situations mainly in terms of the 'pleasantness' and 'involvement' dimensions. When subjects were divided into a high and a low social skill group by Forgas (1983b) on the basis of multiple indices of social skills, it was found that a single dimension of 'social anxiety' dominated the episode representations of the low skill subjects. In contrast, for subjects in the high skill group the dimensions of 'evaluation' and 'intensity' played a much more central role.

In conclusion, research on the cognitive representation of social episodes joins the dimensional studies discussed earlier in this chapter by demonstrating that the interpretation of situational information is determined to a large extent by the psychological characteristics of the situations as opposed to their physical features. Moreover, the last set of studies in particular suggests that there are significant differences in the cognitive representation of situations as a function of specific personality characteristics. These findings clearly support the claim that the study of person–situation interaction can only be expected to yield meaningful results if these characteristic differences are taken into account both conceptually and empirically (cf. also Forgas, 1979a, chapter 9).

While significant contributions have been made towards understanding the consensual or group-specific interpretation of social episodes, the proposed importance of the idiosyncratic nature of episode cognition has received no attention in the available research. All the studies quoted above are based on single sets of situations and rating scales presented to subjects under the implicit assumption that they have the same meaning and relevance for the individuals involved. In contrast, the present approach argues in favour of an idiographic sampling of situations and bipolar attributes, thus implementing a research perspective Forgas proposed in programmatic terms:

> If we want to understand why a particular individual differentiates among social episodes in the way he does, we should begin by looking at his unique life environment, by sampling his 'representative' situations. The most important factors affecting episode perception are likely to reside in the perceiving individual.
> (Forgas, 1979a, 214)

In this vein, the concept of social episodes is adapted in the present research to the individual-centred analysis of the link between situation cognition and behaviour. The aim is to derive a concept-based measure of episode cognition which illuminates the principles underlying the cognitive construction of situational similarities and differences with regard to situations from each individual's personal experience.

Situations as cognitive prototypes

The social episodes model has been concerned primarily with the structural properties of episode cognition through exploring the dimensions underlying the cognitive representation of situations. In contrast, other approaches have been concerned with investigating the *functional* significance of the way in which situational information is cognitively organised. One line of research in this direction is based on the concept of *cognitive prototypes*, referring to the categorisation of social stimuli such as persons, trait-descriptive terms, and situations. Originally developed as a model of the classification of objects in natural language (Mervis & Rosch, 1981; Rosch, 1975; Rosch & Lloyd, 1978, the prototype approach was introduced into social psychology by Cantor & Mischel (1979a, b).

The central tenet of the prototype approach is that cognitive categories, rather than being discrete and mutually exclusive classes, are fuzzy sets with category membership being a function of the degree of similarity between a specific object and the category prototype. In contrast to traditional approaches to classification, the prototype approach regards category membership as a continuous (i.e. quantitive) rather than a dichotomous (i.e. qualitative) variable, insofar as objects may be identified as comparatively 'good' or 'bad' members of the category depending on their similarity to the category prototype. The prototype represents the 'best' or 'most typical' example of a category and is operationally defined in terms of consensual features lists (cf. Cantor 1981). This means that categories are no longer conceived of as discrete and disjunctive classes but as groupings of objects according to their 'family resemblance' (Wittgenstein, 1953) which result in 'fuzzy boundaries' because the less typical exemplars of the category share some of their characteristic features with objects of other 'object families'. The concept of *prototypicality* thus refers to the *degree* of category membership: the more features an object shares with the category prototype and the fewer features it shares with other categories, the higher its prototypicality with regard to the category under consideration.

The comparison of objects in terms of their prototypicality represents the horizontal level of analysis concerned with the internal structure of categories. The complementary vertical perspective is directed at the differentiation of categories at different levels of abstraction. At the highest ('superordinate') level, categories are easy to distinguish (i.e. best meet the criterion of external separation), yet due to the wide range of a superordinate category the similarity of individual members is relatively low (i.e. fails to meet the criterion of internal homogeneity). In contrast, at the lowest ('subordinate') level of abstraction internal homogeneity is high, yet the external separation of categories is problematic. A compromise between the two criteria is provided at the intermediate level of abstraction, somewhat misleadingly called 'basic level', at which categories are both sufficiently homogeneous and separable from each other (Dahlgren, 1985; Shaver, Schwartz, Kirson & O'Connor, 1987).

In a number of studies, the cognitive organisation of social stimuli in the form of prototypes was shown to facilitate the processing of information about objects and persons (cf. Mervis & Rosch, 1981, and Taylor & Crocker, 1981, for reviews). Prototypical objects were found to be associated more frequently with a given category label and recognised more rapidly than less prototypical stimuli (e.g. Brewer, Dull & Lui, 1981; Cohen, 1983). Prototype-consistent information about persons was recalled more accurately than prototype-inconsistent information and led to more differentiated as well as more confident impressions about the persons described (e.g. Cantor &

Mischel, 1979b; Cohen, 1981). Prototypes were also shown to function as a source of bias distorting individuals' perception of other people's behaviour in the direction of the prototype. Rush & Russell (1988) demonstrated that the availability of cognitive prototypes about leadership influenced individuals' descriptions of their supervisors' behaviour in such a way that persons sharing similar prototypic conceptions provided similar behavioural descriptions although they all interacted with a different supervisor. Furthermore, the prototype approach has recently been applied to the issue of behavioural prediction by Niedenthal, Cantor & Kihlstrom (1985). They obtained descriptions of the prototypical residents for certain types of student housing and demonstrated that individual choices of housing options could be predicted as a function of the extent to which the person's self-concept matched the self-concept attributed to the prototypical resident for the different types of housing.

There are only a few studies currently available which have applied the concept of *cognitive prototypes* to the analysis of social situations (Cantor, 1981; Cantor, Mischel & Schwartz, 1982; Eckes, 1986). Cantor, Mischel & Schwartz (1982) presented subjects with a taxonomy of four broad situation categories (social, cultural, stressful and ideological) specified at the three levels of superordinate, basic level and subordinate categories (e.g. 'being in a social situation' – 'being at a party' – 'being at a birthday party'). For each situation category, subjects generated lists of characteristic attributes from which the category prototypes – defined as consensual feature lists – were derived. Comparing the feature lists of different situations, the similarity between situation prototypes can be expressed by the ratio of shared to non-shared attributes in the respective feature lists. This procedure not only provides information about which situations are perceived as being similar to each other but also reveals the criteria, i.e. features, on which the similarity relationship is based. In support of the prototype model, Cantor et al. (1982) demonstrated that situations in each of the four broad classes of the taxonomy were regarded as significantly more similar to other situations within their class than to situations belonging to one of the remaining three general categories.

However, hardly any research is available on the issue of whether the facilitating functions quoted above for prototypes about persons can also be demonstrated for the processing of information about situations. Preliminary evidence suggesting a positive answer comes from a study by Schutte, Kenrick & Sadalla (1985). They constructed a prototypical and a non-prototypical description of each of three situations: in a park, in a bar, and in a job interview. Following the presentation of either set of descriptions, two dependent measures were obtained from the participants: (a) the accuracy with which they recollected the elements of the descriptions in a recognition task, and (b) their predictions of the likelihood that they would show each of a list of fifteen behaviours in each of the three situations described. The hypotheses were that compared to the non-prototypical group, subjects given the prototypical descriptions would (a) tend to falsely recognise highly typical elements *not* given in the original description and (b) show less variability in the range of behaviours which they predicted they would show in these situations. Both hypotheses received clear support from the data, suggesting that the cognitive organisation of situational stimuli as conceptualised in the prototype approach is, indeed, functionally linked to subsequent cognitive operations as well as predicted behavioural responses.

In order to apply the prototype approach to the development of an individual-centred measure of situation cognition which could then be utilised to assess the proposed coherence of situation cognition and behaviour, the current understanding and measurement of prototypes has to be modified. Since prototypes are typically defined in terms of consensual feature lists, a prototype measure of perceived situational similarity can yield valid information about an individual's perception of situations only to the extent that his or her understanding of the characteristic features of the situation is highly similar to the consensual feature list. By definition, non-consensual, i.e. idiosyncratic features are treated as irrelevant in the current version of the prototype approach and, accordingly, are excluded from the prototype. However, it is argued in the present conceptualisation of coherence that it is the subjective situation interpretation of the individual person which affects his or her behavioural patterns. In discussing their findings, Schutte, Kenrick & Sadalla speculated that the influence of situation prototypicality on individual behaviour is greater than revealed by their nomothetic measures of prototypicality: 'To the extent that individuals have idiosyncratic prototypes for situations, then a more idiographic assessment would perhaps result in more powerful effects for any given individual' (Schutte et al., 1985, 127; cf. Eckes, 1986, 159, for a similar point). In line with this reasoning, an individual-centred version of the prototype strategy is implemented in the present research, whereby both the situations and their characteristic features are sampled individually from each person. On this basis, perceived situational similarity may be operationalised in terms of the intraindividual overlap between the feature lists generated for different situations.

Cognitive scripts for situations

Another pertinent line of research exploring the functional significance of the cognitive organisation of situational information is based on the *script concept* (Abelson, 1981; Schank & Abelson, 1977). Cognitive scripts are defined as 'conceptual representations of stereotyped event sequences' (Abelson, 1981, 715), whereby the emphasis is on the dynamic flow of interpretations and inferences in the course of an interaction. The script model postulates that individuals acquire a specific knowledge of event sequences as a result of their experiences in different situations, which enables them to respond quickly and adequately to a situation and to make sense of the behaviour of their interaction partners. This scripted knowledge consists of structures that describe 'appropriate sequences of events in a particular context' (Schank & Abelson, 1977, 41). The basic elements of a script are single actions and events, with strong (as opposed to weak) scripts containing a fixed causal ordering of the different elements. A situation is translated into different scripts according to the role perspectives of the participants. The restaurant script, for example, consists of different elements for the waitress than for the customer. The interpretation of social situations on the basis of scripts entails two basic mechanisms of information processing; (1) the person has to identify the appropriate script applicable to the specific situation and (2) he or she must be able to infer missing information by retrieving stored situational experience. To facilitate the decision as to which script to retrieve from memory, it is proposed that scripts are identified by 'headers', the most essential or 'normative' elements are marked as 'pointers' and those actions of a specific script that are atypical with respect to the generic script are cognitively marked by a 'tag' (Graesser, Gordon & Sawyer, 1979).

Interruptions in the typical course of events within a script can occur in the form of 'interferences' or 'distractions'. Interferences are either external obstacles or interpretative errors by the person which prevent the script from proceeding in the usual way and require corrective action. Distractions typically take the form of unexpected events or actions which induce new goals in the person that carry him or her either temporarily or permanently out of the script (Schank & Abelson, 1977, 52). However, frequently occurring obstacles and mistakes are incorporated as ramifications into the scripted course of events so that usually the structure of scripts becomes more complex as the person gains more experience with the respective situation.

Empirical studies on the cognitive representations of scripted knowledge typically present subjects with sequences of events which they are later asked to reproduce from memory. In this way, it has been demonstrated that people not only show a strong tendency toward false recognition of non-mentioned, but highly typical events (Graesser, Wolls, Kowalski & Smith, 1980), but also tend to rearrange a distorted causal ordering of events when reproducing script-based stories (Bower, Black & Turner, 1979). These results support the basic tenet of the script model that individuals do not store the entire host of information characterising a situation, but confine themselves to only the most characteristic elements (including explicit memory of unusual events) from which the complete sequence of interaction may be reconstructed when required. Unlike the previous studies focussing on consensually shared scripts and their processing, Pryor & Merluzzi (1985, Study 4) investigated individual differences in the cognitive representation of scripted knowledge. They examined the question of whether a person's expertise with a particular script affects the complexity and efficiency of his or her processing of scripted activities. First, consensual scripts were established from two social interaction situations, 'getting a date' and 'going on a first date'. Comparing dating 'experts' and 'novices' they found that while both groups were able to rearrange a distorted sequential ordering of the actions in each of the two scripts, the experts were significantly faster in completing the task. Pryor & Merluzzi (1985, 375) interpret this result as suggesting that 'dating experts apparently found it easier than novices to use their cognitive representations of these scripted activities in imposing an organization upon a random sequence of events'. In personality research, the study by Dworkin & Goldfinger (1985) reported above (cf. p. 76) presents an example of how to apply the script concept to the analysis of individual differences in situation cognition. They asked their subjects to provide scripts for six situations differing in their range of affordances for social interaction. Subsequently, they content-analysed the listed elements in terms of the number of social vs. non-social attributes as well as the responents' anticipation of encountering the two types of affordances when entering the situation. They found that preference for social attributes was significantly correlated with personality measures of sociability.

The impact of cognitive scripts on behavioural intentions and actual behaviour was demonstrated in two studies by Anderson (1983) and Wilson & Capitman (1982). Both studies addressed the hypothesis that the activation of a script increases the likelihood that people will subsequently show script-consistent behaviour. Male subjects in the Wilson & Capitman (1982) study read a detailed version of a 'boy meets girl' script following which they displayed significantly more friendly behaviour towards a female confederate than subjects reading a control story. However, the effect was shown to hold only if the temporal distance between reading the script and interacting with the confederate was minimal. Anderson (1983) showed that imagining a behavioural script, such as donating blood or taking a new part-time job, increased the strength of the person's intention to actually perform the behaviour in question. Here, too, the effect was shown to hold only under specific conditions, namely when subjects imagined the script with themselves rather than another person as protagonists.

Despite these qualifications, it may be concluded from the last two studies that the cognitive availability of situations in the form of scripts is systematically linked to behavioural intentions and performance in those situations. Due to its dynamic nature, scripted knowledge specifies action rules for appropriate behaviour which the person can draw upon immediately as guidelines for behavioural decisions. Cross-situational coherence may thus be conceptualised as a function of the correspondence between 'scripts in understanding' and 'scripts in behaviour' across different situations (Abelson, 1981, 719).

In addressing the issue of the similarity between scripts, Abelson (1981) refers to the prototype approach. A script is considered as a basic category with the single events constituting the characteristic features of the script. Similarity between scripts is thus defined in terms of the number of characteristic actions and events shared by the scripts in question. Adopting this line of reasoning, the present research introduces an individual-centred application of the script approach in which perceived situational similarity is assessed on the basis of comparing the scripts generated by a person for different anxiety-provoking situations from his or her personal experience.

Implications for the present research

None of the three models of situation cognition discussed in the preceding sections was originally developed to address the issue of cross-situational coherence. However, they specify principles of perceived situational similarity which may be applied to this problem. Therefore, they are used in the present research to provide different measures of situation cognition which may than be correlated to behavioural similarities across situations.

Each model focuses on different aspects of the cognitive representation of situational experience. The social episodes model stresses the dimensionality of situation cognition which is reflected in the concept of 'episode space'. Empirical studies modelling the episode spaces of various social groups suggest that situations are represented in terms of the affective, emotional reactions they elicit rather than being characterised by a set of objective, observable characteristics or events. Situational similarity is conceptualised by the social episode model as a function of the dimensional structure underlying the cognitive representation of situational experience. Thus, a major empirical objective of the social episode approach is to identify and interpret the relevant attributes as well as dimensions which determine the psychological meaning of situations for the individual.

The prototype approach is primarily concerned with the aspect of situation categorisation. According to this model, situations are classified into natural, i.e. fuzzy categories based on a comparison of their characteristic features. Perceived situational similarity is regarded as a function of the amount of feature overlap between the respective situations. The emphasis is on how different situations within a given category (e.g. the category of anxiety-provoking situations) are related to one another, rather than on the different types of features (be they persons, objects, behaviours, norms, etc.) by which situations are characterised.

Unlike the prototype model, the script approach emphasises the importance of a particular class of features, namely characteristic actions and events, which define a situation. According to this view, the cognitive representation of situations in terms of causal and temporal sequences of events provides a frame of reference on which the person can rely in subsequent experiences of the same or similar situations. Accordingly, the script model is more concerned with specific elements of situation cognition and their causal and temporal ordering *within* the situation. At the same time, the issue of similarity *between* different situations is of less theoretical concern to the script approach. As an operational definition of similarity between scripts, the idea of feature overlap is adapted from the prototype model.

While the relevance of idiographic analyses of situation cognition is acknowledged in each of the three models, no systematic attempts have been made so far to apply the respective conceptual assumptions to the exploration of situation cognition at the level of the individual person. Therefore, the present research cannot build upon any previous work in its effort to derive concept-based models of situation cognition from the three models to be used in the individual-centred analysis of the correspondence between situation cognition and behaviour. However, at a more general methodological level, there is an increasing body of empirical research stressing the possibility and, indeed, necessity of combining nomothetic and idiographic principles in personality research generally and the search for consistency in particular. These contributions will be discussed in the next chapter with respect to their relevance to the development of an individual-centred methodology for the study of cross-situational coherence.

5   Individual-centred strategies in the search for consistency

While the modern interactionist approach may be regarded as the most prominent *conceptual* response to the challenge of the consistency concept in the late 1960s, another line of response has been directed to developing more adequate *methodological* strategies for demonstrating the cross-situational consistency of behaviour. In this vein, various approaches have been advanced within the nomothetic mainstream aiming to yield more conclusive empirical evidence of consistency.

One prominent strategy consists in the search for *moderator variables* which are supposed to influence the relationship between trait measures and behaviour. Initiated by the well-known study of Bem & Allen (1974), this line of research is guided by the aim to identify subgroups of persons, situations and traits that are characterised by typically high or low levels of behavioural consistency (cf. Baumeister & Tice, 1988; Koestner, Bernieri & Zuckerman, 1989; Paunonen, 1988; and Zuckerman et al., 1988, for recent examples). Furthermore, other authors have recently begun to examine the role of certain cognitive principles, such as the cognitive accessibility of attitudes and self-descriptive contents as moderators of consistency (e.g. Fazio & Williams, 1986). Thus, the identification of moderator variables serves an essential purpose in the attempt to overcome the shortcomings of traditional omnibus models of behaviour prediction by delineating specific types of individuals, traits and situations for which cross-situational consistencies may be expected (Ajzen, 1987).

A second nomothetic approach for providing more convincing evidence of consistency is based on the *principle of aggregation*. Proponents of this approach, most notably Epstein (1979, 1980, 1984), stress that the task of predicting behaviour on the basis of dispositional constructs can only be successful if multiple indices of behaviour are considered, i.e. if trait measures are related not to single instances of behaviour but to aggregated samples of behavioural criteria across time or different situations. Evidence of cross-situational consistencies between trait measures and aggregated behavioural patterns was found in a number of recent studies (e.g. Moskowitz, 1988; Rushton, Brainerd & Pressley, 1983; Rushton & Erdle,

1987). These findings suggest that while single instances of behaviour may be determined to a large extent by the specific features of the situation, stable behavioural patterns can be shown to exist as a function of personality disposition if behavioural acts are aggregated across a representative number of situations and occasions (cf. also Brody, 1988).

Finally, a third strategy aimed to improve the methodological prerequisites for demonstrating consistency relies on *peer ratings* as a source of information about a person's behavioural performance in different situations. The peer rating strategy is also committed to the principle of aggregation, but the focus is on increasing the sample of raters rather than the sample of behavioural criteria. Relying on informed raters, i.e people who are familiar with the persons under study and their characteristic ways of acting in various sections of their social environments, enables the investigators to go beyond self-report data and also to check their validity by comparing them to the data obtained from knowledgeable informants. In this way, evidence of consistency has been obtained by relating subjects' self-reports to information collected from spouses or roommates (e.g. Gormly, 1983; McCrae, 1982; Moskowitz & Schwartz, 1982; Woodruffe, 1984, 1985).

While each of these approaches has generated a large body of empirical evidence within the individual difference paradigm (cf. Krahé, in press for a comprehensive discussion) their relevance to the understanding of *intraindividual* patterns of consistency remains limited. This is true even for the moderator variable approach which in its emphasis on predicting individual differences in consistency sticks mainly to the analysis of data at group level. In contrast, other methodological developments, like the *act frequency approach* (Buss & Craik 1984) and the strategy of *template matching* (Bem, 1983a) are explicitly designed to lend themselves to both nomothetic *and* idiographic inquiry. A more radical perspective rejecting the nomothetic study of consistency is adopted by Lamiell (1982, 1987) in his *idiothetic approach*. Finally, there is a growing number of studies comparing the viability of nomothetic vs. idiographic measures for providing evidence of consistency in personality in a variety of domains. In the following sections, these methodological developments are reviewed as to their significance for the individual-centred conceptualisation and measurement of cross-situational coherence.

The act frequency approach

The conceptual basis of the act frequency approach advanced by Buss & Craik (e.g. 1980, 1981, 1983a, b, c, 1984, 1986, 1989) is the summary view of traits discussed in chapter 2. According to this view, traits are invoked as descriptive categories summarising a person's characteristic ways of acting the past. Applying a trait term, such as 'friendly', to a person thus reflects the observation that over a certain period of time or range of situations, that person has shown a relatively high number of behaviours covered by the term, i.e. a high frequency of friendly acts. At the same time, it involves the expectation that the person is likely to show an equally high frequency of trait-referent behaviours on future occasions. The act frequency approach postulates that a multiple-act index of past behaviours provides the appropriate basis for predicting behavioural trends within the respective trait category. From this conceptualisation of traits, two essential implications derive:

1 If traits are understood as summary labels for *categories* of behavioural acts, then the act frequency approach has to advance propositions about the internal category structure as well as the interrelationships among different categories.

2 If the ascription of a trait to a person means that the person's frequency of trait-referent behaviour is above the average level or 'norm', then this requires evidence of behavioural base rates for the respective trait category against which individual act trends may be compared.

To meet these requirements, the first step consists in establishing a comprehensive range of behavioural indicators representing the trait category in question. This is achieved through the strategy of 'act nominations' in which subjects are asked to list typical behaviours representing the trait category (e.g. typical instances of friendly behaviour).

To conceptualise the internal structure trait categories, Buss & Craik draw upon the prototype approach (cf. chapter 4) in suggesting that trait categories are 'fuzzy sets', with behavioural acts differing in terms of their typicality as members of the category. Some acts may belong to more than one trait category, while others are referents of only one trait (cf. also Borkenau, 1986). Thus, a trait category is composed of a set of behavioural acts, some of which are good (highly typical) and others poor (less typical) members of the category. Consensus among independent raters about the level of typicality is generally used as a criterion for the prototypicality of a given act with respect to the underlying category. In their internal structure, categories differ in terms of the number of behavioural acts they contain as well as the range of typicality covered by the different acts. As far as the relationship between different categories is concerned, two trait categories are regarded the more similar or closer to each other the higher the proportion of behavioural acts that they share in common.

The task of determining individual act trends as well as base rates against which they can be judged is facilitated by the fact that frequency tallies of overt behaviours have an absolute zero point, namely when no trait-referent behaviours are shown during the specified period of observation. By providing an absolute metric for establishing the strength of an act trend, the act frequency approach lends itself to three different modes of analysis:

1 It may be applied to the study of 'modal human tendencies' where different groups of people are compared in terms of the absolute frequency with which they display trait-referent acts. Thus, it is possible to address questions like 'Is the average act trend for friendly behaviour higher for females than for males?'

2 Within defined groups, act trends provide information about individual differences in that they allow one to determine a person's act trend, as well as its stability over time, relative to that of other members of the group.

3 Finally, in an idiographic mode of analysis, the absolute frequencies of an individual's trait-referent behaviours at different times or in different situations may be interpreted as an idiographic index of temporal or cross-situational stability without having to resort to sample-based information about relative act frequencies (cf. Buss, 1985).

The sequence of empirical steps involved in the act frequency approach is illustrated in an early study by Buss & Craik (1980) exploring the category of dominant acts. The aim was to demonstrate that act trends composed of multiple criteria for dominant behaviour can be successfully predicted by traditional trait measures of dominance, provided that the selected behavioural criteria are typical examples of the category of dominant behaviours. In two pilot studies, a sample of 100 dominant acts was generated through the 'act nomination strategy' mentioned above and rated by an independent group of raters in terms of the typicality and social desirability of each act. Subjects participating in the main study received the following instruments:

(a) the dominance scales from two standard personality inventories, the California Psychological Inventory (CPI; Gough, 1957) and the Personality Research Form (PRF; Jackson, 1967);

(b) the total list of 100 dominant acts whereby they were asked to indicate whether or not they had ever performed each of the behaviours, and, if so, how frequently they had performed it in the past;

(c) a global self-rating scale of dominance.

In order to explore the link between the trait measures of dominance and the corresponding act trends, correlations were first computed for each of the 100 acts between the reported act performance as well as frequency and the three traditional trait measures (CPI, PRF and global rating) of dominance. These correlations were in the range of $r = .10$ and $r = .20$, indicating that trait measures of dominance are poor predictors of single dominant acts. In a subsequent analysis, the protypicality ratings elicited in the second pilot study were used to divide the total set of dominant acts into four categories of typicality, whereby the first and last categories comprised the twenty-five most and least typical acts, respectively. Thus, each category provided a multiple act criterion of dominant behaviour, with the different categories representing different levels of typicality of this criterion. By correlating the three traditional measures of dominance with the multiple act trend for each category, it was found that both the CPI and PRF scores were significantly and substantially correlated with the act trend in the category comprising the most typical dominant acts. A linear decrease in the magnitude of correlation coefficients was found as act categories became less typical.

In conjunction with later studies exploring other personality domains (e.g. Buss, 1984; Buss & Craik, 1981), these findings underline two central points. The first is that multiple act trends can be more accurately explained by standard personality measures than single acts, a conclusion that is well in line with the principle of aggregation described above. The second is more peculiar to the act frequency approach, namely that the typicality of the acts chosen to represent a trait category critically determines the success of behavioural predictions. By providing an explicit rationale as well as empirical strategy for establishing the typicality of trait-referent behaviours, the act frequency makes an important contribution to improving the strength of behavioural predictions based on trait measures.

While the Buss & Craik (1980) study illustrates how the act frequency approach may be applied to the (nomothetic) study of individual differences, no empirical work is as yet available which examines its applicability to the (idiographic) study of intraindividual regularities. So far, the authors have confined themselves to general strategies for 'individualising dispositional assessment' by means of the act frequency approach (Buss & Craik, 1984, 280ff.).

The most straightforward application in the service of idiographic inquiry has already been mentioned, namely the recording of act trends for individual persons over time as well as situations. On the basis of such idiographic data patterns it becomes possible to establish individual base rates against which act trends observed in particular 'critical' situations or periods of time may be assessed. Apart from exploring the strength of an act trend, this strategy is also informative, at a descriptive level, of the specific kinds of acts characterising the person under study. It could thus be discovered, for instance, that two individuals who show the same overall act trend for the domain of friendliness, differ substantially with regard to the specific acts of which this trend is composed.

However, from a strictly idiographic point of view the previous strategy suffers from the problem that the behaviours which are counted in the act frequency tallies are nomothetically determined, i.e. selected on the basis of an interindividual consensus about their meaning as well as typicality. In principle, this problem, however, can be resolved by leaving both act nomination and typicality ratings to the individual. Subjects could be asked to sort their behavioural performances in a specified situation or period of time into subjectively appropriate categories as well as rate the different acts for prototypicality according to their own, possibly idiosyncratic, criteria. According to Buss & Craik, 'an ultimate step would be to enlist the individual in segmenting his or her monitored stream of behaviour [. . .] as well as generating categories of acts from it' (1984, 282). As appealing as these suggestions for an idiographic application of the act frequency approach are at a programmatic level, it remains to be seen whether they will eventually prove feasible in empirical research on the consistency of individual act trends across situations.

The template matching approach

The template matching technique advanced by Bem and his associates (Bem, 1983a; Bem & Funder, 1978; Bem & Lord, 1979) is a methodological strategy that reflects the authors' commitment to an interactionist understanding of personality. They claim that in order to understand the interplay between personal and situational determinants of behaviour, it is essential that both person and situation variables become part of a common methodological framework within which they can be studied in relation to each other. The general idea is that regularities in individual behaviour may be conceptualised and explained as a function of the match between the characteristics of the person and those of the situation. Accordingly, what is envisaged by the template matching approach is a strategy for describing persons which also lends itself in the same way to the description of situations.

The general issue which the template matching technique seeks to address may be stated as follows: a given situation typically provides various behavioural alternatives, and the crucial task is to predict which of these alternatives the person will actually choose to perform. In order to solve this task, a two-step procedure is suggested:

1 First, each behavioural alternative is linked to a *template* describing the personality of the hypothetical 'ideal' individual most likely to show that behaviour in the situation. For example, this would involve construing the template, i.e. idealised personality description, of somebody who would typically prefer sociable leisure activities to solitary ones or of the typical person showing dominant as opposed to submissive behaviours in interactions with same-sex peers.

2 In order to predict the behaviour of concrete individuals, personality descriptions of these individuals are obtained and compared with the different templates. The idea is that the person will show the behaviour associated

with the template that corresponds most closely to his or her personality profile. Thus, a person is expected to show dominant behaviours in interactions with same-sex peers to the extent that his or her personality profiles resembles the template corresponding to that behavioural alternative.

For the match between individual personalities and templates to be determined and expressed in quantitative terms in a diverse range of situations, a descriptive instrument is required which can be applied in the same way to hypothetical as well as real persons in relation to a variety of situations. To serve this purpose,

– the descriptive language itself must not be situation-specific or specific to certain trait domains;

– the instrument must be person-centred rather than variable-centred, i.e provide information about the relative importance of personality character-istics within the person rather than about the relative standing of different persons on that characteristic. (This means, for instance, that one would want to know whether 'behaving in a dominant fashion in interacting with same-sex peers' is more characteristic of the person than 'the wish to be liked by others' rather than knowing whether 'behaving in a dominant fashion' is more characterisic of person A than of person B.);

– finally, the instrument must facilitate direct comparisons between two persons, two templates, or a person and a template.

The Q-sort technique first introduced by Butler & Haigh (1954) is a well-established method that meets these requirements, and it has therefore been used in a variety of studies based on the template matching approach. Bem and his colleagues have chosen the California Q-sort, a version constructed by Block (1961), which consists of 100 descriptive personality statements. The standard procedure for the use of Q-sorts asks the subject to sort these statements into nine categories reflecting the extent to which the statements are true for the person's real self as well as ideal self. In this sorting, subjects are typically required to stick to a fixed frequency distribution, so that fewer statements may be sorted in the highly characteristic and uncharacteristic categories than into the intermediate categories. This particular feature of the Q-sort technique results in formally equivalent distributions obtained under different instructions which allow, for example, comparison of self vs. ideal self Q-sorts in terms of the magnitude and the nature of discrepancies between the two.

In template matching, the Q-sort technique is used to elicit both the personality descriptions of the actual subjects and the templates associated with the different behavioural patterns. The former may be obtained either through self-ratings or through peer-ratings. To arrive at the templates pertaining to a given situation, three strategies have been explored so far:

1 Deriving templates from existing data on the relationship between

personality and behaviour in the area under investigation. This approach was illustrated by Bem & Funder (1978) who studied children's behaviour in a situation involving delay of gratification. Apart from recording delay times, Q-sorts for each child were obtained from his or her parents. The templates were constructed by dividing the total sample into long- and short-delaying boys and girls and then collapsing the individual Q-sorts across the members of each group to obtain an average or typical profile of the short- and long-delaying child (cf. Bem & Funder, 1978, 491, for procedural details). The extent to which each child's personal Q-sort is correlated with the template pertaining to his or her group represents the criterion for evaluating the validity of the template matching strategy.

2 A second way of arriving at the templates characterising different responses to a situation is to ask observers to provide Q-sorts for the typical person showing the behaviour in question. The feasibility of this strategy was demonstrated by Bem & Lord (1979). They presented observers with a description of the 'Prisoner's Dilemma Game' and asked them to provide Q-sorts for the typical subject pursuing each of three strategies: maximising the joint gain of both players, maximising his or her absolute gain, and maximising his or her own relative gain. The resulting three templates were then correlated with the Q-sorts obtained from the roommates of participants in an actual Prisoner's Dilemma Game who had followed one of the different strategies. It was found that the individual Q-sorts correlated significantly higher with the templates pertaining to the strategy actually chosen by the person than with the templates pertaining to the two remaining strategies. Adopting a similar reasoning, Niedenthal, Cantor & Kihlstrom (1985) suggested that university students' choices between different housing options may be predicted on the basis of the extent to which the person's self-concept matches that of the prototypical resident in the respective option.

3 A final strategy for defining templates characteristic of a particular situation is to draw upon formal psychological theories. Bem & Funder (1978) provide an example of this strategy applied to forced-compliance situations. They asked a dissonance theorist, a self-perception theorist, and a self-presentation theorist to construct, from their theoretical points of view, templates (i.e. Q-sorts) of the hypothetical persons most likely to show attitude change under forced-compliance conditions. These templates were compared to the Q-sorts as well as attitude change scores obtained from participants in a forced-compliance experiment. The extent to which the similarity of individual Q-sorts with the different theory-specific templates is correlated with the actual attitude change scores indicates the success of each theory in predicting behaviour. The results show that dissonance theory did worst and self-presentation theory did best in this comparison (cf. Funder, 1982, for a conceptual extension of this study).

From what has been said so far, it is clear that the template matching technique facilitates behavioural predictions at both individual and group level. In a study which is directly relevant to the present research, Lord (1982) has offered a comparative analysis of a nomothetic and an idiographic version of the template matching technique applied to the domain of conscientious behaviour. His study was designed to test the hypothesis that persons will consistently show conscientious behaviours in a variety of situations to the extent that the situations involved are perceived as similar. To test this proposition, he employed four different indices of perceived situational similarity:

(a) direct ratings of the extent to which situations were perceived as similar;

(b) goal satisfaction similarities, referring to the extent to which situations were perceived as being instrumental in attaining an important goal in each situation;

(c) self–template similarities, based on the correlations between situation-specific templates and Q-sorts for the individual subject, whereby behaviour was expected to be consistent to the degree that self–template correlations were similar in the situations involved; and finally,

(d) template–template similarities, defining situational similarity in terms of the overlap of the templates pertaining to the respective situations.

Each of these similarity indices was related to a set of behavioural criteria for conscientiousness in an idiographic and nomothetic mode of analysis, whereby the nomothetic measures were obtained by collapsing individual similarity data across subjects. The results show that the idiographic measures of consistency, i.e. correspondence between perceived and behavioural similarities, were substantially higher than the nomothetic measures. This was true, in particular, for the self–template and template–template measures of perceived situational similarity, suggesting that the template matching strategy is, indeed, a promising approach for demonstrating cross-situational regularities at the level of the individual person.

However, the studies reviewed so far suffer from the problem that they are limited to a mechanistic understanding of person–situation interaction. Personality descriptions as provided by the Q-sorts are elicited in global, context-free terms, and it is only afterwards that they are related to the situation-specific templates. The extended strategy of *contextual template matching* proposed by Bem (1983a) is designed to address this shortcoming. The new feature of this version is a set of descriptive attributes referring to situations (S-set) which is formally equivalent to the attributes of the Q-set. Just as the typical Q-sort consists in describing a person through the attributes of the Q-set, the S-sort consists in describing a situation in terms of the attributes of the S-set. Once the characteristic features of a situation have been established in this way (usually through multiple raters), person-related

Q-sorts may be obtained with direct reference to the situational properties. This is done by presenting subjects (or informed others) with the list of relevant S-features and ask them to provide a Q-sort for the person with respect to each successive element of the S-set. Thus, each Q-item is judged in terms of whether it is characteristic of the person being studied in a situation having the described feature. By collapsing these Q-sorts over all S-items, a situation-specific Q-sort for the person is obtained.

In a first test, the contextual template matching technique was applied to a reanalysis of the Bem & Funder study of forced-compliance situations described above. It could be shown that significantly better behavioural predictions were achieved on the basis of a contextual matching of individual characteristics and templates, leading Bem to conclude; 'Contextual template matching, then, implements a stronger version of interactionist thinking. It does not simply add together person information and situation information independently, but rather treats the person-in-context as the fundamental unit of analysis' (1983a, 211). However, apart from the obviously very time-consuming nature of this strategy, a potentially serious conceptual problem remains. This is that in contextual template matching, a situation is first split up into single features and then 're-synthesised' into a global situation profile after the situation-specific Q-sorts have been obtained. Such a procedure is based on the problematic assumption that there is a simple additive relationship between the characteristic features of a situation and leaves no room for taking more complex interdependencies between situation features into account.

In conclusion, the template matching technique provides a flexible language for describing both the person and the situation which facilitates behavioural predictions at an intraindividual as well as an interindividual level of analysis. Like the act frequency approach, it is currently no more than an empirical strategy for discovering consistency, without being embedded in a specific theoretical network. Nevertheless, the two approaches make a significant contribution to personality psychology, particularly because they open up feasible ways of combining both nomothetic and idiographic objectives into a common methodological framework. This perspective is pursued even more rigorously in the work considered in the next section.

The idiothetic approach

The very name of this approach contains, in a nutshell, Lamiell's (1981, 1982, 1987) argument for a perspective on personality which combines the principles of *idio*-graphic measurement with the search for nomo-*thetic* knowledge about personality functioning. His work can be regarded as one of the most prominent albeit deliberately controversial contributions recently made to the field of personality. As Lamiell states at the outset of his latest and most comprehensive account of the idiothetic model, 'much of what I have to say is wholly antithetical to what are, at least to those who answer to the appellation of "personality psychologist", deeply entrenched beliefs' (1987, xvi; cf. also Ross, 1987).

To clarify the epistemological foundations of his approach, Lamiell goes back to the fundamental distinction between *differential psychology* aimed at exploring individual differences with respect to specific personality constructs such as traits, and *personality psychology*, which concentrates on investigating issues of personality structure and development at the level of the individual. He argues that the failure to observe this basic distinction is responsible for the profound crisis in which the field of personality has found itself over much of its recent history. In particular, the argument is that the perennial issue of consistency in individual behaviour, which is essentially a problem of personality psychology, has traditionally been approached through the methods of the individual difference paradigm, leading Lamiell to conclude: 'Knowledge of the sort contained in the empirical findings generated by individual difference research is therefore ill-suited to the task of advancing a theory of personality, however useful the same knowledge may be for other purposes' (1986, 4).

On the basis of this critique, the thrust of Lamiell's argument is directed at highlighting the need for an alternative paradigm for uncovering temporal as well as cross-situational regularities in individual behaviour. Such a paradigm should combine idiographic methods of analysis with the elaboration of general principles of personality:

> The key to any such reconciliation lies in the fact that there is nothing in the search for general principles of personality which logically requires that the status of an individual on a given attribute be defined relative to the measured status of others on the same attribute.
> (Lamiell, 1981, 285)

Thus rejecting individual rank orders as a source of information about single members of a sample, the idiothetic approach is faced, first and foremost, with the task of finding a new frame of reference which would allow one to interpret any pattern of individual behaviour as a weak, average or strong manifestation of an underlying personality characteristic. In the idiothetic model, such a frame of reference is provided by the total range of trait-referent behaviours that the person could, in principle, have chosen to perform. Thus, individual behaviour is interpreted against the standard of what the person could have done, not against the standard of what other people decided to do in the same situation. As an empirical research strategy, this understanding of trait-referent behaviour involves the following steps:

1 For each domain to be studied, a comprehensive list of possible behavioural

options has to be collected. The total number of options contained in this list determines the maximum strength or extremity with which individuals may manifest the underlying attribute in their behaviour. The extent to which a person is characterised by the personality attribute in question depends on how many out of the total range of behavioural indicators he or she performs over a specific period of observation or range of situations. It is clear, though, that the maximum score that can possibly be assigned to an individual is defined by the constraints of this sampling procedure.

2 Not all behaviours thus sampled will be equally central or pertinent to the domain in question. Therefore, an index of relevance applicable to each behavioural item is required which can be used as a weighting factor. Lamiell's preferred strategy here is to have all behavioural items judged in terms of their similarity and subsequently subject them to multidimensional scaling. In this way, the coordinates of each behaviour on the underlying dimension(s) can be used as indicators of its relevance to the domain.

3 Behavioural reports are then obtained from the subject for each of the items representing the domain. In their most straightforward form, these reports take the form of 'yes/no' responses to the question of whether the person has shown that behaviour in a certain period of time.[1]

4 On the basis of these behaviour reports the strength of the behavioural performance and, by implication, the strength of the underlying attribute, is expressed through the ratio between the actual number of behaviours performed and the maximum number of behaviours the person could possibly have performed, whereby the relevance weights attached to each behavioural criterion are taken into account on each side of the ratio (cf. Lamiell, 1982).

In this way, both cross-situational consistency and temporal stability can be conceptualised and measured by comparing the relative strength of behavioural tendencies shown in two or more situations. Such a procedure, shown to be feasible in a study by Lamiell, Trierweiler & Foss (1983), offers an empirical assessment of individual patterns of behaviour which is at the same time informative about the single person and – through aggregation across

---

[1] In its use of multiple act criteria and frequency counts as indicators of the strength of a given personality characteristic, the idiothetic model bears a resemblance to the idiographic version of the 'act frequency approach'. Both approaches interpret the frequency with which an individual exhibits certain behaviours as evidence of the strength of a corresponding disposition. However, they differ in two respects: First, the relevance of single behaviours for the domain in question is determined by typicality ratings in the act frequency approach, whereas judgements of similarity and multidimensional scaling are used in the idiothetic model. As Buss & Craik (1984) are right in pointing out, the latter procedure suffers from the fact that behaviours can be highly similar while being at the same time equally peripheral to the domain in question. The second difference concerns the conceptual status of the personality attributes of which behaviour is assumed to be indicative. Whereas the act frequency approach explicitly adheres to the summary view of traits, the conceptual links between the idiothetic approach and the trait model are less clearly spelled out.

persons – about the validity of general hypotheses on consistency and stability in personality.

The potential application of the idiothetic approach to the study of dynamic person–situation interaction is briefly described by Lamiell (1982). Like the template matching strategy, idiothetic analysis claims to provide a framework in which both the person and the situation are simultaneously considered. At a theoretical level, it is the concept of the 'psychological situation' which corresponds most closely to this objective. From the viewpoint of the idiothetic model, 'a *psychological situation* is defined as an *interval of time* (not necessarily a physical location) during which certain concepts dominate the perception and construal of one's alternative possibilities for action' (Lamiell, 1982, 56). This perspective suggests that personality variables are conceived of not in terms of stable traits but rather in terms of 'mediating cognitive processes' as postulated by modern interactionism.

In their empirical applications of the idiothetic model, Lamiell and his associates have so far concentrated on the question of whether impression formation by naive or 'intuitive' observers actually follows the principles laid down in the idiothetic model, i.e. proceeds along the lines of a 'personal qualities' as opposed to an 'individual difference' approach. More specifically, they argue that the reasoning strategy proposed by the idiothetic model is *dialectical* in nature. This means that observers contrast their observations of others' behaviour with mental negations of those observations (e.g. 'what would the conclusion be if the person had not shown this behaviour?'). In a series of studies, Lamiell and his colleagues (e.g. Lamiell, 1982, Lamiell, Foss, Larsen & Hempel, 1983; Lamiell, Foss, Trierweiler & Leffel, 1983) have shown that personality judgements made by naive observers can, in fact, be attributed to their reliance on dialectical reasoning (cf., however, Conger, 1983, and Woody, 1983, for critical assessments). In contrast, traditional personality research is described as being inappropriately based on a *demonstrative* reasoning strategy whereby observations of one person are compared with and interpreted in relation to observations of other persons' behaviour. This discrepancy in the reasoning strategies underlying intuitive and scientific models of personality is held responsible for the persistence of the consistency paradox. According to Lamiell and his co-workers, therefore, the paradox could eventually be resolved if scientific researchers of personality finally recognised the need to adopt dialectical reasoning as their general methodological rationale.

It is not surprising that a view as provocative as the idiothetic perspective has soon been challenged by members of the nomothetic mainstream, as have been the empirical findings invoked for its support. The most radical rejection comes from Paunonen & Jackson (1986) who identify three deficiencies associated with the way in which behavioural tendencies are conceptualised and compared in the idiothetic model. Firstly, they show that the absolute differences in the behavioural tendencies observed in different situations are not invariant towards changes in the sequence of the situations thus compared. The second objection is that there is no need for idiographic indices of consistency and stability, since corresponding nomo-thetic indices produce almost identical results while avoiding the problems associated with the former. To substantiate this point, they demonstrate in a simulation study that the correlation between the two types of indices is $r = .94$. Paunonen & Jackson's third objection is that idiothetically defined behavioural tendencies fail to give proper consideration to the fact that different behavioural criteria (e.g. instances of verbal vs. physical aggression) may have very different base rates, thus precluding their combination into a single index of the strength of behavioural manifestations.

In responding to these criticisms, Lamiell & Trierweiler (1986) accept some of the points pertaining to their empirical procedure. Yet, they argue that the overall objective of the idiothetic approach is neither properly appreciated by Paunonen & Jackson nor in any way seriously compromised by their criticisms.

In conclusion, the idiothetic approach represents an ambitious pro-gramme for a thorough revision of the traditional foundations of (nomothe-tic) personality measurement. It challenges the appropriateness of the individual difference paradigm for understanding regularities in individual behaviour that would be supportive of the notion of consistency in personality. Instead, a new frame of reference for defining and assessing the strength of individual behavioural tendencies is introduced which interprets manifest behaviour against the potential minimum and maximum levels of behavioural performance and thus presents a rationale which does not rely on comparisons between persons. Compared to its innovative force at a conceptual and methodological level, the specific empirical procedures that have so far been offered as part of the idiothetic approach are far less convincing. As the critique by Paunonen & Jackson has demonstrated, the present ways of defining and computing indices of stability and consistency suffer from various shortcomings which do not make them recommendable for the purposes of empirical research. Thus, the contribution made by the idiothetic approach clearly lies in its presentation of a new outline for an individual-centred analysis of consistency rather than its specific suggestions for translating this outline into empirical research strategies.

Comparing idiographic and nomothetic measures of consistency

The three methodological approaches discussed in the previous sections may be viewed as indications of a change of heart in contemporary personality psychology in favour of lifting the ban on idiographic thinking and research as well as recognising its potential for a better understanding of the regularities in individual behaviour (cf. also Pervin, 1984a; Runyan, 1983). This development is reflected in the increasing number of studies aimed at providing comparative analyses of idiographic and nomothetic strategies in the study of behavioural consistencies. These studies address a variety of personality domains yet are linked together by the aim of determining empirically whether the search for cross-situational consistency requires an idiographic exploration of individual data patterns or whether information aggregated across individuals furnishes a more adequate basis for testing the consistency hypothesis. One study pertaining to this issue, conducted by Lord (1982), has already been discussed in connection with the template matching approach earlier in this chapter. Lord compared different indices of perceived situational similarity in terms of their relationship with patterns of behavioural similarity in the domain of conscientiousness, creating both a nomothetic and an idiographic version of each measure. Across the four indices, he found that the idiographic measures typically produced higher levels of consistency between perceived and behavioural similarity than the nomothetic measures. In a related vein, Klirs & Revelle (1986) showed that the number of subjects for whom significant correlations were found between perceived situational similarity and reported behavioural variability in four trait domains was highest in the idiographic mode of analysis, followed by a combined idiographic/nomothetic index of consistency and a purely nomo-thetic measure. Examining the consistency of coping with daily hassles, Dolan & White (1988) also demonstrated that intraindividual indices of coping reveal significantly higher levels of consistency than coefficients based on the aggregation of coping patterns across subjects.

A strong case for the simultaneous pursuance of idiographic and nomothetic goals is stated by Zevon & Tellegen (1982) who investigated the individual structure of mood ratings over time. They asked subjects to complete daily mood protocols over a period of ninety days and subsequently factor analysed the protocols individually for each participant to explore the structural organisation of mood. These analyses revealed that the two a priori postulated factors, positive and negative mood, were confirmed for the large majority of subjects. Moreover, the individual factor solutions showed a high degree of congruence with a composite factor solution based on the aggregation of factor loadings across subjects. However, the potential of an idiographic complement to nomothetic applications of factor analyses of mood states is best illustrated with respect to those three subjects for whom the expected two-factor solution could not be confirmed. First, it is only due to the idiographic approach adopted by Zevon & Tellegen that these individuals were identified instead of simply contributing to error variance in the group data. Second, the search for explanations of why the data patterns of these subjects fail to go along with the majority of respondents is a potentially fruitful way of illuminating the psychological principles underlying the structure of mood change. In the Zevon & Tellegen study, the authors were prompted to examine whether the members of their sample had shared a semantic consensus on the interpretation of the mood adjectives used in the protocols. In fact, an adjective-sorting task checking whether subjects' categorisations of the mood adjectives corresponded to the a priori classification underlying the mood protocols confirmed that two of the 'deviating' subjects had interpreted the mood adjectives in an idiosyncratic way. Thus, the idiographic analysis of mood protocols not only facilitated the identification of exceptions to the general pattern of a two-factor solution; it also suggested a more thorough analysis of the causes of these exceptions which proved fruitful for interpreting the obtained data as a whole. This study, the authors claim, thus illustrates that 'scientific idiography can be a crucial way station to nomothetic description' (Zevon & Tellegen 1982, 121).

The benefits of combining idiographic and nomothetic measures of personality variables are further illustrated by Hermans (1988). He introduces the concept of 'valuation' referring to the personal meaning assigned by the individual to the experiences encountered in his or her life. While valuation is an idiographic concept inasmuch as it refers to the unique life situation of the person, Hermans argues that affective responses associated with those valuations may be described in a nomothetic fashion since there is a common range of affective states with which people respond to events in their lives. In the technique of 'self-confrontation', subjects are requested to generate a list of valuations from their previous experience and subsequently rate each valuation in terms of a number of affective responses. On the basis of these data, it is possible to carry out idiographic comparisons of the affect profiles pertaining to different valuations named by the person or to the same valuation at different data points. At the same time, individual patterns may be assessed against standard patterns (e.g. the typical 'winner' or 'loser' experience) to arrive at information about whether a person's valuation system contains experiences that are associated with similar affective profiles as those associated with the standard. Thus, Hermans found, for example, that the majority of subjects had named valuations that were associated with the affective responses characteristic of the winning and the losing pattern, yet the contents of those valuations were essentially idiosyncratic. In conclusion, he points out that 'each valuation can be studied within three frames of reference: other people, the person at the present moment, and the person at a preceding moment in time. These three frames of reference are seen as mutually complementary in the biographical study of the individual' (Hermans, 1988, 807).

Chaplin & Buckner (1988) approached the issue of the relationship between nomothetic and idiographic personality measurement from a different angle. They conducted a series of studies aimed to uncover the nature of the standards of comparison invoked by persons in self-ratings of their personal characteristics. Subjects were instructed to rate themselves on a variety of personality attributes adopting three different standards of comparison:

(a) a *normative* standard, requiring them to rate themselves compared to other people of their age and sex;

(b) an *ipsative* standard, whereby they were asked to rate their standing on a particular attribute relative to their standing on other personality attributes; and finally,

(c) an *idiothetic* standard, instructing subjects to rate their average standing on a given trait relative to the possible minimum and maximum of trait-referent behaviours.

Each of these standards was related to subjects' *implicit* self-ratings on the same attributes, i.e. ratings for which no explicit standard was prescribed and which could thus be assumed to reflect subjects' intuitive standards in evaluating their personality characteristics.

These analyses revealed, across three independent studies, that there was a small but consistent tendency for ratings based on normative standards to be less similar to implicit self-ratings than ratings based on the ipsative and idiothetic standards. At the same time, the authors report that each of the three standards was most closely related to implicit self-ratings for a certain number of subjects. This finding illustrates that individuals differ in terms of the standards which they employ when asked to make personality ratings of themselves and, possibly, others, casting doubt on the (mostly tacit) assumption that laypersons rely on the nomothetic standard underlying traditional psychometrics in their ratings of personality.

The previous studies comparing idiographic and nomothetic measures have provided evidence of a significant, though numerically small superiority of individual-centred modes of analysis in the measurement of personality and cross-situational consistency. A more pessimistic note is struck by Asendorpf (1988) about the feasibility of enriching nomothetic procedures by taking idiographic information into account. He conducted a study on the relationship between different behavioural indicators of shyness and dispositional ratings of shyness by self and peers which revealed stable individual differences in subjects' typical behavioural manifestations of shyness. Some subjects, for instance, consistently showed gaze aversion when interacting with strangers and persons in authority, while others responded to these situations with pauses in speech. This finding suggested creating an index of consistency based on these idiosyncratic response patterns by selecting each person's most typical response as a predictor of dispositional shyness ratings. Yet, when trait-behaviour consistency was examined by relating behavioural profiles to trait ratings of the subjects' shyness by themselves and observers, no support was found for the empirical superiority of this 'salient response' index over nomothetically defined criteria (either by aggregating across response modes or by selecting the single most valid response for the sample as a whole). To explain these findings, Asendorpf argues that measurements of behavioural manifestation of latent dispositions are potentially subject to at least three errors: lack of reliability due to unsystematic errors, a systematic error due to selecting less valid trait indicators and a 'nomothetic' error due to ignoring differential preferences for certain behavioural indicators by the subjects. If behavioural measurement is about equally liable to each of the three sources of error, the potential benefit of avoiding the nomothetic error by selecting each subject's most salient response is likely to be wiped out through the simultaneous increase in the effect of remaining sources, e.g. decrease in reliability due to considering just one behavioural act. Thus, Asendorpf (1988, 165) concludes: 'As convincing as the call for more respect for the individual case may be from a theoretical stance, it is difficult to realize with real behavioural data for real people in real situations.'

A much more rigorous position is adopted by Paunonen & Jackson (1985) who altogether reject the idea that idiographic approaches in personality measurement have anything to offer in terms of alternative strategies for discovering consistency. Essentially, their argument is that nomothetic measures provide explanations and predictions of behaviour which are just as good and often show strong agreement with corresponding idiographic indices. The reason why nomothetic research strategies should be preferred, according to Paunonen & Jackson, lies in the fact that they are more generally applicable and allow wider generalisations than idiographic analyses.

However, this argument suffers from two problems. Firstly, it is based on the assumption that nomothetic and idiographic approaches are by their very nature irreconcilable, a view that bars the way to a constructive combination of both perspectives advocated by an increasing number of personality theorists (e.g. Brody, 1988; Lamiell, 1981; Pervin, 1984a; Hermans, 1988). Secondly, the argument derives from comparisons between the two strategies which rely on identical types of data and differ only with respect to the statistical analyses to which these data are subjected. However, it is an essential requirement for idiographic research that the information entered into the analysis is valid for the individual subject. For example, administering a standard personality questionnaire in a typical nomothetic study assumes that the items in the questionnaire are equally applicable to and interpreted in the same way by all respondents. Otherwise, interindividual comparisons would be precluded. But this assumption is questionable from an idiographic point of view, claiming that it is essential for the research instruments to be able to access contents (traits, behaviours, etc.) that are subjectively meaningful for the individual person. As far as the issue of cross-situational consistency is concerned, a nomothetic analysis typically examines subjects' behaviour across a range of situations that is preselected by the investigator and identical for all subjects. In contrast, from an idiographic point of view, the appropriate strategy for addressing this problem requires that the relevance of the situations across which behaviour is assumed to be consistent is ascertained individually for each participant. Thus, a comparative evaluation of idiographic and nomothetic research strategies can only be expected to yield valid results if each approach is operationalised strictly according to its underlying methodological stipulations.

In this context, Mischel's (1977; 1983) distinction between norm-centred and person-centred measurement is highly pertinent. He argues that a norm-centred focus aimed at comparisons between individuals in terms of their standing on a particular personality variable calls for a distinctly different methodological rationale than a person-centred focus aimed at describing individual persons in relation to their particular psychological situations and to other aspects of their own behaviour. In drawing this distinction Mischel, unlike Paunonen & Jackson (1985), does not pit one perspective against the other, but acknowledges their complementary significance: 'Both vantage points are useful, depending on one's purpose' (Mischel, 1983, 591).

The research reported in this volume is based on the attempt to integrate the two vantage points in the identification and explanation of cross-situational regularities in individual behaviour. The basic proposition is that in order to arrive at generalising conclusions about the principles underlying coherent patterns of behaviour across situations, one has to begin by adopting an *individual-centred perspective* in which each person is studied in relation to his or her realm of situational experiences as well as their cognitive appraisals.[2] It is only if the validity of the consistency measures is ensured at the level of the individual person that there is a basis for integrating individual data patterns into a broader perspective designed to evaluate nomothetic hypotheses about the cross-situational covariation of situation cognition and behaviour.

The conceptual foundations of the present individual-centred approach to the study of cross-situational coherence are elaborated in the next chapter against the background of the current state of the consistency debate in personality research.

---

[2] In characterising the present approach, the term 'individual-centred' rather than 'person-centred' is used in order to emphasise that the focus is on the *individual* person as opposed to the study of aggregates of persons.

6 Reconceptualising consistency: the coherence of situation cognition and behaviour

Based on an interactionist understanding of personality, the present approach to the study of consistency concentrates on the analysis of perceived situational similarities and their relationship to behaviour. What is central to the proposed model is the conceptualisation of this relationship in terms of *intraindividual* regularities. In addressing the problem of consistency from an individual-centred perspective, our research is grounded in the belief that the debate about cross-situational consistency of behaviour is bound to stagnate so long as the personality variables which are supposed to manifest themselves consistently in overt behaviour are defined and measured independently of the situations involved.

In the concept of *absolute consistency*, trait-referent behaviour is regarded as largely invariant across situations. The more widely accepted understanding of *relative consistency*, while acknowledging the impact of situational influences on trait-specific behaviours, still assumes the impact of situational factors to be constant across individuals. In clear contrast to both of these views, the present search for *coherent* patterns of behaviour across situations is directed at identifying characteristic patterns of similarity and change in individual behaviour due to the cognitive appraisal of the situational framework within which the behavioural decisions are made. Such a perspective on the consistency issue requires that person variables are defined with explicit reference to the situational conditions under which those variables are supposed to have an impact on behaviour. Therefore, cross-situational coherence is defined here as the systematic, intraindividual relationship between the perception of situational similarity on the one hand and the similarity of behavioural responses to those situations on the other. Highlighting the importance of the subjective meaning of situational factors in explaining behavioural regularities reflects a commitment to the reciprocal, dynamic meaning of *interaction* so strongly advocated, yet empirically neglected by the proponents of the modern interactionist view (cf. chapter 3). The cognitive representation of situational meaning, introduced as a key concept for the study of coherence, in a truly reciprocal-interactive concept in that it refers to the individual's interpretation of situations against the background of his or her unique learning history and according to his or her characteristic, possibly idiosyncratic criteria.

As far as the traditional antagonism between idiographic and nomothetic research strategies is concerned, the present approach offers an integrative perspective based on the differentiation between structural and substantive, i.e. content-bound, hypotheses about personality functioning. The present coherence model may be described as nomothetic insofar as it involves a *general* hypothesis about the covariation of perceived situational similarity and behavioural similarity across situations. This hypothesis refers to the structural link between two variables, namely situation cognition and behaviour, which is conceptualised independently of specific personality domains. However, the appropriate empirical assessment of this general proposition involves not only focusing on the intraindividual relationship between the two variables but also selecting a particular personality domain in which both situation cognition and behaviour are operationalised in terms of subjectively valid contents. Thus, it is argued that the nomothetic hypothesis about cross-situational coherence can only be properly examined in the framework of an idiographic research strategy. This line of reasoning and the research programme derived from it are presented in detail in the next chapter.

Before turning to this task, the current stand of the consistency controversy will be briefly summarised to clarify the point of departure for the present studies. As Houts, Cook & Shadish (1986) note, a number of conceptual agreements have emerged in the more recent course of the consistency controversy, reflecting a kind of 'ad hoc multiplism' as a consequence of the converging views of researchers who framed the issue in different terms. At the same time, Houts et al. identify a core of common shortcomings that run through these different perspectives and prevent research on consistency from yielding more valid and reliable results:

> If the current debate about cross-situational consistency is to be
> enlightened by data, studies are required that (1) systematically include a
> broad and heterogeneous array of traits, behaviours, settings, occasions of
> measurement, and types of respondents, (2) systematically unconfound
> discrete, molecular behaviors and situations so that a potential bias in
> past studies is eliminated, and (3) present convincing evidence that the
> different molecular behaviors sampled in different situations are equally
> prototypical representations of the same latent trait.
> (Houts, Cook & Shadish, 1986, 78–9)

From the perspective of the present research, this description of the current state of the consistency debate and its methodological shortcomings needs to be complemented by four more specific points which are particularly pertinent to the proposed coherence model and its methodological foundations:

1 The main force of the consistency debate is still directed at the issue of the maximum magnitude of 'personality coefficients', i.e. correlations between trait measures and behavioural indicators across different situations. In the attempt to improve the evidence of consistent relationships between traits and behaviour, the search for moderator variables of consistency, such as global self-assessed consistency or self-monitoring, has become increasingly prominent (e.g. Bem & Allen, 1974; Chaplin & Goldberg, 1985; Tellegen, Kamp & Watson, 1982; Wymer & Penner, 1985; Zuckerman et al., 1988). At the same time, Epstein's (1979, 1980; 1983b; Epstein & O'Brien, 1985) forceful argument in favour of the aggregation of behavioural information across time and situations has instigated a controversial discussion on the distinction between temporal stability and cross-situational consistency (e.g. Bem, 1983b; Conley, 1984b; Diener & Larsen, 1984; Epstein, 1983a; Funder, 1983; Mischel & Peake, 1982a, b; Houts, Cook & Shadish, 1986). The diverse attempts at salvaging the concept of consistency are based, however, on a nomothetic research perspective in which the validity of the methodological instruments with respect to the individual person is not considered a critical issue.

2 Despite the interactionist elaboration of the consistency concept in terms of *coherence* or systematic cross-situational variability in individual behaviour, the vast majority of empirical studies are based on information aggregated across individuals, leading to data patterns in which the personality-specific patterns of individual behaviour are no longer discernible. This lack of correspondence between the theoretical and operational definitions of coherence may be regarded as compromising the validity of the obtained results. As Mischel (1983, 591) notes with regard to this state of affairs: 'The aim of studying individuals in a person-centred rather than in a norm-centred way seems a most important goal to retain and cultivate, and I share the conviction that correlations for group data are not the appropriate road for that aim.' Furthermore, the commitment to the analysis of group data precludes the sampling of individually relevant situations. Instead, investigators typically rely on situation samples that are, for the most part, selected on the basis of ad hoc criteria of plausibility, without devoting attention to the issue of whether the situations are indeed part of the individual's experience and are interpreted in about the same way by the members of the sample.

3 With few exceptions (e.g. Magnusson & Ekehammar, 1978), the interactionist plea for the consideration of individual, subjective definitions of situational similarity, which derives from the postulated significance of the 'psychological meaning of situations for the individual' (cf. chapter 3), has not been translated into empirical research strategies. In seeking support for

the consistency hypothesis, it is still typically the case that the extent to which situations are regarded as similar or different is defined by the investigator rather than by the participants, either consensually or individually. This neglect of the subjects' perspective poses a threat to the validity of conclusions about cross-situational consistency inferred from studies of this kind, so that Bem & Allen's criticism, raised fifteen years ago, has not lost any of its relevance: 'A sample of individuals is inconsistent to the degree that their behaviors do not sort into the equivalence class which the investigator imposes by his choice of behaviors and situations to sample' (Bem & Allen, 1974, 509). If and when a subject's definitions of situational equivalencies and similarities coincide with those of the investigator and/or those of the remaining members of the sample has not been much of an issue for empirical research. By collecting individual samples of anxiety-provoking situations within four broad situation categories, the present research offers at least a partial answer to this question by revealing the amount of overlap or distinctiveness in the situational experiences considered relevant or 'central' by the participants involved as well as the cognitive representations of those situations as similar or dissimilar (cf. also Gruen, Folkman & Lazarus, 1988).

4 A final feature characterising the current state of the consistency debate refers to the growing recognition of the parallels and commonalities of social and personality psychology, in particular regarding the link between dispositional constructs, such as traits and attitudes, and behavioural performance (e.g. Blass, 1984; Carlson, 1984; Sherman & Fazio, 1983). Nevertheless, empirical efforts to bring social psychological concepts to bear on problems in personality research are still rare. In this light, it may not be surprising to find that none of the social psychological conceptualisations of situation cognition discussed in chapter 4 has so far been applied to the problem of cross-situational consistency. Therefore, to forge a link between recent models of situation cognition and the study of cross-situational coherence in individual behaviour, the present research is faced with the task of specifying the different approaches with regard to their potential contribution to the consistency issue in personality psychology. Such a conceptual as well as methodological extension is guided by the aim to explore the principles underlying the cognitive construction of situational similarities and differences, which is regarded as an essential prerequisite for understanding intraindividual patterns of behavioural variability across situations.

In summary, this brief recapitulation has shown that the consistency controversy as it currently stands is still rooted firmly in the nomothetic research tradition. However, as became apparent at various points in the preceding chapters, critical voices claiming an alternative individual-centred perspective on this central issue of personality psychology are gaining momentum. It is in the spirit of this claim that the empirical research presented in the second part of this volume was designed.

Part 2
Empirical investigations

7 An individual-centred approach to the study of cross-situational coherence in anxiety-provoking situations

The previous chapters were devoted to a critical analysis of the issues involved in the consistency controversy. As part of this analysis, a number of conceptual as well as methodological problems were identified which have so far prevented a convincing resolution of the debate.

In this part of the volume, a research strategy is presented which aims to address some of these inadequacies and present a new perspective on the operational definition and empirical measurement of consistency in personality. Based on the reconceptualisation of the consistency problem in terms of coherence, advanced in the preceding chapter, an individual-centred methodology for analysing the covariation of situation cognition and behaviour in the domain of anxiety was developed and put to the test in a series of three empirical investigations. Before these studies are described in detail in the next three chapters, a general introduction is in order to explain the aims and procedure of the present approach.

An outline of the research programme

From our review of the evidence pertaining to the cross-situational consistency of behaviour, it has become clear that the attempt to predict absolute or relative consistency of *individual* behaviour across different situations is neither conceptually plausible nor empirically feasible. Therefore, the present research adopts a different understanding of consistency. This understanding is embodied in the concept of *coherence*, advanced as part of the modern interactionist perspective on personality, referring to a person's *systematic, individually predictable variability of behaviour in different situations*. Such a conception of consistency implies that observed variations in a person's behaviour across different situations do not necessarily reflect 'inconsistency' due to the impact of situational determinants. Rather, so long as behavioural variability is systematically related to other person variables, it is regarded as a reflection of cross-situational coherence.

In the present approach, the cognitive appraisal of situational features is regarded as the crucial person variable covarying with behavioural varia- bility across situations. Coherence is thus defined more specifically in terms of the *covariation of situation cognition and behaviour*. Empirical evidence in support of this conception requires that patterns of individual behaviour in different situations can be shown to be similar to the extent that the situations involved are assigned similar meanings by the person.

Therefore, the central hypothesis examined in the present research is as follows:

> *There is coherence in personality in the form of systematic, intraindividual covariations of situation cognition and behaviour across different situations; these covariations can be operationally defined in terms of the intraindividual correlations between similarity profiles in the perception of and behaviour in those situations.*

So far, few attempts have been made to substantiate the concept of coherence in empirical research. Therefore, no established approaches to the collection and analysis of data are available so that the task faced by the present research is best described as exploratory. It is for this reason that the link between situation cognition and behaviour has been cautiously formulated in terms of a correlational relationship in the above definition. Ultimately, however, the validity of the coherence concept will depend on whether it facilitates the *prediction* of behavioural patterns on the basis of perceived situational meaning. For such predictions to be successful, an essential prerequisite is to know more about the principles underlying the perceptual construction of situational similarities. The predominant strategy of interac- tionist studies (cf. chapter 3) to elicit global ratings of perceived similarity between situations and subsequently relate them to behavioural profiles is unable to provide this type of information. Instead, measures need to be developed which refer explicitly to conceptual models of situation cognition containing specific assumptions about the cognitive organisation of situ- ational meaning.

Therefore, one of the objectives of the present research was to search for conceptualisations of situation cognition which would provide a theoretical basis for deriving specific measures of perceived situational meaning to be employed in the individual-centred study of coherence in personality. As discussed in chapter 4, cognitive social psychology offers three recent approaches which are potentially suitable for this task: the *prototype* approach to situation categorisation (Cantor et al., 1982), the *social episodes* model (Forgas, 1982) and the *script* approach to the cognitive representation of dynamic event sequences (Abelson, 1981). To reiterate briefly, the main features of each of the three approaches with respect to the aims and requirements of the present research are summarised below.

Developed as a model of natural language classification, the *prototype approach* defines the similarity between objects or instances of a given category in terms of the number of characteristic features which the objects or instances share in common. Situational similarity may thus be conceptualised as the result of a comparison process in which the person looks at the characteristic features of the respective situations. The greater the number of shared features, the higher the similarity.

The *social episode* model (Forgas, 1979a, 1982) is concerned with discovering the dimensions underlying both individual and cultural representations of stereotypic interaction sequences. The cognitive structure of this implicit situational knowledge is represented in the episode space. The major empirical objective of episode research therefore lies in the modelling of cognitive episode paces.

Finally, the *script* concept (Abelson, 1981) postulates that situational information is stored and processed in the form of scripts which individuals develop in the course of their experiences with the situation. This scripted knowledge specifies 'appropriate sequences of events in a particular context' (Schank & Abelson, 1977, 41). According to the script model, social situations are cognitively represented in terms of characteristic (inter-) actions rather than characteristic features or attributes.

By introducing measures of situation cognition which are derived from theoretical models of social cognition, the present research contributes to a conceptual analysis of the *psychological meaning of situations for the individual*. Due to their differences in theoretical focus, the measures of situation cognition derived from each of the three models are likely to be differentially related to behavioural patterns across situations. Therefore, it is important to note that the three studies reported in the next chapters also explore the differences between the three models in terms of their covariation with behaviour across situations.

Since the conceptual and operational definitions of *coherence* both refer to intraindividual regularities in personality functioning, obtaining empirical evidence for cross-situational covariations of situation cognition and behaviour presupposes a methodology which facilitates the interpretation of data at the level of the individual person. As noted earlier on, such a methodology must satisfy two essential requirements:
1 It has to ensure that the situations across which coherence is expected to be found are representative samples from each participant's personal experience; and
2 It has to furnish inferences about individual participants which are not affected by the responses of other members of the sample.

To meet these two demands, an individual-centred methodology was developed for the purposes of the present reconceptualisation of the consistency issue. What is characteristic of this approach is that measures are designed in such a way that their *contents* are allowed to vary from person to person while an identical measurement format is employed to ensure the *structural* comparability of the obtained data. The distinction involved here is between general propositions about the processes of personality functioning on the one hand and the contents (be they trait domains, behaviours, or cognitions) on which these processes are assumed to operate on the other hand. As many critics of the traditional individual difference paradigm have pointed out, there is no compelling reason why one should assume the specific contents of personality measures tapping the substance of an individual's personality to be universally relevant or applicable to all individuals in the same way (cf., for instance, Lamiell, 1981, 285). To examine the nomothetic hypothesis that there is a systematic relationship between perceived situational similarity and behavioural similarity across situations, neither the situations nor the meaning attached to them need be identical for all participants. The only requirement is that the format of the perceptual and behavioural data is the same, ensuring that individual data patterns are formally equivalent and hence comparable across subjects.

This is not to deny that the specific content of hypothetical constructs is of theoretical interest in many areas of personality theory, as for instance in investigating different facets of trait anxiety or distinguishing between public and private aspects of self-consciousness. However, when the aim is to examine broader structural hypotheses, such as the covariation hypothesis entailed in the coherence concept, content is not a conceptually relevant dimension, and the interindividual comparability of the contents of the obtained data is not essential.

While some critics of idiographic research strategies have ignored this basic distinction (e.g. Paunonen & Jackson, 1985), the above line of reasoning is also shared by other authors, such as Bem (1983a, 216), who suggests that one should 'formalize in nomothetic ways some of the *processes* of personality while treating the idiographic *content* of personality as extratheoretical'. The synthesis between nomothetic and idiographic perspectives on cross-situational coherence implied in the present individual-centred approach is summarised in Figure 7.1.

Like the traditional understanding of consistency, the present conceptualisation of coherence involves general propositions about personality and behaviour which should apply, in principle, not only to a large number of persons but also to a wide range of personality constructs and domains. Therefore, the choice of a particular domain in which to seek support for the proposed link between situation cognition and behaviour is to some extent arbitrary from a conceptual point of view. However, from a methodological and pragmatic point of view, certain requirements should be met by the content domain to be chosen for the present research.

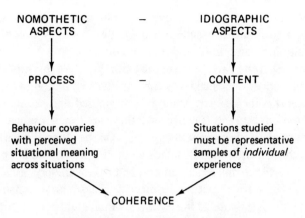

NOMOTHETIC   —   IDIOGRAPHIC
ASPECTS   ASPECTS

PROCESS   —   CONTENT

Behaviour covaries   Situations studied
with perceived   must be representative
situational meaning   samples of *individual*
across situations   experience

COHERENCE

'Behaviour varies from situation to situation
in a lawful, systematic, and idiographically
predictable way' (Magnusson, 1976, 257).

7.1 Features of the individual-centred methodology

Firstly, it should be a domain comprising personally relevant situations, experiences, and reactions so that participants would be motivated to invest time and effort in the cognitive processing of those situations over several data points.

Secondly, the range of feasible and likely behaviours in the respective situations has to be wide enough to allow a sufficient degree of individual variance. This means that those classes of situations are unsuitable where the range of behavioural options is typically limited by social norms and other constraints or where the nature of the situations is such that only few behavioural alternatives are available.

Thirdly, it should be a domain which has been investigated by previous research addressing the issue of cross-situational consistency so that the results from the present studies may be compared with evidence based on the traditional understanding of consistency as well as findings from other studies within the modern interactionist framework.

One domain which meets all three requirements is the field of *anxiety*. Anxiety-provoking situations represent a diverse category of universal, personally involving experiences. At the same time, there is a relatively wide range of behavioural responses which may vary from person to person and from situation to situation and thus affords the manifestation of systematic variabilities in individual behaviour as proposed by the coherence concept. Finally, as illustrated in chapter 3, the domain of anxiety has been one of the prime areas of theorising and research based on the interactionist model of personality. Most prominently, Endler's (1975; 1983) multidimensional mode of trait anxiety distinguishes between different facets of dispositional anxiety and postulates that individual differences in responding to a given anxiety-provoking situation are determined jointly by the type of threat inherent in the situation and the strength of the corresponding A-trait facet. Since the present research shares some of the assumptions of this model, yet differs in terms of its overall objectives, a comparative evaluation of the two approaches is of particular interest. As far as the proposed significance of the perception of situational threats is concerned, there are conceptual parallels between Endler's model and the present approach. On the other hand, a basic difference lies in the fact that unlike Endler's work, the present studies do *not* aim to predict individual differences in responding to anxiety-provoking situations and explain them with reference to dispositional constructs. Instead, the aim is to investigate, at the level of the individual person, the link between perceived situational meaning and behavioural responses.

For these reasons the domain of anxiety-provoking situations was selected as an exemplary field of application for the coherence model. If support is found in this domain for the proposed covariation of situation cognition and behaviour as well as the validity of the three concept-based measures of situation cognition described above, then further research would appear warranted extending the present research programme to other personality domains and seeking to provide further support for the generality of the model.

Sampling anxiety-provoking situations: the 'situation grid'

In keeping with the individual-centred approach underlying the present studies, the first step in the empirical investigation of the link between situation cognition and behaviour consists in developing a strategy for sampling anxiety-provoking situation from the individual's past experience. As has been argued earlier on, coherence of situation cognition and behaviour can only be expected for those situations which are perceived by the person as anxiety-provoking by his or her subjective standards. Therefore, the prevalent approach of exploring consistency or coherence on the basis of nomothetically defined samples of anxiety-provoking situations (e.g. Magnusson & Ekehammar, 1975; 1978; Klirs & Revelle, 1986) has to be rejected for its inability to take the possibly idiosyncratic perception and interpretation of potentially anxiety-provoking stimuli into account.

The task of obtaining individual samples of anxiety-provoking experiences is of central importance to the present approach as it provides the 'input' for all subsequent measures of situation cognition and behaviour. It is at this stage that the situations are generated across which the covariation of perceived similarity and behavioural similarity is to be examined later on. The sampling of anxiety-provoking situations for each participant thus requires a methodological device which is characterised by a high degree of objectivity and formal standardisation while at the same time facilitating the coverage of a diverse range of individual experiences.

It is not surprising that the traditional stock of research methods in personality with its heavy emphasis on the individual difference paradigm does not provide an instrument which would meet these demands. However, if one looks at methodological developments in the cognitive tradition of personality research, Kelly's (1955) *Repertory Grid Technique*, developed in the context of his theory of personal constructs (cf. chapter 2), offers a strategy which lends itself immediately to the objectives of the present research. Kelly's understanding of personal constructs as revealing the individual's characteristic mode of interpreting and organising his or her world of experience may be interpreted as a kind of superordinate concept in which the two constituents of the present approach, namely situation cognition and behaviour, are integrally linked. The subjective construction of similarities and differences which is central to our conceptualisation of cross-situational coherence is regarded in the theory of personal constructs as the fundamental principle of cognitive organisation (Kelly, 1955, 9).

Reflecting Kelly's core assumption that construct systems are unique to each individual, the repertory grid technique was developed explicitly as an *idiographic* measure facilitating a fine-grained analysis of personal construct systems. As such, it was employed and elaborated in a large number of studies (cf. Adams-Webber, 1979; Adams-Webber & Mancuso, 1983; Slater, 1977). Essentially, the grid technique is a structured free response measure in which both the *elements*, i.e. the objects of a person's thoughts, and the *constructs*, i.e. the qualities that the person attributes to those objects, are elicited from the person whose construct system is to be explored (Phillips, 1989; cf. also Fransella & Bannister, 1977). Its name derives from the graphic arrangement of the elements and constructs as columns and rows of a matrix which results in the emergence of a grid-like pattern.

Within the framework of Kelly's personality theory, the grid technique has been used primarily to elicit personal constructs referring to other persons as 'elements' in the respondent's social environment. However, various studies have demonstrated that it can easily be adapted to the elicitation of constructs pertaining to other elements, such as situations (e.g. Cochran, 1978; Furnham, 1981; van Heck, 1981; Wysor, 1983) and physical environments (Harrison & Sarre, 1976; Honikman, 1976; Stringer, 1976).

In the present research, the grid technique is adapted to the task of eliciting anxiety-provoking situations as well as the person's central constructs reflecting his or her cognitive representation of those situations. The procedural details involved in this measure will be described in the context of Study 2 where the 'situation grid' was first applied (cf. chapter 9). At this point, it should be noted that the principal advantage of the grid technique for the study of cross-situational coherence lies in its ability to elicit samples of anxiety-provoking experiences which are unique to each person in terms of their specific contents yet measured in a formally identical way across respondents. Thus, the situation grid provides just the kind of information that is required as input data for the individual-centred study of coherence.

Overview of the studies

The search for empirical corroboration of the proposed covariation of situation cognition and behaviour in the domain of anxiety involves the development of an entirely new set of instruments tailored to the requirements of the individual-centred approach outlined above. Therefore, the primary aim of Study 1 consists in an exploratory examination of the various new measures. In particular, this refers to determining the exact format of the Situation Grid, but also includes pilot tests of the newly developed Script, Prototype, and Social Episode measures of situation cognition. Furthermore, Study 1 is designed to seek tentative evidence in support of the proposed intraindividual covariation of situation cognition and behaviour which forms the basis for a more thorough analysis in the subsequent studies.

Study 2 is devoted to a more comprehensive analysis of the central question whether systematic relationships between situation cognition and behaviour can be demonstrated across different anxiety-provoking situations. A more complex design is employed facilitating intraindividual comparisons between the different measures of situation cognition and their correspondence with behavioural responses across situations. Following the elicitation of individual samples of anxiety-provoking situations through the Situation Grid, each participant is required to complete the three concept-based measures of situation cognition as well as a global rating measure of perceived situational similarity. On the behavioural side, two different measures are employed. The proposed cross-situational regularities are operationally defined in terms of intraindividual correlations between the different measures of behavioural and perceived similarities.

Study 3 is designed to corroborate and extend the previous findings by providing another test of the coherence model involving a further refinement of the instruments. While the exploratory nature of the present research initially required the different measures to impose as few restrictions as possible on the respondents, the results from the previous studies permit a greater formal standardisation of the instruments in Study 3. Moreover, a more complex measure of behavioural responses to anxiety-provoking situations is introduced to replace the traditional response-scale measures of anxiety used in the preceding studies. Altogether, the aim of this final study is to provide further evidence in support of the coherence model by extending the scope of the behavioural measure and further improving the methodology employed in the present research.

8   Study 1: Developing an individual-centred methodology

Within the framework of the present strategy for investigating coherence in personality, this study is designed to provide a pilot test of the different measures developed for the individual-centred analysis of situation cognition and behaviour. In particular, the aim is to advance a strategy for constructing the Situation Grid designed to elicit idiographic samples of anxiety-provoking situations. Moreover, the feasibility of the newly developed Prototype, Script and Social Episode measures of situation cognition is tested and each measure is related to behavioural patterns across a select sample of situations to provide a tentative test of the covariation hypothesis.

As far as the Situation Grid is concerned, a crucial stage in the development of this measure consists in deciding about the *elements*, i.e. situation categories, presented to the respondents in order to elicit the specific situations for which they are then asked to generate constructs. In the standard version of the grid technique applied to the analysis of construct systems referring to persons, the elements of the grid consist in a set of *role titles* (e.g. mother, sister, closest friend). This list is presented to the respondents with the instruction to designate the personal identities of the people in their own realm of experience who fit those different roles, and it is to these individuals that the subsequent generation of constructs refers. In the same way, the Situation Grid requires a list of *situation titles* for which respondents then supply specific situations from their personal experience.

Obviously, the generality of the findings derived from grid data depends on the extent to which the elements provided by the investigator represent a comprehensive range of individual experiences in the respective domain. So, in order to explore a person's construct system pertaining to the cognitive representation of interpersonal relationships, like in the standard grid, it is important that a wide range of different relationships is covered by the elements of the grid. In the same way, it is essential that the elements included in the situation grid represent a broad spectrum of anxiety-provoking situations.

The issue of how to select the elements of a grid and to ensure that they are representative of the domain in question has received only marginal attention in the theory of personal constructs. Kelly himself treated this problem in rather general terms:

> If the test is to indicate how the subject develops his role in the light of his understanding of other people, it is necessary that the other people appearing in the test be sufficiently representative of all the people with whom the subject must relate his self-construed role. The list of role titles is designed with this in mind. Representative figures, with respect to whom people seem normally to have formed the most crucial personal role constructs, are incorporated in the list.
> (Kelly, 1955, 230)

Even pragmatic descriptions of the grid technique, such as Fransella & Bannister's (1977) 'Manual for Repertory Grid Technique', touch only briefly on the issue without providing any explicit guidelines for the selection of elements. Thus it would appear that research using the grid technique typically relies on implicit, intuitively plausible criteria in deciding upon the elements of a grid.

In contrast, an explicit strategy is employed in the present study to ensure that the *situation titles* included in the grid provide a comprehensive coverage of the domain of anxiety-provoking situations. Ideally, this task would have been made superfluous by the availability of a well-established taxonomy of anxiety-provoking situations. In the absence of such a taxonomy, however, the comprehensive delineation of the domain of anxiety-provoking situations remains an empirical problem. To address this problem, the present study refers to the categories of Endler's (1980, 1983) interactionist model of anxiety, described in chapter 3, as a starting point. In the first part of the study, an open-ended questionnaire is administered to determine whether the range of anxiety-provoking situations covered by the categories of Endler's model is broad enough to elicit comprehensive samples of specific situations from the individual participants. To the extent that these categories can be shown to accommodate the majority of situations spontaneously generated by subjects in a free response format, it would appear justified to employ them as situation titles in the grid measure.

The second objective of the present study is to conduct pilot tests of the measures of situation cognition and behaviour as well as provide preliminary evidence on the proposed covariation of situation cognition and behaviour. Free-response measures of perceived situational meaning are derived from the prototype, script, and social episode models by asking subjects to generate characteristic features, events, and evaluative judgements for the situations elicited through the open-ended questionnaire described above. Profiles of perceived situational similarity are derived from these measures and related to measures of behavioural responses obtained on a separate occasion.

Sample and overview

Twenty-five psychology undergraduates at the University of Sussex participated in the study on a voluntary basis. Respondents were required to attend three separate data points scheduled at weekly intervals. In the first session, they were asked to generate a list of anxiety-provoking situations which they had encountered in the past. In the second session, they described their behavioural responses to each of those situations. In the final session, the cognitive representations of the same set of situations were measured. Two respondents failed to attend the second data point so that the findings reported below concerning the covariation of situation cognition and behaviour are based on a total of twenty-three subjects.

Eliciting anxiety-provoking situations

The first data point was devoted to examining the following four categories, specified by Endler (1980) in his multidimensional model of anxiety, in terms of their suitability as *elements* of the situation grid:

- Social evaluation situations
- Physical danger situations
- Interpersonal situations
- Ambiguous situations

These four categories were presented to subjects in a free-response question-naire instructing them to write down as many specific, concrete situations from their personal experience as they associated with each category.[1] An undefined residual category was additionally provided to comprise those situations which the respondents felt could not be grouped under any of the four preceding categories. The format of this 'Situation Experience Question-naire' is illustrated in Figure 8.1.

Since the primary aim of this measure consisted in examining whether the four categories specified above would be broad enough to represent the entire spectrum of anxiety-provoking situations, the situations listed by the participants were subjected to a quantitative as well as qualitative analysis. First, the average frequency of nominations was computed for each category. This revealed that the greatest number of situations had been named in the 'social evaluation' category while the residual category had received the smallest number of nominations. The means and standard deviations for each category are presented in Table 8.1.

Pair-wise t-tests of each of the four defined categories and the residual category showed that significantly fewer situations were listed in the residual category than in all other categories (t-values ranging from 2.98 to 5.98, p's ranging from $<.01$ to $<.001$).

---

[1] The fifth category introduced by Endler, referring to innocuous or daily routine situations, was omitted since the model does not specify exactly how the anxiety-provoking nature of this type of situations is conceptualised (cf. chapter 3).

Situation Experience Questionnaire

This questionnaire is part of a larger study investigating the ways people look at a number of different situations in which they might find themselves. In particular, we are concerned with situations which people find to be stressful or anxiety-provoking. In today's task, which constitutes the first part of the study, our aim is to explore the diversity of different anxiety-provoking situations persons encounter in their everyday lives. Therefore, we would like to ask *you* to list those situations from your personal experience which gave and may still give rise to some sort of stress or anxiety.

On the following pages you will find a number of general headings referring to situations which you will probably have encountered, in one form or another. Your task is:

TO GO THROUGH THESE GENERAL HEADINGS ONE AT A TIME AND TO WRITE DOWN AS MANY SPECIFIC, CONCRETE SITUATIONS FROM YOUR PERSONAL EXPERIENCE AS YOU ASSOCIATE WITH THESE GENERAL HEADINGS.

You may list as many or as few instances as you wish under each general heading. You should provide the essential and necessary detail in describing each event so that another person who is unfamiliar with it gets a basic idea of what was going on. This should, however, not normally require more than two or three sentences.

Please try to think about situations carefully, but do not feel pressured to list situations which might be only of little significance to you personally.

I Please think of situations you encountered where you were being *evaluated, judged or observed* by other people.

II Please think of situations where you were about to or actually did encounter *physical danger*.

III Please think of situations that were *new, ambiguous or unfamiliar* to you, that is, situations in which you did not know or were uncertain as to what to expect.

IV Please think of situations involving *interaction with other people* in which you felt uncomfortable.

V Please think of situations in which you felt *uncomfortable or even frightened*, which cannot be grouped under any of the previous general headings.

8.1 Situation experience questionnaire

Table 8.1. *Means and standard deviations of the*
number of situations listed per category (N = 25)

	Nominations of situations per category	
	M	s
Social evaluation	4.05	1.412
Physical danger	3.37	2.022
Ambiguous situations	3.15	1.537
Interpersonal situations	3.56	1.888
Residual	1.82	1.882

From these data it may be concluded that the four categories of the Situation Experience Questionnaire exhaustively cover the total range of anxiety-provoking situations typically experienced by a student sample. Thus, the present findings provide an empirical foundation for using the four categories as elements in the Situation Grid to be employed as a structured measure for eliciting idiographic samples of situations in the next two studies.

Beyond this quantitative analysis, interesting findings emerged from the qualitative inspection of the specific situations named by the responents. When the rationale of the present individual-centred methodology was outlined earlier on, it was argued that a serious shortcoming of traditional nomothetic strategies for exploring cross-situational consistency lies in their reliance on preselected lists of situations which are assumed to be equally relevant to and have identical meanings for all subjects involved. If this assumption were correct, then one would expect a relatively high degree of convergence or consensus in the specific situations named in a free-response measure by a homogeneous sample such as the present one. In order to examine the extent to which a consensual list of situations emerged from the Situation Experience Questionnaire, the frequency with which specific situations had been named by different subjects was computed for each of the five categories. Table 8.2 presents the results of this frequency count by listing all situations named by five or more of the twenty-five participants as well as indicating their proportion of the total number of situations listed per category.

This analysis clearly shows that there is a wide range of specific situations experienced as anxiety-provoking by a student sample. Even in the category displaying the highest degree of consensus, i.e. the category of 'social evaluation' situations, less than half of the situations were named by at least 20% of the subjects. In the remaining categories, that overlap is substantially lower. Across the five categories, the proportion of situations named by five or

Table 8.2. *Anxiety-provoking situations with five or more nominations*

Social evaluation
- Being in a (job) interview (N = 17)
- Being in a seminar meeting (N = 15)
- Giving a stage performance (N = 6)
- Talking in front of an audience (N = 6)
- Participating in a psychological experiment (N = 5)
(47.6% of the total number of situations in this category)

Physical danger
- Being involved in a road accident (N = 6)
- Being attacked by member of the family (N = 5)
(13.3% of the total number of situations in this category)

Ambiguous situations
- Coming to university (N = 13)
- Meeting new people (N = 5)
(23.1% of the total number of situations in this category)

Interpersonal situations
- Visiting the doctor (N = 6)
(6.7% of the total number of situations in this category)

Residual
No single situation in this category was listed by at least five participants

more subjects is just 22.7%. It is also worth noting that the list presented in Table 8.2 contains situations which are unlikely to appear in any a priori defined sample of situations yet emerged from the present data as relatively common experiences (e.g. 'being attacked by member of the family', or 'visiting the doctor' as being perceived primarily as an interpersonally threatening situation).

Altogether, the findings from the Situation Experience Questionnaire suggest that the vast majority of situations experienced as anxiety-provoking by the present sample could be grouped under one of the four categories specified as part of Endler's interactionist model of anxiety. Thus, these categories can be assumed to be representative of the domain of anxiety-provoking situations as a whole, which recommends them as 'elements' for the Situation Grid. At the same time, an inspection of the listed situations in terms of their contents clearly supports the claim of the present research that the search for cross-situational regularities in behaviour has to be based on situations which are ascertained, not just assumed, to be of personal relevance to the individual. The present results demonstrate that if people are given the opportunity to generate their own samples of situations, the range of situations named as anxiety-provoking displays considerable diversity as well as idiosyncrasy. This finding presents an empirical challenge to conventional nomothetic strategies of sampling situations for the study of consistency.

A preliminary test of the coherence model

Following the elicitation of idiographic samples of anxiety-provoking situations, the remaining two data points were devoted to collecting the behavioural and cognitive measures required for a preliminary examination of the coherence model. A further aim of this part of the study was to provide a comparative test between traditional analyses of the congruence of perceived and behavioural similarity based on a nomothetic set of anxiety-provoking situations, exemplified by the Magnusson & Ekehammar (1978) study described in chapter 3, and the same analysis based on idiographic samples of anxiety-provoking situations as obtained in the present research.

To begin with, situation samples were established individually for each participant by selecting the first two situations named for each category of the Situation Experience Questionaire. This resulted in a total of eight situations which formed the basis for the different measures of situation cognition and behaviour.

Behavioural measure

At the second data point, behavioural profiles were collected for each person with respect to his or her eight situations. The 'Present Affect Reactions Questionnaire' (PARQ, Endler, 1980, 1983), which is a well-established instrument for eliciting self-reports of behavioural responses to anxiety-provoking situations, was employed to this end. The PARQ consists of twenty reaction scales, half of which address 'autonomic-emotional' responses while the other half refers to 'cognitive worry' responses. For each subject, a questionnaire was prepared containing his or her eight situations, each followed by the twenty items of the PARQ. For each item, respondents were asked to indicate on a five-point scale the extent to which they had shown the respective response in each situation. The items of the PARQ are listed in Figure 8.2 which illustrates the general format of the behavioural measure with a 'physical danger' situation named by one participant.

Cognitive measures

When the subjects arrived for the third data point, designed to collect the cognitive measures, they were presented with a questionnaire consisting of two parts: one to elicit global ratings of perceived situational similarity and

Coming close to an accident

Please circle a number from 1 to 5 on this sheet for each of the 20 items to indicate

How you feel in this particular situation

(A)[a] 1 Hands feels moist
        1 2 3 4 5
        Not at all   Very much

(C)[a] 2 Distrust myself

(A) 3 Breathing is irregular

(C) 4 Unable to focus on task

(A) 5 Have tense feeling in stomach

(A) 6 Heart beats faster

(C) 7 Feel helpless

(C) 8 Unable to concentrate

(A) 9 Perspire

(C) 10 Fear defeat

(A) 11 Mouth feels dry
        1 2 3 4 5
        Not at all   Very much

(C) 12 Self-preoccupied

(C) 13 Feel uncertain

(A) 14 Feel tense

(C) 15 Feel inadequate

(A) 16 Hands feel unsteady

(A) 17 Feel flushed

(C) 18 Feel self-conscious

(C) 19 Feel incompetent

(A) 20 Feel lump in throat

---

[a] (A) = autonomic-emotional items
   (C) = cognitive-worry items

8.2 Example of the behavioural measure

the other to obtain one of the three concept-based measures of situation cognitions, i.e. prototype, script, or social episode.

Global similarity rating: For this measure, subjects' sets of eight situations were entered into a matrix facilitating pairwise ratings of perceived similarity for all twenty-eight possible pairs of situations on a five-point scale ranging from 0 = not at all similar to 4 = completely similar.[2] Each participant received a custom-tailored version of the questionnaire referring to his or her sample of situations. The format of this measure is illustrated in Figure 8.3 for the situations listed by one respondent.

To elicit the measures of situation cognition derived from the *script, prototype* and *social episode* models, subjects were divided into three groups.

---

[2] The same response scale was used in the Magnusson & Ekehammar (1978) study.

In this part of today's questionnaire you are asked to rate the similarity between all eight situations on a five-point scale ranging from

0———1———2———3———4

not at all   completely
similar   similar

Please enter a score between 0 and 4 in each cell of the matrix provided below to indicate the degree of similarity between each pair of situations.

		(S2)	(S3)	(S4)	(S5)	(S6)	(S7)	(S8)
Being in an interview situation	(S1)	[ ]	[ ]	[ ]	[ ]	[ ]	[ ]	[ ]
Being in a setting involving a number of people	(S2)		[ ]	[ ]	[ ]	[ ]	[ ]	[ ]
Facing physical danger in a traffic situation	(S3)			[ ]	[ ]	[ ]	[ ]	[ ]
Visiting the doctor	(S4)				[ ]	[ ]	[ ]	[ ]
Being in an experimental situation which involves three or more experimenters	(S5)					[ ]	[ ]	[ ]
Interacting with authorities	(S6)						[ ]	[ ]
Coming to university	(S7)							[ ]
Witnessing a scuffle in a dance hall involving physical violence	(S8)							

8.3 Format for eliciting global ratings of perceived similarity

Prototype measure: Of the twenty-five subjects, nine completed this measure eliciting the characteristic features of each of the eight situations. Subjects were instructed to

> [. . .] list, for each of the situations, all the characteristics that come to your mind when you consider being in that particular situation. Features may be adjectives, specific acts, persons involved, etc., and you should include all those features you consider important as characterising the situation.

Again, individually tailored versions were prepared with each situation being presented on a separate page and followed by blank lines on which to write down the characteristic features. Figure 8.4 illustrates the format of the Prototype measure with the features listed by the respondent who had named the experience of 'Coming close to an accident' as a physical danger situation.

Social Episode measure: Eight subjects provided the Social Episode data. They were presented with individual versions of the questionnaire asking them to rate each of their eight situations on seven bipolar evaluative scales. In accordance with the requirements of an individual-centred methodology, the selection of evaluative dimensions should also be based on idiographic information rather than being determined a priori by the investigator. In Studies 2 and 3, this requirement was met by selecting individual lists of evaluative attributes from the constructs supplied by each respondent as part of the Situation Grid. For the present preliminary test of the coherence model, however, this procedure was not feasible. Instead, seven scales were selected which had emerged as central descriptive features of social episodes in previous studies by Forgas (e.g. 1983a). The format of the Social Episode measure including the seven scales is illustrated in Figure 8.5.

Script measure: Finally, eight subjects completed the Script measure which asked them to provide a description of the course of events in each of the eight situations by listing its main actions and events. They received the following instruction:

> You should regard each of the brief situation headings presented on the following pages as *the title of a script* (like a film script) which carefully describes the events going on in the situation.
>
> Please list, for each of the 'script titles', every relevant event or action by any of the persons involved in the situation. The final list of actions and events for each situation should provide a kind of basic framework for some who would actually want to set up a 'script' to enact the situation. Therefore, you should list as many events as you consider necessary for another person to understand what was going on.

Figure 8.6 illustrates the type of information generated by the Script measure with the list of events named by one subject for a situation from the 'social evaluation' category.

To summarise, two measures of situation cognition were obtained for each subject at the third data point. One provided global ratings of perceived

Coming close to an accident

Please visualize the situation carefully:
What are its characteristic features?

1   *noise*
2   *panic*
3   *rush*
4   *crowded cars*
5   *hostility of other drivers*
6   *traffic signals*
7   *feeling nauseous*

8.4 Example of the prototype measure

Coming close to an accident

Please use the following rating scales to describe your feelings about this situation:

Informal	0——0——0——0——0——0——0	Formal
Simple	0——0——0——0——0——0——0	Complex
Constrained	0——0——0——0——0——0——0	Unconstrained
Predictable	0——0——0——0——0——0——0	Unpredictable
Know how to behave	0——0——0——0——0——0——0	Don't know how to behave
Uninvolved	0——0——0——0——0——0——0	Involved
Non-intimate	0——0——0——0——0——0——0	Intimate

8.5 Example of the social episode measure

Doing a psychology test

Please to try to imagine the situation carefully:
What are the main actions and events taking place?

1   *I went into the room.*
2   *The test was explained.*
3   *I did the test.*
4   *They opened the door and let me out.*
5   *I went away.*

8.6 Example of the script measure

similarity between all possible pairs of situations, while the other was explicitly derived from a theoretical conceptualisation of situation cognition, i.e. the script, prototype or social episode model.

Results

As prescribed by the present individual-centred methodology, the data were analysed individually for each subject. Since the Script and Social Episodes groups each contained one subject who had failed to complete the behavioural measure, the total number of subjects for the remaining analyses was reduced to twenty-three.

The first step in examining the correspondence between perceived similarity and behavioural similarity across each participant's eight anxiety-provoking situations consisted in deriving indices of similarity from the PARQ as well as the Prototype, Script, and Social Episode measures.

To arrive at a measure of *behavioural similarity*, Euclidian distances between the eight situations across the twenty PARQ reaction scales were computed for each subject. The Euclidian distance index was selected as a similarity index for these data, mainly because it was the first and most comprehensive of four indices employed in Magnusson & Ekehammar's study to compute the similarity between behavioural profiles across situations (cf. Magnusson & Ekehammar, 1978, 44). By using this index, the results of the present study are immediately comparable to the findings of their investigation. In the present analysis of individual reaction profiles, Euclidian distances between each possible pair of situations were computed across the twenty reaction scales, resulting in a rank order of behavioural similarity for the twenty-eight situation pairs.

The same strategy was adopted to arrive at an index of cognitive similarity based on the *Social Episode measure*. Euclidian distances between each of the twenty-eight situation pairs were computed across the seven bipolar adjective scales on which each situation had been rated. In this way, a rank order of situational similarity was derived from the Social Episode measure for each subject.

In accordance with the procedure commonly adopted in prototype research (e.g. Cantor, Mischel & Schwartz, 1982), cognitive similarity based on the *Prototype measure* was operationally defined in terms of the common features in the feature lists generated by each subject for each of the eight situations. This involved, first of all, pairwise comparisons between the situations to establish the number of shared features in the lists of characteristics generated by the respondent. An index of feature overlap, i.e. similarity, was then computed for each pair of situations by relating the number of shared features to the total number of features listed for the two situations according to the following formula:[3]

$$r(i, j) = \frac{nc}{\sqrt{n(i) \times n(j)}}$$

A stringent criterion of feature overlap was adopted, whereby only those characteristics which were worded in exactly the same way were counted as 'shared features'. This analysis provided individual rank orders of perceived similarity derived from the prototype model.

The pairwise similarities between the *scripts* generated by each subject in this group for his or her eight situations was defined, as in the prototype measure, by the amount of overlap between the scripted events generated for each situation. By adopting this operationalisation of similarity between scripts, the present study follows a suggestion by Abelson (1981). Again, only those actions and events which were identically worded were regarded as 'shared elements'.

The global ratings of perceived similarity between each possible pair of situations provided an additional, straightforward rank order of perceived similarity for each subject.

As a result of the above analyses, three similarity rank orders of the twenty-eight situation pairs were obtained for each subject: one reflecting behavioural similarity based on the PARQ ratings, one reflecting global similarity perceptions based on the rating scale measure, and one based on the more complex measure of cognitive similarity (either Scripts, Prototypes, or Social Episodes).

To test the proposed covariation between situation cognition and behaviour across situations, intraindividual correlations were calculated between the behavioural and the cognitive similarity rank orders. Two coefficients were computed for each subject; the correlation between behaviour and global cognitive similarity ratings *and* the correlation between behaviour and Script, Prototype or Social Episode measures, respectively.

Table 8.3 presents a summary of the results pertaining to the correlations between global similarity ratings and reaction profiles aggregated across subjects. These figures are directly comparable to the findings obtained by Magnusson & Ekehammar (1978) on the correspondence between perceived and behavioural similarity across a nomothetic sample of anxiety-provoking situations.

[3] r (i, j) = similarity between situations i and j; varies between 0 and 1. nc (i, j) = number of features shared by situations i and j; n(i) = number of features for situation i; n(j) = number of features for situation j.

Table 8.3. *Correlations between situation perception and behaviour:*
Aggregated findings (N = 23)

Average correlations between global similarity ratings and behaviour	$r = .37$	(.15)
Average z-transformed correlations between global similarity ratings and behaviour	$r = .40$	(not reported)
Percentage of correlations in expected direction	91%	(77%)
Percentage of significant correlations in expected direction	65%	(44%)

Note:
Figures in parentheses refer to data reported by Magnusson & Ekehammar (1978) based on the
Euclidian distance index of profile similarity.

As Table 8.3 shows, each of the present indices reflects a substantially
higher level of correspondence between perceived and behavioural similarity
than obtained in the Magnusson & Ekehammar study. In particular, the
average correlation of $r = .37$ represents an increase of .22 over Magnusson
& Ekehammar's figure that was based on an identical set of situations for all
subjects. Likewise, the percentage of positive correlations between situation
perception and behavioural profiles increased from 77% to 91%, and the
percentage of significant correlations increased from 44% to 65%. In line
with the conceptual framework of the present individual-centred approach, it
may be concluded from these findings that the idiographic sampling of
situations for each participant is a more adequate basis for investigating
cross-situational coherence, resulting in considerably higher levels of
correspondence between situation cognition and behaviour than comparable research based on identical sets of situations for all subjects. At the same
time, the present analysis illustrates the feasibility of combining the
requirements of idiographic research strategies with the testing of general,
i.e. nomothetic hypotheses. Due to the identical format of the data provided
by each subject, it was possible to combine the obtained correlations into an
aggregate score of cross-situational coherence, notwithstanding the fact that
each of those correlations referred to different samples of anxiety-provoking
situations as well as their cognitive appraisal.

Further support for the claim to study coherence at the level of the
individual person comes from an inspection of Table 8.4 which provides the
individual correlations for each subject between global perceptual similarity
and behaviour along with those between the concept-based measures of
perceptual similarity and behaviour.

Both global ratings and more fine-grained measures of perceptual
similarity correlate significantly with behaviour for most of the subjects. A

Table 8.4. *Individual correlations between situation perception and behaviour*

1 Prototypes

Subject No.	Prototype/ behaviour	Global similarity/ behaviour
1	.33*	.41*
2	.63***	.67***
3	.64***	.49**
4	.13	.01
5	.49**	.56***
6	.56***	.63***
7	.32*	.34*
8	.42*	.38*
9	.28	−.01
M (z-transformed) =	.46	.43

2 Social episodes

	Episode/ behaviour	Global similarity/ behaviour
10	.32*	.28
11	.53**	.52**
12	−.36*	.29
13	.54**	.36*
14	.52**	.12
15	.07	.64***
16	.24	.32
M (z-transformed) =	.29	.39

3 Scripts

	Scripts/ behaviour	Global similarity/ behaviour
17	.35*	.27
18	.36*	.38*
19	.32*	.12
20	.23	.42*
21	.42*	.24
22	.56**	.63***
23	.61**	.49**
M (z-transformed) =	.44	.39

Note:
* $p<.05$ ** $p<.01$ *** $p<.001$

substantial proportion of the coefficients obtained exceeds the magic limit of $r=.30$ for 'personality coefficients' identified by Mischel (1968). At the same time, Table 8.4 reveals that the strength of the relationship between situation cognition and behaviour varies considerably among subjects. In a conventional nomothetic study on behavioural consistency, this variation would have been no longer discernible, yet it would have affected the overall pattern of results in such a way that any interpretation of the findings with respect to individual members of the sample had been precluded. Finally, it should be noted that differences between the average correlations for global and concept-based measures were non-significant for each of the three groups of Prototype, Social Episode, and Script measures, respectively.

Discussion

The findings from this preliminary test of the coherence model lend clear support to the hypothesis that cognition–behaviour correlation are substantially higher when subjects judge idiographically sampled situations in contrast to preselected situations determined by the investigators, as in the Magnusson & Ekehammar (1978) study. Congruence between perceived situational meanings and behavioural patterns across situations is shown to increase as a function of including situations which represent valid samples from an individual's personal experience. Congruence in this sense reflects precisely the systematic, though variable relationship between situation perception and behaviour proposed in the conceptualisation of coherence advanced by the present research. Behavioural patterns are expected to vary across situations which are perceived as being different, and they are expected to be similar to the extent that the situations involved are attributed similar meanings by the individual. This understanding of coherence implies that, on the behavioural side, low cross-situational correlations between behavioural profiles must not be interpreted in terms of a lack of consistency but rather as a person's flexible interaction with their environment which is mediated by the cognitive representation of situational cues.

While global ratings of situational similarity are adequate for demonstrating the link between situation perception and behaviour postulated by the concept of coherence, they are mute with regard to other important conceptual issues: how an individual's experience of situations is cognitively organised and how different forms of cognitive representation affect the link between situation cognition and behaviour. These questions, which are core issues of the present research, were tentatively addressed in this study on the basis of more complex measures of situational similarity. These were derived from recent theoretical models of situation cognition and applied to an idiographic analysis of cognition–behaviour relationships across eight anxiety-provoking situations. The Script, Prototype, and Social Episode measures of situation cognition were shown to be applicable to the issue of cross-situational coherence in that each measure was significantly correlated to behaviour for the majority of subjects. Although it would not appear warranted to conclude, on the basis of the present data, that the more complex measures of situation cognition produced higher levels of cognition–behaviour covariations than global ratings, they were at least shown to be equally well-suited to reflect cross-situational coherence. Their main advantage over global rating measures is that they illuminate the structural principles by which situations are cognitively construed as similar or different. A clearer understanding of these principles is essential for the task of predicting individual behaviour as a function of the dynamic interaction between person and situation.

In conclusion, the results of Study 1 lend encouraging support to the proposition that individual behaviour in response to anxiety-provoking situations covaries systematically with the perceived similarity in meaning of those situations. However, due to their exploratory nature, the present findings constitute no more than preliminary evidence. In order to provide a more comprehensive examination of the cross-situational coherence of situation cognition and behaviour, two further studies were designed to improve the present methodology: In Study 2, intraindividual comparisons between the three cognitive measures of Script, Prototype, and Social Episodes are facilitated by presenting all three measures to each subject. On the basis of the intercorrelations between the three measures it is possible to arrive at comparative conclusions about their contributions to a theoretical elaboration of the 'psychological situation' along with assessing the extent to which each measure addresses different aspects of situational similarity. In Study 3, the methodological scope is extended further by employing behavioural measures which are able to cover more complex reactions to and behavioural patterns in stressful situations. These studies are presented in detail in the next two chapters.

9 Study 2: Coherence of situation cognition and behavioural ratings

Building upon the methodological devices developed in Study 1, this study is designed to provide a more comprehensive analysis of the coherence of situation cognition and behaviour. At the centre of this analysis is the hypothesis that *individual patterns of behaviour in anxiety-provoking situations vary systematically as a function of the perceived similarity between the situations.* In view of the inadequacies of many previous nomothetic studies of cross-situational consistency, the operational definition of the three basic constituents of this hypothesis, i.e. behavioural patterns, perceived similarity, and the relationship between the two, is a particularly crucial stage in the empirical examination. In line with the conceptual foundations of the present research outlined in chapter 6 and the corresponding individual-centred methodology introduced in chapter 7, the elements of the above hypothesis are operationalised in such a way that

– the analysis of the proposed coherence refers to individual samples of anxiety-provoking situations obtained from each participant on the basis of a structured, free-response instrument, the Situation Grid;

– two different measures of behavioural responses are employed, one of which is the 'Present Affect Reactions Questionnaire' used in the previous study, while the other is a global rating of the extent to which the person's behaviour is similar in two situations;

– four different measures of situation cognition are presented to each participant. In addition to a global rating of similarity between pairs of situations , the Prototype, Script, and Social Episode measures developed in the first study are administered, each yielding a different picture of the perceived similarity between situations; and finally,

– the covariation of behavioural similarity and perceived similarity is examined on the basis of *intraindividual* correlations which provide information about patterns of coherence for every participant as well as reveal the extent to which individuals differ in terms of their levels of coherence on each of the different measures.

Sample and overview

Thirty first-year psychology undergraduates (22 females and 8 males) at the University of Sussex participated in this study. Two female subjects dropped out in the course of the study. Participants received a single payment of £6.00.

Participants in this study were informed that they would be requested to attend five data points. The five sessions were scheduled over a period of six months with intervals of approximately five weeks. In the first session, subjects completed the Situation Grid to elicit idiographic samples of anxiety-provoking situations. In the subsequent three data points, the cognitive measures were administered. Behavioural data were collected in the fifth session. In advance of each session, all participants were contacted individually and offered a choice of dates on which to report for the study. Except for the first session where individual appointments were made to administer the Situation Grid, subjects completed the different measures in groups of two to six.

It is noteworthy that twenty-eight out of the original thirty subjects completed the study, i.e. took part in all five data points. In light of the demanding and time-consuming nature of the data collection, this can be regarded as an extremely low 'drop-out' rate. One reason why subjects were prepared to invest a substantial amount of time and effort into the study, which offered only little financial incentive, undoubtedly lies in the fact that they were asked to work on personally significant material and were interested in the reflective processes about their own experiences stimulated by the study. Compared to the traditional nomothetic methodologies prevalent in personality and social psychology, an individual-centred approach such as the present one has the potential to offer an immediate personal benefit to the participants by focusing on individually relevant themes.

After completion of the data analysis, each subject received a detailed description of the aims and major results of the study, including his or her personal correlations between situation cognition and behaviour.

The Situation Grid

Based on the findings of Study 1, a Situation Grid was developed building upon the four categories of Endler's multidimensional model of trait anxiety: social evaluation, physical danger, interpersonal and ambiguous situations. The Situation Grid was designed to provide a structured, free-response format for eliciting a sample of anxiety-provoking situations from each participant. At the same time, personal constructs describing those situations were elicited in the form of bipolar attributes. Within the context of Kelly's (1955) personality theory, the rationale for operationalising personal constructs in terms of bipolar attributes is grounded on the so-called *dichotomy corollary* stating that 'a person's construct system is composed of a finite number of dichotomous constructs' (Kelly, 1955, 59). For the present research, the main advantage of this aspect of the grid technique is that the bipolar constructs thus elicited can be employed as individually sampled attributes required by the Social Episode measure of situation cognition.

Subjects participated in this data point in individual sessions. In administering the Situation Grid, the procedural details involved in the standard Repertory Grid Technique referring to the cognitive construction of *persons* were closely followed (cf. Fransella & Bannister, 1977). First, participants were presented with the four situation categories named above as representing the 'elements' of the grid. For each category of social evaluation, physical danger, interpersonal and ambiguous situations, they were asked to list three specific situations from their personal experience. This resulted in a list of twelve situations for each subject which constituted the basic material for all subsequent stages of the data collection process.[1] The sequence of the four categories was systematically varied across subjects.

After eliciting the situations, the method of triadic comparisons was used to generate ten constructs describing the twelve situations. In the successive unfolding of their construct systems, the respondents' task consisted in comparing selected triads of situations in terms of their similarities and differences by naming the feature that two situations shared in common ('construct pole' or 'emergent pole') as well as identifying the opposite of that feature ('contrast pole' or 'implicit pole'). Thus, by organising the situations as columns of a matrix and the constructs as rows, a grid-like pattern emerged. Finally, the respondent was asked to go through the list of situations once again and indicate whether or not the construct poles previously generated for the specified triads of situations were applicable to other situations as well. Thus, the final matrix of twelve situations and ten constructs contained a dichotomous judgement (applies/does not apply) for each construct with respect to each situation. Altogether, completing the grid took approximately thirty minutes. The format of the Situation Grid is illustrated in Figure 9.1, while examples of the type of data collected in this

---

[1] The decision on the number of elements and constructs elicited as part of a grid is essentially a-theoretical, guided by the practical necessity to reach a compromise between obtaining comprehensive samples from the respondents' construct systems and not overstretching their time and concentration. Kelly himself included twenty-four role titles in the version of the grid designed for clinical testing, but he also developed a group version containing fifteen elements. Given that more recent studies using the Repertory Grid Technique typically employ between ten and fifteen elements and constructs, it was decided to include a total number of twelve situations and ten constructs in the Situation Grid.

Please think of three situations involving *interaction with other people* in which you felt uncomfortable.

Please think of three situations you encountered where you were being *evaluated, judged or observed* by other people.

Please think of three situations where you were about to or did encounter *physical danger*

Please think of three situations that were *new, ambiguous or unfamiliar* to you, that is, situations in which you did not know or were uncertain what to expect.

1	2	3	4	5	6	7	8	9	10	11	12	Common feature	Contrast
	O						O				O	1.	—
		O		O					O			2.	—
O			O		O							3.	—
					O		O			O		4.	—
				O			O				O	5.	—
O		O						O				6.	—
	O		O						O			7.	—
					O	O				O		8.	—
O								O			O	9.	—
			O			O			O			10.	—

9.1 Format of the situation grid

Situations

Social evaluation
– A new lover looking at me while we are both in a group of 5–6 people
– Doing a radio show
– Visiting relatives

Physical danger
– Capsizing while canoeing in whitewater
– Being hit in the stomach while walking out of a disco
– Hitching with a drunk driver

Ambiguous situations
– Being in my first psychology experiment
– Hitch-hiking abroad for the first time
– Sleeping rough on my own or the first time

Interpersonal situations
– Talking to my Dad when I'd crashed his car
– Having tea with some very posh people I used to work for
– When two different groups of people I know meet

Constructs

The figures in parentheses indicate the number of situations to which the construct pole was applicable.

– enjoyment not expected – enjoyment expected (8)
– time to think about what's happening – no time to think (10)
– not wanting to be disliked – wanting to be disliked (6)
– dislike the experience – like the experience (7)
– I have a lot of control over the situation – very little control (7)
– anxious to please – want to upset (6)
– other people involved – do not care what happens (5)
– no physical danger expected – physical danger expected (6)
– very high anxiety – very low anxiety (3)

9.2 Situation grid data (Respondent A, male)

way are presented in Figures 9.2 and 9.3 by quoting the situations and constructs named by a male and a female respondent.

Situation cognition measures

About four weeks after completing the Situation Grid, participants were invited to the first of three consecutive sessions designed to collect the different measures of situation cognition. Altogether, each participant

Situations

Social evaluation
- Giving a short talk
- Being interviewed for a university place
- Attending court in Bahrain

Physical danger
- Riding a runaway horse
- Being on a very small overloaded boat in a storm out at sea
- Facing a major operation

Ambiguous situations
- Coming to Sussex
- Starting my first job at seventeen
- Having my first sexual experience

Interpersonal situations
- Going to a cocktail party
- Going to my mother's funeral
- Being in my first tutorial

Constructs

The figures in parentheses indicate the number of situations to which the construct pole was applicable.

- feeling uncomfortable – feeling at ease (9)
- need for mental preparation – something that just happens (8)
- shyness – confidence (6)
- fear of looking stupid – awareness of one's abilities (5)
- fearful of unknown – routine, often experienced situations (10)
- not easy to escape – flexible situations (8)
- stressful – relaxed (8)
- first time experiences – situations about which I have some knowledge (8)
- experience controlled by a man – autonomy (8)
- trivial events – important events (2)

9.3 Situation grid data (Respondent B, female)

completed four instruments: the Prototype, Script, and Social Episode measures along with a global rating of the extent to which each pair of situations was perceived as being similar. For the three concept-based measures, the order of presentation was systematically varied across the three data points, while the global measure of perceived situational similarity was presented to all subjects at the third data point.

Prototype measure

For this measure, each subject's twelve situations were entered into an open-ended questionnaire. Using the format illustrated in Figure 8.4, respondents were asked to generate a list of characteristic features for each situation, whereby they were free to list as few or as many features as they considered appropriate. The average number of features aggregated across subjects and situations was 8.11.

Social Episode measure

For this measure, questionnaires were prepared containing each subject's sample of situations along with a set of bipolar scales on which to rate the situations. Unlike Study 1, where a preselected and identical set of scales was presented to all subjects, idiographically sampled scales were included in each subject's questionnaire. These scales were derived from the Situation Grids by selecting those seven constructs with the highest rate of applicability to the total range of situations (cf. the figures in parentheses in Figures 9.2 and 9.3). The constructs and their respective contrasts were arranged as seven-point bipolar scales according to the format displayed in Figure 8.5. The order of presentation of the scales and the sequence of the two poles were randomly varied across the twelve situations.

Script measure

To arrive at individual measures of the cognitive representation of situations in terms of scripts, subjects were asked to provide detailed descriptions of the characteristic sequence of actions and events in each situation. The format of this measure was the same as in Study 1, illustrated in Figure 8.6. Frequency analyses of the number of events named for each situation revealed an average of 8.37 across subjects and situations.

Global measure of perceived similarity

In addition to these specific measures of situation cognition, all subjects were asked to provide global ratings of perceived similarity between all pairs of situations using the format illustrated in Figure 8.3.

On each of the measures, the twelve situations were presented in random orders.

Figures 9.4 and 9.5 illustrate the scope of the data collected in this stage of the study. For the three concept-based measures of situation cognition, Figure 9.4 presents a male respondent's data for an *interpersonal situation*

Being in a seminar with lots of people who were very knowledgeable and I couldn't contribute anything

Prototype measure
1 Small enclosed space
2 Shelves of books
3 Silence
4 Lecturer waiting for you to speak
5 Embarrassing feeling
6 Hot sun through the blinds
7 Looking at the books on the shelves
8 Soft leather seats
9 Strange pictures on the wall

Social Episode measure

1 being on guard	X—o—o—o—o—o—o	relaxed
2 unfriendly atmosphere	o—X—o—o—o—o—o	friendly atmosphere
3 unexpected reactions	o—o—o—X—o—o—o	expected reactions
4 in control	o—o—o—o—o—o—X	not in control
5 feeling confident	o—o—o—o—o—o—X	feeling inadequate
6 unfamiliar people	o—o—X—o—o—o—o	familiar people
7 having to put on an act	o—X—o—o—o—o—o	being able to say what I think

Script measure
1 Walking into a small room with 3 or 4 people in it
2 Sitting down
3 Arranging my books and papers
4 Tutor begins discussion
5 People contribute a lot to the discussion
6 Trying to avoid the gaze of the tutor
7 Feeling prickly and hot, feeling like I want to get up and leave

9.4 Example of the situation cognition data (Respondent C, male)

from his Situation Grid, and Figure 9.5 illustrates a female respondent's data pertaining to an *ambiguous situation*.

Behavioural measures

At the fifth and final data point, the behavioural profiles of each person with respect to his or her twelve situations were measured. Two separate methods were employed.

Arriving at the scene of a road accident

Prototype measure
1 Broken glass
2 Liquid on the floor
3 Darkness
4 Tangled metal
5 Lifeless bodies
6 Astonished impressions
7 Lots of people standing around

Social Episode measure
1 dangerous	X—o—o—o—o—o—o	not really dangerous
2 in control	o—o—o—o—o—o—X	not in control
3 need to make an impression	o—o—o—o—o—o—X	no need to make an impression
4 long-term effects	X—o—o—o—o—o—o	short-term effects
5 active	o—o—o—o—X—o—o	powerless
6 others don't appear superior	o—o—o—X—o—o—o	faced with superior people
7 concentrating intently	o—o—X—o—o—o—o	difficult to concentrate

Script measure
1 I pull up behind a stream of cars
2 I realise there has been an accident and get out to investigate
3 Two cars face each other, bonnets thoroughly dented, and a third has ploughed into the side of both
4 I see four passengers in one car, one in the other, none in the sideways one
5 I ask if fire brigade and ambulance have been called
6 I walk around the cars. All the passengers are trapped
7 All are alive. I check for signs of serious injuries
8 I see a fluid trickling out of a car
9 I tell people not to smoke and feel this was a very inane thing to say
10 I walk round and round the cars, and my heart is beating fast

9.5 Example of the situation cognition data (Respondent D, female, a trained nurse)

Present Affect Reactions Questionnaire

For each situation, subjects were first presented with the twenty reaction scales of the PARQ (Endler, 1980) used in Study 1 (cf. Figure 8.2). On a five-point scale, they indicated for each item the extent to which they had shown the respective response in that situation.

Global measure of behavioural similarity

Since the PARQ is focused on specific, mainly physiological reactions to anxiety-provoking situations it does not take more complex behaviours into account. Therefore, subjects were asked in the second part of the behavioural measure to rate the similarity of their behavioural patterns in each pair of situations. In order to clarify the relationship between the two measures for the subjects, they received the following instruction:

> On the preceding pages, you described your reactions to each of the situations on a very specific, rather more physiological level. In order to get a comprehensive impression of your behaviour in each situation, we have included a further measure in this questionnaire. Here you are asked to think about your behaviour in more general terms, considering all the different actions and reactions you remember showing in each situation. [. . .]

The global ratings of behavioural similarity were made on a five-point scale ranging from 0 = behaviour not at all similar to 4 = behaviour completely similar.

Employing two different behavioural measures offers the possibility of analysing both the agreement between the two measures and their potential differences in terms of the correspondence between situation cognition and behaviour.

Results

The three concept-based measures of situation cognition as well as the PARQ asked subjects to describe each situation in its own right rather than providing comparative judgements between pairs of situations. Therefore, similarity relationships between all possible combinations of situations had to be derived from these measures as a prerequisite for the analysis of the proposed covariation of situation cognition and behaviour. The same similarity indices as in Study 1 were used towards this end.

For the Prototype measure, similarity between each pair of situations was operationally defined in terms of the ratio of shared features to the total number of features generated for the two situations. To compute the extent of feature overlap, the formula introduced in chapter 8 was employed.

In the same way, pairwise scores of situational similarity were derived from the Script measure by relating the number of shared events to the total number of events named for the two situations involved.

For the Social Episode measure, similarity between each pair of situations was expressed as the Euclidian distance between them computed across the seven bipolar scales.

Finally, Euclidian distances across the twenty reaction scales were computed between all pairs of situations to arrive at indices of behavioural similarity based on the PARQ.

The global ratings of perceived and behavioural similarity provided the required information about similarity relationships without any further tranformations.

Following these analyses, six similarity matrices were available for each subject with respect to the twelve anxiety-provoking situations named in his or her Situation Grid. These similarity measures referred to the following variables:

For the cognitive measures:

1 Characteristic *features* (Prototype measure)
2 Characteristic *events and actions* (Script measure)
3 Central *evaluative* dimensions (Social Episode measure)
4 *Global* perceived similarity

For the behavioural measures:

5 Characterisic *reactions* (PARQ measure)
6 *Global* behavioural similarity

To test the hypothesis that individual patterns of situation cognition and behaviour covary across situations and thus reflect coherence in personality, intraindividual or 'within-subject' correlations between the four measures of perceived similarity and the two measures of behavioural similarity were computed for each subject. In these analyses, the sixty-six possible pairs of situations were regarded as 'cases', with the cognitive and behavioural similarity indices being treated as 'variables' (cf. Michela, 1990). This procedure is based on the premise that the situation pairs are independent elements of a sample drawn from each individual's population of anxiety-provoking situations. The intraindividual correlations between situation cognition and behaviour are shown in Table 9.1. The intercorrelations between the four cognitive measures can be found in Table 9.2. Finally, Table 9.3 contains the intercorrelations between the two behavioural measures for the twenty-eight participants.

An inspection of the individual correlations between the cognitive and the behavioural measures reveals substantial differences between subjects in the magnitude of the obtained correlations as well as the overall pattern of results. Some participants showed consistently high (e.g. Subject no. 15), medium (e.g. Subject no. 4), or moderate (e.g. Subject no. 20) correlations between perceived similarity and behavioural similarity across the eight indices. Others were characterised by particularly high or low coefficients on only one or two of the measures. For Subject no. 1, for instance, the correlations of the four cognitive measures with the PARQ were minimal, while each of the correlations with the global measure of behavioural

Table 9.1. *Individual correlations between situation cognition and behaviour*

Subject no.	gl/r	ep/r	pr/r	sc/r	gl/p	ep/p	pr/p	sc/p
1	.45***	.42***	.23*	.48***	.03	−.02	−.04	.17
2	.82***	.56***	.46***	.44***	.46***	.49***	.29**	.36***
3	.42***	.20	.15	.24*	.10	.15	.00	.18
4	.35**	.21*	.41***	.35**	.15	.34**	.27*	.51***
5	.93***	.42***	.39***	.50***	.54***	.62***	.16	.17
6	.66***	.55***	.22*	.21*	.00	.23*	.09	.21*
7	.67***	.30**	.65***	.65***	.19	.29**	.22*	.52***
8	.95***	.57***	.73***	.48***	.79***	.41***	.57***	.41***
9	.87***	.73***	.19	.24*	.77***	.65***	.17	.09
10	.77***	.70***	.48***	.12	.51***	.56***	.50***	.12
11	.51***	.25*	.22*	.40***	.33**	.45***	.36**	.58***
12	.86***	.42***	.46***	.20	.59***	.43***	.36**	.02
13	.38**	.19	.11	.28*	.44***	.22*	.21*	.42***
14	.83***	.12	.46***	.34**	.59***	.22*	.43***	.17
15	.88***	.74***	.54***	.48***	.57***	.64***	.33**	.27*
16	.50***	.26*	.40***	.30**	.38***	.08	.20	.04
17	.85***	−.10	.30**	.55***	.45***	−.04	.24*	.40***
18	.72***	.37***	.47***	.40***	.09	.38***	.03	.14
19	.89***	.67***	.38***	.37***	.73***	.52***	.38***	.39***
20	.32**	.34**	.27*	.15	.29**	.35**	.11	.02
21	.77***	.46***	.16	.15	.65***	.67***	.16	.33**
22	.57***	.34**	.39***	.47***	.41***	.33**	.23*	.41***
23	.67***	.21*	.55***	.39***	.36**	.31**	.33**	.19
24	.57***	−.02	.33**	.38***	.39***	.31**	−.03	−.01
25	.61***	.49***	.10	.29**	.48***	.51***	.14	.46***
26	.43***	.07	.17	.23*	.16	.34**	−.07	.02
27	.79***	.24*	.45***	.43***	.45**	−.10	.14	.35**
28	.49***	.48***	.47***	.36**	.20	.27*	.43***	.01

Notes:
gl = Global rating of perceived similarity
 r = Global rating of behavioural similarity
ep = Social Episode measure
pr = Prototype measure
sc = Script measure
 p = PARQ behavioural measure
*p < .05   **p < .01   ***p < .001

similarity were significant. A different pattern emerged for Subject no. 17, where the Social Episode measure was negatively correlated with both behavioural measures, while all remaining cognition–behaviour correlations were significantly positive. Even though the present data do not suggest specific hypotheses about individual differences in cross-situational coherence, we would argue that a decisive advantage of the present individual-centred methodology lies in the fact that those differences are made apparent rather than being averaged out or treated as error variance as would be the case in a nomothetic study of cross-situational consistency. The task of identifying systematic patterns of individual differences in the type and magnitude of cross-situational coherence, possibly in the vein of the

Table 9.2. *Intercorrelations between the cognitive measures*

Subject no.	gl/ep	gl/pr	gl/sc	ep/pr	ep/sc	pr/sc
1	.33**	.19	.23*	.35**	.31**	.14
2	.50***	.52***	.52***	.54***	.30**	.48***
3	.42***	.42***	.42***	.10	.32**	.38***
4	.25*	.31**	.24*	.21*	.24*	.29**
5	.39***	.36**	.52***	.18	.22*	.13
6	.52***	.26*	.24*	.33**	.27*	.03
7	.23*	.59***	.49***	.31**	.18	.59***
8	.54***	.68***	.46***	.58***	.30**	.23*
9	.68***	.14	.24*	.06	.04	.22*
10	.56***	.60***	.05	.34	−.04	.22*
11	.25*	.26*	.29*	.31**	.26*	.21*
12	.51***	.38***	.34**	.30**	.24*	−.01
13	.37***	.21*	.40***	.39***	.14	.13
14	.12	.64***	.33**	.02	.05	.32**
15	.70***	.57***	.38***	.50***	.46***	.31**
16	.31**	.61***	.32**	.39***	.27*	.46***
17	.08	.34**	.46***	−.30**	.02	.19
18	.32**	.56***	.36**	.19	.23*	.22*
19	.61***	.47***	.44***	.17	.35**	.52***
20	.34**	.26*	.24*	.15	.16	.20*
21	.42***	.17	.13	−.01	.19	−.08
22	.43***	.56***	.27*	.28*	.20*	.38***
23	.04	.59***	.57***	.01	.04	.44***
24	.36**	.20*	.11	.02	.06	.43***
25	.29**	.19	.27**	.07	.17	.26*
26	.04	−.01	.55***	−.10	.15	.04
27	.13	.33**	.42***	.18	.11	.30**
28	.48***	.53***	.46***	.46***	.23*	.31**

Notes:
gl = Global rating of perceived similarity
ep = Social Episode measure
pr = Prototype measure
sc = Script measure
*p < .05   **p < .01   ***p < .001

Table 9.3. *Intraindividual correlations between the two behavioural measures*

Subject no.	r	Subject no.	r	Subject no.	r	Subject no.	r
1	−.01	8	.81***	15	.59***	22	.44***
2	.57***	9	.82***	16	.02	23	.45***
3	.11	10	.60***	17	.56***	24	.05
4	.35**	11	.49***	18	.17	25	.37***
5	.56***	12	.68***	19	.71***	26	.33**
6	.10	13	.32**	20	.35**	27	.48***
7	.43***	14	.61***	21	.69***	28	.32**

Note:
*p < .05   **p < .01   ***p < .001

Table 9.4. *Average correlations between cognitive similarity and behavioural similarity across twelve anxiety-provoking situations (N = 28)*

	Global behavioural similarity	PARQ	Global perceived similarity	Episode measure	Prototype measure
Global Behavioural Similarity					
PARQ	.46**				
Global Perceived Similarity	.72*** [a]	.43* [e]			
Episode measure	.38* [b]	.37* [f]	.37*		
Prototype measure	.38* [c]	.24 [g]	.41*	.24	
Script measure	.36* [d]	.26 [h]	.36*	.20	.26

Percentage of significant correlations

	[a]	[b]	[c]	[d]	[e]	[f]	[g]	[h]
$p < .001$	89.3	50.0	57.1	53.7	60.7	46.6	17.8	35.6
$p < .01$	10.7	10.4	7.2	10.7	10.7	21.4	17.8	7.2
$p < .05$	0.0	18.5	14.3	21.4	0.0	14.2	17.8	7.2
n.s.	0.0	21.1	21.4	14.2	28.6	17.8	46.6	50.0

Notes:
*$p < .05$ **$p < .01$ ***$p < .001$

moderator variable strategy (cf. chapter 5), could be one of the conceptual as well as empirical extensions of the present approach.

To arrive at a comparative appraisal of the findings for the total sample, the individual correlations were z-transformed and then averaged across subjects. The results from this analysis are presented in Table 9.4 along with the percentage of intraindividual correlations for each index that reached statistical significance.[2]

Both individual and aggregated data lend convincing support to the hypothesis that coherence in personality is reflected in the intraindividual covariation of perceived similarity and behavioural similarity across anxiety-provoking situations. With a score of $r = .72$ the average correlation between the two global measures of perceived and behavioural similarity accounts for 51.8% of the total variance. The magnitude of this figure is all the more noteworthy as the two measures were not collected at the same data point, as

---

[2] When comparing individual and aggregated scores in terms of their statistical significance, it should be borne in mind that the two sets of coefficients are based on different sample sizes. In the individual analyses, the N = 66 situation pairs are treated as 'cases', while the aggregated scores are based on the total number of N = 28 respondents.

as in most studies of cross-situational consistency, but were separated by an interval of approximately three months. Although the average correlations of the three theory-based measures of situation cognition with the behavioural measures are lower, the majority of them are still statistically significant. A comparison of the three concept-based measures of situation cognition does not identify a single measure as being superior or inferior with regard to its correlation with the behavioural measures.[3]

The behavioural profiles created on the basis of the PARQ clearly emerged as corresponding less with the different measures of situation cognition than the global measure of behavioural similarity. Different explanations suggest themselves to account for this finding. First, the PARQ consists of a well-established, yet nomothetic set of response scales, while the cognitive measures relied exclusively on idiographically sampled data. Thus, there is a discrepancy between the two types of data in terms of their immediate reference to individual experiences which may have resulted in relatively low correlations between them. Moreover, the PARQ covers only short-term, primarily physiological responses to anxiety-provoking situations, leaving aside more complex patterns of behaviour which may be of higher psychological significance to the person. The moderate correlation between the PARQ and the global rating of behavioural similarity, specifically instructing subjects to take the whole range of their behaviours into account, reflects this difference between the two measures.

Finally, it should be noted that the average correlations among the cognitive measures are relatively low. The correlations of each of the three concept-based measures of situation cognition with the global measure of perceived situational similarity are moderate, but statistically significant. Among themselves, the intercorrelations of the three concept-based measures are non-significant, with scores ranging from $r = .20$ to $r = .24$. These findings permit the conclusion that the three measures employed in the present study, as well as the theoretical models from which they were

[3] The order of presentation of the three measures had been ruled out as a potential source of bias by balancing the sequence in which the measures were administered over the three data points. Nevertheless, one might argue that the long intervals between the data points could have produced a linear relationship between the temporal proximity of the cognitive and behavioural measures and the magnitude of their correlations to the effect that cognition–behaviour correlations would be highest for those cognitive measures collected in the final of the three data points devoted to the measurement of situation cognition. Without implying a systematic bias in favour of one of the methods, such a possibility would nevertheless lead to a distorted picture in evaluating the feasibility of the three measures as correlates of behavioural profiles across situations. Therefore, to address this issue, correlations across subjects were computed for each measure between the magnitude of its correlation with behaviour and its position in the sequence of presentation of the three measures. These correlations ranged from $r = -.17$ to $r = .26$, none being statistically significant. Thus, there are no indications of a systematic relationship between the magnitude of cognition–behaviour correlations and the order of presentation of the three concept-based measures of situation cognition.

derived, refer to different aspects of the cognitive representation of situations, thus warranting their use as independent operationalisations of the concept of situation cognition.

Discussion

The aim of this study was to obtain empirical support for the concept of coherence in personality. Coherence was defined in terms of systematic variabilities in behaviour across situations as a function of the perceived similarity or dissimilarity of those situations. Special emphasis was placed on the analysis of concept-based measures of perceived situational similarity in terms of their covariation with behavioural profiles across a diverse range of anxiety-provoking situations sampled individually for each participant.

Looking first at the relationship between situation cognition and behaviour reflected in the aggregated data, perceived situational similarity and behavioural similarity are shown to be most strongly related if similarity is measured on the basis of global ratings: more than 50% of the variance in individual behaviour across a wide range of anxiety-provoking situations is accounted for by the cognitive representation of those situations in terms of their perceived similarity or difference. As far as the pessimistic conclusions of critics of the consistency concept are concerned (e.g. Mischel & Peake, 1982a, b), the present findings demonstrate that individual behaviour may well be shown to follow a systematic pattern attributable to the subjective meaning assigned by the person to the situations encountered in his or her everyday life. For this pattern to be discovered empirically, however, it is essential that the methodological strategies are adequate to the theoretical assumptions inherent in the concept of cross-situational coherence. An adequate operationalisation of coherence requires that
– the situations across which coherence is expected to be found are valid samples from the individual's personal experience;
– judgements of situational similarity are not made a priori by the investigator but left to the individual, and finally,
– the idea is abandoned that the contents of situations and their meaning have to be comparable, or even identical, across individuals.

The intraindividual correlations between global measures of situation cognition and behaviour, which are above $r = .80$ for some subjects, demonstrate along with the aggregated findings that conclusive evidence of coherent behavioural patterns can be found if these requirements are met. However, they do not yield information about the criteria the subjects relied on in their ratings of similarity. Therefore, three concept-based measures of situation cognition, derived from the prototype, social episode and script approaches in cognitive psychology, were employed in this study. These approaches contain specific assumptions about the principles underlying the cognitive representation of situations and thus suggest themselves as building blocks in the search for a theoretical foundation of the concept of 'psychological situation'. In the Prototype measure, perceived situational similarity is conceptualised in terms of shared characteristic features. The Script measure defines situational similarity in terms of shared actions and event sequences. Finally, in the Social Episode measure situational similarity is established through subjects' ratings of situations on relevant evaluative dimensions.

Each of the three concept-based measures of perceived situational similarity shows significant average correlations with the global measure of behavioural similarity. The magnitude of these correlations is approximately the same, yielding no indication for the superiority or inferiority of any one measure. Bearing in mind that the models underlying these measures were not explicitly designed to address the issue of cross-situational coherence but had to be adapted to the purposes of the present research, the obtained findings may be regarded as encouraging. One reason for the lower correlations of the concept-based measures with behaviour as compared to the global measure of perceived similarity can be seen in the fact that they each refer to different aspects of situational meaning, all of which may be considered simultaneously by the subjects in their global ratings. The low correlations among the Prototype, Script and Social Episode measures lend support to this line of reasoning. Another reason why average correlations between situation cognition and behaviour were lower for the three concept-based measures than for the global rating has to do with differences in the tasks involved in the two types of measures. In the Prototype, Script and Social Episode measures, subjects were asked to describe each situation individually, and similarity relationships between situations were sub-sequently derived from these descriptions as part of the data analysis. In contrast, for the global rating of perceived similarity, subjects were instructed explicitly to think about the similarity of situation pairs. Since it is reasonable to assume that measures of situational similarity derived from independent descriptions of situations are likely to attenuate similarity scores compared to direct comparisons between situations, the concept-based measures can be regarded as providing a more stringent test of the covariation hypothesis, and the magnitude of their correlations with behaviour should be interpreted with this possibility in mind.

Altogether, the findings from the present study corroborate the tentative evidence in support of the coherence concept found in Study 1. An inspection of the relevant tables (Table 8.3 and Table 9.4) reveals highly similar average correlations of $r = .40$ and $r = .43$ between the global measures of perceived and behavioural similarity in the two studies. As far as the Prototype, Script, and Episode measures are concerned, differences in sample size permit no more than cautious comparisons. Nevertheless, these comparisons also suggest that the newly developed research strategy is capable of producing replicable findings in support of the concept of coherence in personality. At the same time, the present findings join those of the previous study in demonstrating the practicability of the individual-centred methodology aimed at combining idiographic principles of data collection and analysis with the examination of nomothetic hypotheses about personality functioning.

Yet, even though the evidence obtained thus far is encouraging from both a conceptual and a methodological point of view, the empirical strategies used in the first two studies were not entirely unproblematic. Two problems in particular emerged in the course of the analyses.

1 The first problem refers to the collection of behavioural information with regard to anxiety-provoking situations. As outlined above, somewhat disappointing results were obtained for the PARQ as a behavioural measure, possibly due to its nomothetic character as well as the relatively narrow of behavioural responses captured by this meassure. Therefore, a more stringent application of the individual-centred methodology would require to replace the PARQ by an idiographic measure of complex behavioural patterns in response to anxiety-provoking situations.

2 The second problem that emerged from the first two studies has to do with the individual differences of the obtained findings. An inspection of the intraindividual correlations reveals considerable variance across respondents which may be interpreted in at least two different ways. One possibility is that this variance could be indicative of stable individual differences in the extent to which people are consistent in their behaviour across situations. This explanation would be in line with Bem & Allen's (1974) and others' research on self-reported level consistency as a moderator of empirically observed consistency across situations (cf. chapter 5). However, an alternative explanation could be that part of the variance in cognition–behaviour correlations is due to the open-ended and relatively unstandardised format of the present measures, prescribed by the novelty of the individual-centred methodology. For instance, this format allowed subjects to decide upon the number of characteristics and events included in the Prototype and Script measures so that the subsequent patterns of situational similarity were based on information which was differentially comprehensive across respondents. On the basis of the previous experiences with these new measures, it is now possible to unify their format in order to reduce the impact of method variance on the interindividual comparison of the findings. This is an essential prerequisite for addressing the more relevant issue of whether stable individual differences can be found in the level of coherence across situations.

10 Study 3: Coherence of situation cognition and behavioural self-reports

This study is designed to corroborate the validity of the present approach to the study of coherence by replicating the findings from the first two studies. At the same time, modifications are introduced to the individual-centred methodology aimed at enhancing its generalisability as an empirical strategy for the study of coherence in personality. As in the previous studies, the basic hypothesis states that coherence in personality is reflected in the covariation of perceived situational similarity and behavioural similarity across anxiety-provoking situations, provided that the situations, behaviours and perceptions of situational similarity are valid samples from the individual's personal experience.

Whilst the present study thus shares the overall design and objectives of Studies 1 and 2, the format of the individual-centred measures developed and applied successfully in the first two studies was tightened and unified. The rationale behind these modifications was to allow a more conclusive comparison of the different measures as well as clarify the meaning of individual differences with respect to the concept of coherence. In addition, a new free-response measure of behaviour was developed capturing more complex reactions to anxiety-provoking situations than those addressed by the 'Present Affect Reactions Questionnaire'.

Altogether, the study is aimed at providing further evidence of the proposed link between behavioural profiles across anxiety-provoking situations and the individual's cognitive representation of situational similarity.

Sample and overview

A new group of thirty-three first year undergraduates at the University of Sussex volunteered to participate in this study. After the first data point, eight subjects dropped out so that the final sample comprised twenty-five participants, seventeen females and five males. After the final session, they received a payment of £13.00 along with a detailed report about the aims and findings of the study.

The study required subjects to attend six data points extending over a period of six months. In the first data point, individual samples of anxiety-provoking situations were obtained through the Situation Grid. The second data point introduced the behavioural measures, while the third, fourth, and fifth sessions were required to collect the cognitive measures. A sixth session was scheduled in this study to examine the reliability of the new behavioural measure through a re-test.

Measures of situation cognition and behaviour

Sampling anxiety-provoking situations

As in Study 2, the Situation Grid was employed in the first session to elicit a sample of anxiety-provoking situations from each participant. To limit the temporal range of the situations sampled from the participants, the instructions were modified in such a way that subjects were asked to supply, for each of the four categories (physical danger, interpersonal, social evaluation and ambiguous situations), three situations from their personal experience *they had encountered in the course of the past twelve months.*[1] Otherwise, the format of the Situation Grid was the same as in Study 2 (cf. Figure 9.1).

Behavioural measures

The second data point in this study was devoted to collecting the behavioural information. In view of the limitations of the PARQ as a measure of behaviour in anxiety-provoking situations, which had become apparent in the first two studies, alternative strategies were considered to replace it. Eventually, a new and more complex self-report measure of behaviour was developed after an attempt had failed to implement a strategy for arriving at behavioural data without reliance on self-reports. Before the new measure is introduced, this failed attempt will be described briefly in the light of the particular problems involved in the measurement of behavioural regularities across different situations.

A crucial problem confronting any study on the cross-situational consistency of behaviour lies in the fact that information about a person's behaviour is required on multiple occasions and situations. For a variety of reasons, this information is difficult to obtain by experimental manipulation

---

[1] It might be argued that introducing a time span of twelve months is still not sufficient to ensure that the sampled situations are comparable in terms of their proximity to the respondents' completion of the Situation Grid. On the other hand, the previous studies revealed that some situation categories, especially the physical danger category, were encountered so infrequently that any further limitation of the timeframe for supplying situations would have involved the risk of forcing respondents to refer to relatively trivial or 'blown-up' situations in their grids.

or direct observation. Therefore, investigators are often forced to rely on self-report information despite the well-known susceptibility of such information to a variety of deliberate or unwitting distortions (Pryor, 1980). With respect to anxiety-provoking situations, there is not only a plethora of practical problems associated with collecting idiographic behavioural data on multiple occasions through experimental manipulations or planned observation. Even more importantly, ethical concerns preclude the intentional exposure of subjects to anxiety-provoking circumstances of any severity.

Since the recording of overt behaviour in a large number of anxiety-provoking situations, differing from person to person, appeared neither feasible nor ethically acceptable, an alternative strategy was contemplated along the lines suggested by the 'peer rating' strategy mentioned in chapter 5 (e.g. Moskowitz, 1986; Woodruffe, 1985). This strategy requires subjects to name a number of peers or other knowledgeable informants who would be able to report on their behaviour in a particular situation. By aggregating reports obtained from different informants, it is possible to arrive at consensual indices of the subject's behaviour in a given situation.

A pilot test was conducted to test the feasibility of collecting behavioural information through peer ratings. An independent sample of twenty undergraduates was asked to complete a questionnaire instructing them to list a total of eight anxiety-provoking situations from their personal experience (two for each of the four categories used in the Situation Grid). Following each situation, they were asked to nominate at least two persons who had been present in that situation to serve as raters on their behaviour. The outcome of this pilot study revealed that such a procedure would not be workable for three main reasons:

1 A substantial number of anxiety-provoking situations which respondents might have named had happened without the presence of observers who could act as 'witnesses' on the respondent's behaviour;

2 Many subjects refused to nominate observers because they did not want to disclose to the informants that they had experienced the situation in question as being anxiety-provoking; and, finally,

3 They were unwilling to enlist the other persons' cooperation without their prior consent.

Altogether, the pilot sample's responses to the questionnaire clearly showed that reliance on peer ratings as a source of information about individual behaviour in a sensitive domain like anxiety would not be feasible, suggesting that attempts at broadening the scope of the behavioural measure in the present study would have to remain located within the boundaries of self-report data.

In view of this conclusion, a free-response, idiographic measure was designed in which respondents were asked to supply, for each situation from their Situation Grid, a list of eight behaviours they had shown in that situation. For each behaviour, they were also asked to rate the likelihood that they would show it again given that they were in the same situation once more. These likelihood ratings, which were made on a five-point scale, provided the basis for the re-test of the behavioural measure at the sixth data point. In particular, subjects received the following instructions:

> On the following pages, you will be asked to list, for each situation, eight different behaviours and reactions you showed in that situation. These may be more 'overt' reactions, such as trying to get out of the situation, saying or doing something in particular, etc. or more 'covert' ones, such as having butterflies in the stomach, heart beating faster, etc. You are free to write down whatever you actually did or experienced during the situation, but please *do not include thoughts or emotional feelings*, but concentrate on actual behaviour.
>
> Following each of the behaviours you list, you will be asked to indicate the likelihood that you would show the same behaviour again if you were in the same situation once more. To do this, you are provided with a five-point rating scale. Endorsing '0' means that it is very unlikely that you would show the same behaviour again, while endorsing '4' indicates that it is very likely that you would show the behaviour again.

The format of the new behavioural measure is illustrated in Figures 10.1 and 10.2 with the data provided by a male respondent for a situation from the *social evaluation* category and a female respondent for a situation from the *interpersonal* category.

In addition to providing a list of eight specific behaviours for each of the twelve situations, subjects were provided with a matrix of all sixty-six pairs of situations and asked to make pairwise ratings of the extent to which their behaviour had been similar in the two situations. As in the previous study, these ratings were made on a five-point scale ranging from '0 = behaviour not at all similar' to '4 = behaviour completely similar'.

Cognitive measures

In the third, fourth and fifth data points, subjects completed the three concept-based measures of situation cognition along with providing global ratings of perceived situational similarity. The order of presentation of the Prototype, Social Episode and Script measures was balanced across subjects, while the global ratings were obtained from all participants at the fourth session.

The overall format of the cognitive measures was identical to the previous studies. For the Prototype measure, subjects were asked to describe each situation in terms of its characteristic features using the format illustrated in chapter 8 (cf. Figure 8.4). In line with the aim of the present study to

Being interviewed for Sussex university

Please list eight different behaviours you showed in this situation and rate each behaviour on the rating scale provided below.

1 Talked to other interviewees
   How likely is it that you will show this behaviour again given that you are in the same situation once more?

   0———1———2———3———4
   very unlikely   very likely

2 Very aware of heartbeat – palpitations
   How likely is it that you will show this behaviour again given that you are in the same situation once more?

   0———1———2———3———4
   very unlikely   very likely

3 Breathed deliberately and deeply
4 Avoided biting nails
5 Bit nails
6 Remained tense in interview
7 Checked self-image
8 Drank coffee

10.1 Example of the behavioural self-report measure (Respondent E, male)

Being disciplined unfairly in my job

Please list eight different behaviours you showed in this situation and rate each behaviour on the rating scale provided below.

1 Had a dry mouth
   How likely is it that you will show this behaviour again given that you are in the same situation once more?

   0———1———2———3———4
   very unlikely   very likely

2 Perspiring palms of hands
   How likely is it that you will show this behaviour again given that you are in the same situation once more?

   0———1———2———3———4
   very unlikely   very likely

3 Palpitations
4 Butterflies in stomach
5 Spoke in calm but angry voice
6 Sat rigidly in chair
7 Slammed door
8 Nausea

10.2 Example of the behavioural self-report measure (Respondent F, female)

standardise the different measures as far as possible, all subjects were instructed to generate a fixed number of eight features for every situation.[2] Similarly, the Script measure was modified in such a way that respondents were required to supply a total of eight characteristic events for each situation. Otherwise, the format of the Script measure remained the same (cf. Figure 8.6; chapter 8). One respondent failed to complete the Script measure. In the Social Episode measure, each situation was rated on a set of seven evaluative scales derived from the constructs generated by the participants in their Situation Grids (cf. Figures 9.4 and 9.5, chapter 9). In addition, to arrive at the global ratings of perceived similarity, subjects judged each pair of situations on a five-point scale ranging from '0 = not at all similar' to '4 = completely similar'.

Re-test of the behavioural measure

In order to examine the reliability of the new behavioural measure, a sixth data point was introduced. For the re-test, subjects were presented once more with the list of behaviours they had previously supplied for each situation and asked to repeat their ratings of the likelihood that they would show the behaviour again if the same situation recurred in the future. The correlations between the two ratings, which were separated by an interval of four months, were interpreted as an index of the reliability of the self-reported behavioural patterns.

Since the previous studies had revealed a substantial amount of individual variability in the level of coherence across situations, an additional aim of the present study was to clarify the causes of those differences. By tightening the format of the different measures so as to reduce the impact of their open-ended design on correlations between situation cognition and behaviour, a more conclusive examination of an alternative explanation became possible suggesting that a person's actual level of consistency may be predicted on the basis of his or her self-reported variability (Bem & Allen, 1974). To address this latter hypothesis, ratings of self-perceived consistency were elicited on the basis of the following question adapted from the Bem & Allen study: 'How much do you vary from one situation to another in how much anxiety you feel?' Responses were made on a seven-point scale ranging from '1 = not at all variable' to '7 = extremely variable'.

Upon completion of the sixth data point, subjects were paid and promised a detailed report of the aims and findings of the study, including their own pattern of results.

---

[2] The decision to set the number of characteristics at N = 8 for the Prototype and Script measures was made on the basis of the findings from Study 2 where an average number of 8.11 features and 8.37 events, respectively, had been named.

Results

To examine the proposed covariation of perceived situational similarity and behavioural similarity, the first step of the analysis consisted in converting the data obtained from the three concept-based measures of situation cognition as well as the behavioural self-reports into similarity rank orders for each participant. For the Prototype, Script, and Behaviour measures, situational similarity was established through identifying the amount of overlap between the information provided for all pairs of situations. Formally, this overlap was defined in terms of the ratio of shared elements (i.e. characteristic features, events and behaviours) in relation to the total number of elements, using the formula introduced in chapter 8. For the Social Episode measure, ratings were averaged across the seven bipolar scales for each situation, and Euclidian distances between all pairs of situations were then computed on that basis. No further transformations were required by the global ratings of perceived and behavioural similarity.

This part of the data analysis yielded the following similarity profiles for the idiographic set of anxiety-provoking situations provided by each of the twenty-five participants.

On the situation cognition side, perceived similarity was operationalised in four different ways, based on

1 eight characteristic features supplied for each situation (Prototype measure)
2 ratings of each situation on seven idiographically sampled dimensions (Social Episode measure)
3 eight actions and events supplied for each situation (Script measure)
4 global ratings of perceived similarity for all pairs of situations

On the behavioural side, two measures of similarity were available, based on

1 a list of eight behaviours shown in each situation
2 global ratings of behavioural similarity for all pairwise combinations of situations.

Before examining the link between the cognitive and behavioural measures of situational similarity, the reliability of the new behavioural measure was established by correlating the likelihood ratings obtained at the second and sixth data points. The re-test correlations for the individual participants as well as for the total sample are presented in Table 10.1.

In view of the fact that the two measurements were separated by an interval of four months, the aggregated score of $r = .77$, as well as the majority of individual coefficients, speak to the reliability of this measure, warranting its use in the subsequent examination of the covariation hypothesis.

Table 10.1. *Intraindividual correlations between the ratings of behaviour probability at the second and sixth data points*

Subject no.	r	Subject no.	r	Subject no.	r	Subject no.	r
1	.43	8	.35	15	.14	22	.81
2	.34	9	.95	16	.74	23	.83
3	.69	10	.85	17	.58	24	.93
4	.51	11	.69	18	.56	25	.85
5	.76	12	.93	19	.85		
6	.79	13	.64	20	.99	M	.77
7	.95	14	.28	21	.77		

Table 10.2. *Individual correlations between situation cognition and behaviour*

Subject no.	gl/r	ep/r	pr/r	sc/r	gl/s	ep/s	pr/s	sc/s
1	.70***	.17	.28*	.40***	.43***	.28*	.24*	.25*
2	.49***	.23*	.13	.12	.38***	.16	.49***	.48***
3	.87***	.23*	.13	.10	.23*	.18	.31**	.56***
4	.82***	.45***	.20	.19	.33**	.26*	.34**	.50***
5	.79***	.27*	.28*	.33**	.31*	.03	.39***	.34**
6	.55***	.48***	.15	−.12	.32**	.24*	.23*	.24*
7	.72***	.45***	.34**	.45***	.43***	.42***	.22*	.44***
8	.78***	.60***	.64***	.44***	.41***	.34**	.43***	.47***
9	.69***	.39***	.27*	.37***	.32**	.27*	.45***	.35**
10	.53***	.09	.28*	.30**	.37***	.29**	.39***	.19
11	.73***	.40***	.34**	.18	.58***	.16	.58***	.38***
12	.59***	.21*	.31**	.50***	.36**	.41***	.34**	.29**
13	.76***	.44***	.27*	.28*	.33**	.13	.49***	.49***
14	−.07	.67***	.46***	.50***	.04	.44***	.23*	.43***
15	.71***	.60***	.19	.36**	.30**	.49***	.29**	.17
16	.66***	.53***	.29**	.30**	.35**	.46***	.43***	.45***
17	.52**	.27*	.37***	.28*	.36**	−.09	.34**	.37***
18	.52***	.16	−.06	.19	.34**	.13	.10	.34***
19	.76***	.22*	.42***	.55***	.29**	.18	.51***	.52***
20	.83***	.62***	.37***	.50***	.46***	.46***	.34**	.39***
21	.74***	.72***	.50***	.41***	.40***	.47***	.44***	.51***
22	.48***	.41***	.05	.33***	.25*	.37***	.40***	.51***
23	.61***	.28*	.05	.16	.29**	.45***	.37**	.50***
24	.53***	.13	.45***	—	.26*	−.07	.23*	—
25	.57***	−.12	.40***	.53***	.17	−17	.59***	.69***

Notes:

gl = Global rating of perceived similarity
r = Global rating of behavioural similarity
ep = Social Episodes measure
pr = Prototype measure
sc = Script measure
s = Self-generated behavioural reports

*p < .05   **p < .01   ***p < .001

In the main part of the data analysis, individual correlations were computed between the four cognitive measures and the two behavioural measures. Table 10.2 presents the results of these analyses. The intercorrelations between the cognitive measures are given in Table 10.3. Finally, Table 10.4 displays the correlations between the two behavioural measures.

Looking first at the individual correlations between the different measures of situation cognition and behaviour, it is obvious that for most of the participants the majority of correlations were significant. The overall pattern of the results displayed in Table 10.2 clearly supports the hypothesis that behaviour is similar across situations to the extent that the situations are assigned similar meanings by the person. With one exception, correlations between the two global measures of perceived similarity and behavioural similarity were highly significant for all participants, ranging from $r = .48$ to $r = .87$. Correlations between the three concept-based measures and each of the two behavioural measures, despite being generally lower, were also significant for the majority of subjects.

A closer inspection of the results reveals that there are again substantial individual differences in terms of the magnitude as well as the pattern of the obtained coefficients. First of all, it is noteworthy that there is not a single respondent who showed consistently low correlations across the total range of measures. For a sizable proportion of respondents, all measures of situation cognition were significantly correlated with behavioural profiles (e.g. Subjects no. 7, 8, 16, 20 and 21). From this evidence, it may be concluded that for these individuals the different modes of cognitive representation of situations captured by the four measures are largely equivalent as far as their relevance to the person's behaviour in the respective situations is concerned. This is further reflected in the finding that consistently high intercorrelations between the cognitive measures were typically found for these subjects. In contrast, the data of other respondents reflect the differential impact of the four cognitive measures on behaviour in anxiety-provoking situations. There is one group of subjects (e.g. no. 4, 6, 13 and 23) for whom the global measure of perceived similarity and the Social Episode measure were significantly correlated with the global measure of behavioural similarity, but not with the more complex measure of self-generated behaviours. For the same group, the Prototype and Script measures were related more closely to the self-generated behaviours than the global behavioural measure. Finally, a third group of subjects can be identified for whom single measures of situation cognition stand out as performing particularly well, or poorly, as correlates of behaviour. This is true, for instance, for Subject no. 14 whose global ratings of perceived similarity failed to correlate with both measures of behaviour, while significant coefficients were obtained on all remaining indices. Likewise, in the pattern of results obtained for Subject no. 25, the

Table 10.3. *Intercorrelations between the cognitive measures*

Subject no.	gl/ep	gl/pr	gl/sc	ep/pr	ep/sc	pr/sc
1	.27*	.24*	.46***	.26*	.12	.14
2	.35**	.51***	.35**	.04	.10	.50***
3	.18	.24*	.17	.02	.20	.23*
4	.48***	.36**	.34**	.32**	.22*	.29**
5	.28*	.28*	.40***	.21*	.14	.46***
6	.61***	.29**	.21*	.13	.03	.17
7	.24*	.51***	.35**	.17	.24*	.43***
8	.69***	.68***	.51***	.51***	.33***	.55***
9	.40***	.44***	.39***	.16	.28*	.29**
10	.20	.33**	.37**	.29**	.23*	.41***
11	.23*	.51***	.22*	.33**	.07	.21*
12	.17	.41***	.70***	.18	.09	.32**
13	.36**	.41***	.31**	.18	.11	.47***
14	−.05	.00	.00	.47***	.39***	.26*
15	.45***	.21*	.44***	.36**	.35**	.18
16	.49***	.38**	.35**	.31**	.57***	.40***
17	.35**	.30**	.26*	.20	.24*	.28*
18	.21*	.10	.34**	−.08	.12	.35**
19	.16	.44***	.52***	−.03	.02	.59***
20	.63***	.36**	.46***	.35**	.35**	.15
21	.57***	.49***	.38**	.37**	.36**	.32**
22	.33**	.16	.27*	.05	.25*	.31**
23	.36***	.30**	.37***	.28*	.36**	.68***
24	.25*	.23*	—	.18	—	—
25	.16	.25*	.39***	−.16	−.12	.77***

Notes:
gl = Global rating of perceived similarity
ep = Social Episodes measure
pr = Prototype measure
sc = Script measure

*p < .05   **p < .01   ***p < .001

Table 10.4. *Intraindividual correlations between the behavioural measures*

Subject no.	r	Subject no.	r	Subject no.	r	Subject no.	r
1	.51***	8	.36**	15	.33*	22	.26*
2	.13	9	.32**	16	.43***	23	.30**
3	.13	10	.30**	17	.34**	24	.36**
4	.31**	11	.49***	18	.31**	25	.55***
5	.30**	12	.38**	19	.38**		
6	.06	13	.24*	20	.52***	M	.37
7	.59***	14	.49***	21	.56***		

Notes:
*p < .05   **p < .01   ***p < .001

Social Episode measure clearly emerged as being irrelevant to the behavioural patterns of that person.

Looking at the intercorrelations between the four measures of situation cognition, it is revealed that for most participants correlations between the global measure of perceived similarity and the three concept-based measures were significant. In view of the conceptual overlap between the global measure and the remaining measures, this finding was expected. However, the correlations presented in Table 10.3 are of a magnitude which suggests that each measure was distinctive enough to be used as an independent operationalisation of the concept of situation cognition. A greater proportion of nonsignificant coefficients was found for the correlations among the three concept-based measures, suggesting that for a number of participants these measures referred to distinctly different aspects of situational meaning. A similar picture is conveyed by Table 10.4 of the correlations between the two behavioural measures. While the two measures are significantly related for most of the participants, the magnitude of the correlations suggests that each refers to specific facets of behavioural responses to anxiety-provoking situations.

As a next step in the analysis, the correlations between situation cognition and behaviour were related to the self-ratings of consistency vs. variability in the domain of anxiety which had been collected at the sixth data point. Against the background of the continuing search for moderator variables which would be able to explain individual differences in consistency (cf. chapter 5), this analysis was directed at assessing the hypothesis that cross-situational coherence is moderated by the extent to which the person rates of him- or herself as being generally consistent or variable in the domain in question (Bem & Allen, 1974). For this purpose, the eight indices of cognition–behaviour correlation were correlated with the self-ratings of consistency across participants. The results from this analysis are presented in Table 10.5.

As far as the impact of self-rated consistency as a moderator of cross-situational coherence is concerned, the results reported in Table 10.6 fail to support the hypothesis that a person's level of cross-situational coherence is systematically related to his or her self-perceived consistency. Apart from the significant, though moderate correlations involving the Social Episode measure, the correlations between the indices of coherence and the subjects' self-rated consistency are minimal and nonsignificant. Thus, the present findings joined earlier research in casting doubts on the view that a 'differential psychology' of cross-situational consistency may be established on the basis of straightforward self-ratings of consistency (e.g. Chaplin & Goldberg, 1985; Wymer & Penner, 1985).

In view of the wide range of individual differences in intraindividual

Table 10.5. *Correlations between cognition–behaviour correlations and self-rated consistency*

gl/r	ep/r	pr/r	sc/r	gl/s	ep/s	pr/s	sc/s
.10	.48*	−.21	−.10	−.16	.35*	.04	.03

Notes:
gl = Global rating of perceived similarity
 r = Global rating of behavioural similarity
ep = Social episodes measure
pr = Prototype measure
sc = Script measure
 s = Self-generated behavioural reports

*p < .05

correlations between situation cognition and behaviour, it is difficult to arrive at a general evaluation of the present findings with respect to the proposed coherence model on the basis of the individual data alone. Therefore, the individual coefficients were z-transformed and subsequently aggregated across the respondents so as to facilitate a comprehensive assessment of the different measures. It is important to note, however, that these scores differ from traditional nomothetic evidence on consistency in that the data were first analysed individually for each participant and subsequently aggregated rather than being aggregated first and then analysed as group data.[3] The resulting average indices of cross-situational coherence are displayed in Table 10.6.

First of all, the aggregated findings show that by far the highest correspondence between situation cognition and behaviour was obtained for the two global measures of perceived and behavioural similarity. The average correlation of r = .66 was highly significant, accounting for almost 44% of the total variance. While the global measures allowed subjects to take all possible factors into account, the more specific measures of situation cognition focused their attention on a particular perspective. This may account for the generally lower levels of cognition–behaviour correlations involving the three concept-based measures. Two of the aggregated coefficients reached significance in this study. One is the average correlation between the Social Episode measure and the global ratings of behavioural similarity. The other is the correlation between the Script measure and the new measure of self-generated behavioural reports. The latter substantial

[3] As in Study 2, it should be noted that the two sets of coefficients are based on different sample sizes. In the individual analyses, the N = 66 situation pairs are treated as 'cases', while the aggregated scores are based on the total number of N = 25 respondents.

Table 10.6. *Average correlations between the cognitive and behavioural measures (N=25)*

	Global behavioural similarity	Self-generated behavioural reports	Global perceived similarity	Episode measure	Prototype measure
Global behavioural similarity					
Self-generated behavioural reports	.37				
Global perceived similarity	.66*** [a]	.34 [e]			
Episode measure	.38* [b]	.26 [f]	.35		
Prototype measure	.29 [c]	.37 [g]	.35	.21	
Script measure	.33 [d]	.42* [h]	.37	.22	.38*

Percentage of significant correlations

	[a]	[b]	[c]	[d]	[e]	[f]	[g]	[h]
p<.001	96.0	52.0	32.0	45.8	32.0	36.0	52.0	68.0
p<.01	4.0	0.0	16.0	16.7	44.0	8.0	24.0	12.0
p<.05	0.0	28.0	20.0	8.3	16.0	16.0	20.0	8.0
n.s.	0.0	20.0	32.0	29.2	8.0	40.0	4.0	8.0

Notes:
*p<.05   ***p<.001

correlation of $r = .43$ suggests that the cognitive representation of situations in terms of their characteristic actions and events is closely related to actual behavioural patterns in these situations, a finding which supports not only the validity of the present approach but also the general assumptions advanced within script theory about the functional impact of cognitive scripts on actual behaviour.

Finally, Table 10.6 reveals only moderate intercorrelations between the cognitive measures as well as the behavioural measures, suggesting that the different measures do indeed capture different aspects of both the cognitive representation of situational information and the pertinent behavioural responses.

Discussion

This study was conducted to corroborate the evidence from the first two investigations in support of the concept of coherence in personality. More specifically, the aim was to demonstrate significant intraindividual relationships between different measures of perceived situational similarity and behavioural similarity over a range of anxiety-provoking situations whereby the situations involved were supplied by each respondent from his or her personal experience.

The proposed covariation of situation cognition and behaviour receives conclusive support from the present findings. When both perceived similarity and behavioural similarity are measured in terms of global ratings, highly significant correlations emerge from the individual analyses of the data. These findings suggest that a person's behaviour is similar across different anxiety-provoking situations to the extent that he or she assigns similar meanings to those situations.

Yet, how are these meanings construed by the person, i.e. which aspects of the specific situations are most important in forming an impression about the situation which determines how the person will react behaviourally to it? This question cannot be answered conclusively on the basis of global ratings of situational similarity. Instead, measures of situation cognition are required which are derived explicitly from conceptual models specifying different principles of the cognitive representation of situations. Therefore, the three concept-based measures of situation cognition introduced in the first two studies were elaborated further so as to illuminate the judgemental process underlying the subjective construction of situational similarities and differences. The present results join those of the previous studies in demonstrating that measures of perceived situational similarity derived from the prototype, script, and social episode models are significantly related to behavioural profiles for the majority of subjects. In conjunction with the moderate correlations among the three measures, these findings permit the conclusion that the measures capture different aspects of situational meaning, each of which is shown to be pertinent to the person's behavioural responses.

Measuring individual behaviour across different anxiety-provoking situations was a particularly difficult task in the search for coherence. In view of the limitations of traditional measures of state anxiety as well as the ethical and practical reasons precluding the manipulation and/or observation of behaviour in anxiety-provoking situations, a measure of self-generated behavioural reports was developed in the present study. The satisfactory re-test correlations after four months demonstrate that this method of eliciting comprehensive behavioural self-reports is a feasible strategy for arriving at reliable information about how individuals behave in anxiety-provoking situations.

While the overall pattern of results presents conclusive evidence in support of the proposed covariation of situation cognition and behaviour as well as of the suitability of the Prototype, Script, and Social Episode measures for exploring the cognitive representation of situations, further insights may be gained from an inspection of the individual differences apparent in the cognition–behaviour correlations.

Due to the further formal standardisation of the situation cognition measures across participants introduced in the present study, differences in subjects' patterns of results can be interpreted more conclusively with respect to the concept of coherence. Basically, three distinct patterns are discernible in the distribution of cognition–behaviour correlations. First, there is one group of subjects who show high coefficients on all of the eight indices of coherence. These individuals appear to have a stable and unequivocal representation of their perception of and behaviour in the respective situations that is manifested in much the same way across the different measures and is also reflected in consistently high correlations among the cognitive and behavioural measures. A second group of subjects is character-ised by high cognition–behaviour correlations for certain measures only. Among the measures that stand out, there is a clear dichotomy between those instruments requiring subjects to make judgements on provided response scales (i.e. the global measures of perceived and behavioural similarity as well as the Social Episode measure) and those involving the elicitation of free responses (i.e. the Prototype and Script measures as well as the self-generated behavioural reports). This suggests that for the subjects in this group the formal correspondence of the cognitive and behavioural measures is a crucial factor determining their interrelations. Finally, a third group may be identified who display particularly high or low correlations on just one of the eight indices of cognition–behaviour correlations. However, this pattern cannot be interpreted conclusively on the basis of the present data because there is no evidence of the consistent superiority or inferiority of a single measure across the sample as a whole.

Altogether, the clear-cut individual differences in the level as well as patterning of cross-situational coherence underline once more the necessity to adopt an individual-centred strategy for understanding the regularities in individual behaviour. Furthermore, it is only by uncovering these differences instead of obliterating them through aggregation early in the data analysis that the identification of moderator variables of consistency may ultimately prove successful. The search for moderator variables of the relationship between perceived similarity and behavioural similarity across different anxiety-provoking situations was not among the primary aims of the present study. Nevertheless, the design of the study permitted the inclusion of a measure of self-rated consistency used with varying success by a number of previous studies to differentiate between consistent and inconsistent indi-viduals. No evidence was found in the present data for the hypothesis that respondents' self-ratings of variability vs. consistency in the domain of anxiety are significantly correlated with their actual levels of cross-situational coherence.

In conclusion, the findings from Study 3 provide further confirmation for the basic proposition of the present approach that systematic links may be found between situation cognition and behaviour on the basis of an individual-centred methodology. The obtained patterns of coherence are highly similar to the results from the first two studies, underlining the feasibility of the methodological strategy implemented in this series of investigations.

11 Beyond the 'nomothetic vs. idiographic' controversy in the search for cross-situational consistency

In the present volume, the conceptual as well as methodological history of the consistency debate was traced from the early work of Hartshorne & May (1928) and Allport (1937) through the days of hard-line situationism culminating in Mischel's *Personality and Assessment* (1968), to the emergence of the modern interactionist approach to personality in the course of the 1970s. By emphasising the joint impact of personal dispositions and situational influences on individual behaviour, modern interactionism offered an integrative perspective on the consistency issue that has become widely accepted in personality research, if only, as noted somewhat disparagingly by some critics, as 'a happy compromise that allows both parties in a dispute to conclude that they were right after all' (Kenrick & Dantchik, 1983, 292).

A pervasive problem that has been running through the consistency controversy from the beginning and accounts for much of its longevity has to do with the way in which the problem of consistency has been approached empirically within the trait model and its corresponding individual difference paradigm. Even though the concept of consistency has been used at a general theoretical level to refer to regularities in individual behaviour across different situations, it has typically been operationalised in terms of the stability of individual *differences* across situations. This strategy implies that hypotheses about consistency are tested at the level of aggregated data, a procedure which does not allow inferences about individual persons (Ozer & Gjerde, 1989). Yet there is a tendency among personality psychologists to derive statements about the psychological functioning of individual persons from group-based correlational findings, as various authors have criticised (e.g. Epstein, 1983b; Lamiell, 1982; Valsiner, 1986). It is in view of such problems that West & Graziano (1989, 187) emphasise the need for statistical models that 'represent adequately the nature of the process under investigation'.

The modern interactionist approach, while rejecting the idea of relative consistency in favour of the concept of coherence, has equally fallen short of meeting the methodological requirements implied in its understanding of coherence in terms of intraindividual, idiographically predictable regularities in behaviour (Magnusson, 1976). The predominant strategies of interactionist research are clearly those of the nomothetic tradition in personality measurement, including the strong reliance on the 'analysis of variance' model in substantiating the proposed significance of person–situation interactions. At the same time, in view of the central importance assigned to the subjective meaning of situations, the progress of theoretical and empirical work on the cognitive representation of situations can only be described as slow even by a committed interactionist like Magnusson (1981b).

This analysis of the course of the consistency controversy, and particularly of the way in which the consistency issue has been treated within the modern interactionist model, provided the background for the research presented in the preceding chapters.

At the most general level, the present research was motivated by the attempt to develop a new perspective on the study of cross-situational consistency, a perspective that would combine the elaboration of the central constructs implied in the meaning of consistency with the search for a methodological framework in which the theoretical propositions about consistency are adequately translated into empirical research strategies. More specifically, this attempt involved the following tasks.

1 Building upon the interactionist concept of *coherence*, the first task consisted in advancing a more precise conceptual definition of the proposed intraindividual regularities of behaviour across situations. This definition focused on the covariation of situation cognition and behaviour, suggesting that behavioural patterns should be similar across situations to the extent that the situations are assigned similar subjective meanings by the individual.

2 Deriving directly from the conceptualisation of consistency in terms of coherence, the second task was to advance a methodological framework for studying patterns of situation cognition and behaviour at the level of the individual. Of necessity, this framework had to be individual-centred rather than variable-centred, facilitating conclusions about the level of consistency displayed by individual persons with respect to situations from their specific biographical backgrounds.

3 An equally important task referred to the more precise analysis of the psychological meaning of situations for the individual, proposed as a key variable in the modern interactionist model. In particular, it was argued that a clearer understanding of how situations are cognitively represented and related to each other in terms of similarities and differences is required to

establish the 'psychological situation' as a meaningful concept in the study of cross-situational coherence and also other aspects of the person–situation interaction. Unlike the field of personality psychology where the analysis of situations and their perceived significance has been largely neglected, recent work in social psychology offers different perspectives on the cognitive organisation of situational meaning that were discussed with regard to their applicability to the study of coherence.

4 The final aim of the present research was to illustrate a possibility for reconciling the principles of idiographic inquiry with the pursuance of nomothetic questions about personality. In the present individual-centred methodology, the idiographic study of cross-situational coherence was combined with the examination of general hypotheses about the link between situation cognition and behaviour by distinguishing between the idiographic treatment of the *contents* and the nomothetic treatment of the *processes* involved in the dynamics of consistency. In proposing this distinction, the present approach shares the view of other recent authors that it is possible, in principle, for idiographic and nomothetic approaches to join forces so as to contribute to a more comprehensive analysis of the issues of personality psychology. As Lamiell, for instance, points out:

> There is no logical a priori reason to reject a paradigm for the scientific study of personality in which generality is sought with reference to the *process* of personality development but in which comparability in the *substance* of individuals' personalities is neither presumed nor precluded.
> (Lamiell, 1981, 285)

In the same vein, Pervin pleads for a revision of the traditional antagonism between the nomothetic and the idiographic approach, arguing that 'the utility of the idiographic approach lies not in contradistinction to the nomothetic approach, but in its compatibility with it, and not in contradistinction to science, but in its commitment to it' (Pervin, 1984a, 279; cf. also Brody, 1988, 121, for a similar point).

In addressing these tasks, the three studies reported in this volume used a variety of measures of situation cognition and behaviour to provide empirical support for the proposed intraindividual covariation of perceived situational similarity and behavioural similarity in the domain of anxiety-provoking situations.

What distinguishes the present studies from previous work on the issue of coherence is that they are based on a strictly idiographic methodology in which not only the situations but also the relevant cognitions and behaviours are sampled individually from each participant. With respect to the controversial issue, rekindled by Mischel & Peake (1982a), whether or not to dismiss the idea that behaviour is consistent not only over time but also across situations, the present results clearly suggest that evidence of cross-situational regularities can be found in individual behaviour provided that the concept of coherence is properly translated into analytical designs. Strong support for the coherence concept derives in particular from those correlations between perceived situational similarity and behavioural similarity that are based on the individuals' global judgements of similarity. Correlations between situation cognition and behaviour based on the more specific concept-based measures of perceived situational similarity, while being generally lower, are still substantial. They suggest that each of the Prototype, Script, and Social Episode measures captures significant aspects of the cognitive representation of situations proposed in the covariation hypothesis.

While the overall pattern of results thus reveals moderate to high levels of coherence for the majority of participants, an equally important aspect of the present methodology lies in its highlighting the variability of individual patterns of coherence both within and across the different measures. Unlike nomothetic or variable-centred designs in which such variability is no longer discernible following the aggregation of data, the individual-centred analysis of coherence shows that individuals differ considerably in the extent to which their perceptions of situational similarity covary with behavioural similarities on the different measures of situation cognition and behaviour. For some participants, pervasively high or moderate correlations are obtained, while others are characterised by particularly high or low coherence scores on specific measures.

The range of individual differences in the level of consistency displayed *across situations* that was found in the present studies fits in well with the pattern of results reported by Ozer & Gjerde (1989) with respect to the stability of personality *over time*. Guided by the aim to illustrate the benefits of a person-centred approach to the issue of personality development, they analysed patterns of personality stability and change between the ages of three and eighteen as reflected in Q-sorts obtained at five data points from observers who were familiar with the subject at each time (e.g. nursery staff; school teachers).

Although revealing generally high levels of stability across the four age periods covered by the study, their data also reflect a substantial variability in the distribution of intraindividual correlations. In order to obtain a more precise picture of this variability, they performed a cluster analysis on the intraindividual correlations to identify subgroups of participants with similar patterns of stability and change. This analysis, carried out separately for male and female subjects, revealed that the largest cluster in each sex comprised subjects who were characterised by high levels of stability across all four age periods. The second largest group consisted of those subjects who showed consistently moderate levels of consistency. The remaining groups (two for the male and three for the female sample) contained subjects who showed distinctively lower stability levels for at least one age period.[1]

Thus, similar to the present study, a substantial group of subjects was characterised by consistently high levels of stability, lending empirical support to the concept of temporal stability in personality. In contrast to the present studies which employed self-report measures of situation cognition and behaviour, indices of consistency were derived in the Ozer & Gjerde study from observer ratings at the different measurement points. The fact that a similar picture of the range of individual differences in the level of consistency emerged in the two sets of data attests to the generality of those differences across S- and R- data (Block, 1977; cf. also chapter 2). At the same time, the wide range of individual variability that was shown to exist both in the Ozer & Gjerde study and in the present research underlines the need to approach the issue of consistency from an individual- or person-centred perspective in order to do justice to the conceptual definition of consistency in terms of intraindividual regularities rather than individual differences.

Returning to the studies reported in the present volume, it should be noted that there was a high degree of correspondence between the findings from the three independent studies which speaks in favour of the reliability of the different measures of situation cognition and behaviour that had to be developed specifically for the purposes of the present research.

At the same time, this convergence of results from the three studies also highlights several limitations of the present empirical strategy for demonstrating coherence in individual behaviour.

The first limitation of the present results lies in their correlational nature which, although providing information about systematic relationships between situation cognition and behaviour at the descriptive level, does not facilitate the prediction of those relationships.

Secondly, the present studies were faced with the problem of having to rely on self-report methods in collecting the behavioural data, thus restricting the generality of the obtained findings to that type of behavioural evidence. As explained earlier, attempts at referring to other sources of behavioural

---

[1] It should be noted that membership in a given cluster was determined exclusively by the magnitude of the correlations between the Q-sorts obtained at the different data points and was completely independent of the contents of the Q-sort items. As Ozer & Gjerde (p. 496) point out, 'two subjects could show very large Q-correlations across time and be grouped into the same cluster; yet these subjects might be quite dissimilar to each other'. Thus, their approach to the analysis of stability implies the same distinction between contents and processes of personality functioning that is assigned crucial importance in the present individual-centred methodology. To obtain (nomothetic) evidence of stability over time, the only requirement is that the data obtained for different subjects are structurally comparable, i.e. have an identical Q-sort format, yet the contents of the Q-items can be allowed to vary idiographically from participant to participant.

information, such as ratings by knowledgeable informants or direct observation in experimentally created situations, were precluded by the specific
constraints involved in the study of anxiety-provoking situations. While
some of these constraints, in particular referring to ethical concerns about
deliberately exposing subjects to anxiety-provoking situations may be
avoided by studying cross-situational coherence in other personality
domains, attempts at replacing behavioural self-reports by alternative types
of data are always faced with the enormous task of collecting reliable
measures for a large number of individuals on a substantial number of
different situations and/or points in time.

A final limitation revealed by the convergent pattern of results emerging
from the three studies refers to the maximum levels of coherence obtainable
on the basis of the present methodology. In particular, correlations obtained
for those indices involving measures derived from explicit models of situation
cognition, i.e. the Prototype, Social Episode and Script measures, did not
exceed the moderate range for the majority of subjects in the three studies.
Two complementary directions for future research are suggested by this
pattern of results. The first is to embark on the development of conceptualisations of situation cognition that would be geared more specifically to the
issue of cross-situational consistency, allowing us to derive measures of
perceived situational similarity that might turn out to be more closely related
to behavioural patterns across situations. The second line to follow from the
present results would be to seek to identify further variables that determine
individual patterns of behaviour across situations over and above the impact
of perceived situational meaning. Such an extension of the theoretical basis of
the coherence concept could start from the interindividual variability in
consistency observed in the present research as well as other individual-
centred analyses of consistency. If it was possible to pinpoint the central
respects in which individuals showing high levels of coherence differed from
those characterised by less systematic patterns, then this would provide a
clue for identifying critical determinants of the extent to which a person's
behaviour is coherent across different situations. This line of reasoning has
long been pursued by the moderator variable strategy. Yet the evidence
generated so far by this approach does not provide a conclusive answer to the
question of which variables moderate the level of cross-situational consistencies (Zuckerman et al., 1988), suggesting that the task of delineating more
specifically the determinants of consistency will continue to be high on the
agenda of personality research.

While the problems outlined above clearly need to be tackled before the
proposed individual-centred analysis of cross-situational coherence can be
established as a genuine alternative to the prevailing nomothetic study of
consistency, a key advantage of this methodological approach has already

become apparent in the present research. This advantage lies in the active role assigned to the participants as experts on their own personalities which turns the investigation of coherence into a joint venture of the subjects and the investigator. The success of this venture was demonstrated in the present research by the extremely low drop-out rates in spite of the extensive and time-consuming nature of the data collection process. Zevon & Tellegen (1982, 113), who asked their subjects to complete daily mood ratings over a period of ninety days, arrived at a very similar conclusion:

> The above procedures generated a high degree of cooperation and personal involvement in the subjects. In our opinion, this factor contributed most to the success of the study. The responsibility for data collection became a shared burden, and the completion of the study became a goal for both subjects and investigators.
> (Zevon & Tellegen, 1982, 113)

Thus, by suggesting an individual-centred approach to the study of coherence, the present research also illustrated a general strategy for enhancing the readiness of research participants to cooperate in complex and demanding investigations. Whether this strategy will prove successful in other areas of personality research as well depends to a large extent on designing empirical studies in such a way that participants believe they can draw a personal benefit from their cooperation that goes beyond the accumulation of course credits (cf. also Mischel, 1984b, 273).

In conclusion, the work described in this volume was guided by the aim to provide a perspective on the consistency issue in which the objectives of nomothetic and idiographic inquiry are reconciled within an individual-centred framework and theoretical developments in social psychology are brought to bear on a crucial problem in personality research. This perspective seeks to combine the study of the uniqueness and complexity of individual experience with the search for general principles of personality functioning, thus pursuing a goal that was outlined as early as 1937 by Allport and has remained a challenge for personality psychology ever since:

> The psychologist, while studying the single case, is never content until he himself has made appropriate generalizations. The generalizations are not, or should not be, concerned only with the operations of a hypothetical 'average' mind. The aim is rather to state explicitly the principles by virtue of which unique personalities are created by nature and understood by men.
> (Allport, 1937, 61)

References

Abelson, R.P. (1981). The psychological status of the script concept. *American Psychologist*, 36, 715–29.

Ackerman, C.A. & Endler, N.S. (1985). The interaction model of anxiety and dental treatment. *Journal of Research in Personality*, 19, 78–88.

Acock, A.C. & Scott, W.J. (1980). A model for predicting behavior: The effect of attitude and social class on high and low visibility political participation. *Social Psychology Quarterly*, 43, 59–72.

Adams-Webber, J. (1979). *Personal Construct Theory*. New York: Wiley.

Adams-Webber, J. & Mancuso, J.C. (1983). *Applications of Personal Construct Theory*. Toronto: Academic Press.

Ajzen, I. (1987). Attitudes, traits, and actions: Dispositional prediction of behavior in personality and social psychology. In: L. Berkowitz (ed.)., *Advances in Experimental Social Psychology* (vol. 20). San Diego, CA: Academic Press, pp. 1–63.

(1988). *Attitudes, Personality and Behavior*. Milton Keynes: Open University Press.

Alker, H.A. (1977). Beyond ANOVA psychology in the study of person–situation interactions. In: D. Magnusson & N.S. Endler (eds.). *Personality at the Crossroads*. Hillsdale, NJ: L. Erlbaum, 243–56.

Allen, B.P. & Potkay, C.R. (1981). On the arbitrary distinction between states and traits. *Journal of Personality and Social Psychology*, 41, 916–28.

(1983). Just as arbitrary as ever: Comments on Zuckerman's rejoinder. *Journal of Personality and Social Psychology*, 44, 1087–98.

Allport, G.W. (1937). *Personality: A Psychological Interpretation*. New York: Holt.

(1966). Traits revisited. *American Psychologist*, 21, 1–107.

Amato, P.R. & Pearce, P. (1983). A cognitively-based taxonomy of helping. In: M. Smithson, P.R. Amato & P. Pearce, *Dimensions of Helping Behaviour*. Oxford: Pergamon, pp. 22–36.

Amato, P.R. & Saunders, J. (1985). The perceived dimensions of help-seeking episodes. *Social Psychology Quarterly*, 48, 130–8.

Anderson, C.A. (1983). Imagination and expectation: The effect of imagining behavioral scripts on personal intentions. *Journal of Personality and Social Psychology*, 45, 293–305.

Andrews, K.H. & Kandel, D.B. (1979). Attitude and behavior: A specification of the contingent consistency hypothesis. *American Sociological Review*, 44, 298–310.

Argyle, M., Furnham, A. & Graham, J.A. (1981). *Social Situations*. Cambridge University Press.

Argyle, M., Graham, J.A., Campbell, A. & White, P. (1979). The rules of different situations. *New Zealand Psychology*, 8, 13–22.

Argyle, M. & Little, B.R. (1972). Do personality traits apply to social behaviour? *Journal for the Theory of Social Behaviour*, 2, 1–35.

Aronoff, J. & Wilson, J.P. (1985). *Personality and the Social Process.* Hillsdale, NJ: L. Erlbaum.

Asendorpf, J.B. (1988). Individual response profiles in the behavioural assessment of personality. *European Journal of Personality*, 2, 155–67.

Athay, M. & Darley, J.M. (1981). Toward an interaction-centered theory of personality. In: N. Cantor & J.F. Kihlstrom (eds). *Personality, Cognition, and Social Interaction.* Hillsdale, NJ: L. Erlbaum, pp. 281–303.

Backteman, G. & Magnusson, D. (1981). Longitudinal stability of personality characteristics. *Journal of Personality*, 49, 148–60.

Ball, D.W. (1972). 'The definition of situation': Some theoretical and methodological consequences of taking W.I. Thomas seriously. *Journal for the Theory of Social Behaviour*, 2, 61–82.

Bandura, A. (1969). *Principles of Behavior Modification.* New York: Holt, Rinehart & Winston.

   (1986). *Social Foundations of Thought and Action.* Englewood Cliffs, NJ: Prentice-Hall.

Baron, R.M. & Boudreau, L.A. (1987). An ecological perspective on integrating personality and social psychology. *Journal of Personality and Social Psychology*, 53, 1222–8.

Baron, R.M. & Kenny, D.A. (1986). The moderator–mediator variable distinction in social psychological research: Conceptual, strategic, and statistical considerations. *Journal of Personality and Social Psychology*, 51, 1173–82.

Battistich, V.A. & Thompson, E.G. (1980). Students' perceptions of the college milieu: a multidimensional scaling analysis. *Personality and Social Psychology Bulletin*, 6, 74–82.

Baumeister, R.F. & Tice, D.M. (1985). Toward a theory of situational structure. *Environment and Behavior*, 17, 147–92.

   (1988). Metratraits. *Journal of Personality*, 56, 571–98.

Beail, N. (ed.) (1985). *Repertory Grid Technique and Personal Constructs: Applications in Clinical and Educational Settings.* London: Croom Helm.

Bem, D.J. (1983a). Toward a response style theory of persons in situations. In: M.M. Page (ed.) *Personality – Current Theory and Research.* 1982 Nebraska Symposium on Motivation. Lincoln, NB: University of Nebraska Press, pp. 201–31.

   (1983b). Further déjà vu in the search for cross-situational consistency. A response to Mischel and Peake. *Psychological Review*, 90, 390–93.

   (1983c). Constructing a theory of the triple typology: Some (second) thoughts on nomothetic and idiographic approaches to personality. *Journal of Personality*, 51, 566–77.

Bem, D.J. & Allen, A. (1974). On predicting some of the people some of the time: The search for cross-situational consistencies in behavior. *Psychological Review*, 81, 506–20.

Bem, D.J. & Funder, D.C. (1978). Predicting more of the people more of the time: Assessing the personality of situations. *Psychological Review*, 85, 485–502.

Bem, D.J. & Lord, C.G. (1979). Template matching: A proposal for probing the ecological validity of experimental settings in social psychology. *Journal of Personality and Social Psychology*, 37, 833–46.

Bishop, D.W. & Witt, P.A. (1970). Sources of behavioral variance during leisure time. *Journal of Personality and Social Psychology,* 16, 352–60.

Blass, T. (1984). Social psychology and personality: Towards a convergence. *Journal of Personality and Social Psychology,* 47, 1013–27.

Block, J. (1961). *The Q-Sort Method in Personality Assessment and Psychiatric Research.* Springfield, IL: Thomas.

(1968). Some reasons for the apparent inconsistency of personality. *Psychological Bulletin,* 70, 210–12.

(1977). Advancing the psychology of personality; Paradigmatic shift or improvement of the quality of research. In: D. Magnusson & N.S. Endler (eds.). *Personality at the Crossroads.* Hillsdale, NJ: L. Erlbaum, pp. 37–63.

Block, J., Buss, D.M., Block, J.H. & Gjerde, P.F. (1981). The cognitive style of breadth of categorization: Longitudinal consistency of personality correlates. *Journal of Personality and Social Psychology,* 40, 770–9.

Borkenau, P. (1986). Towards an understanding of trait interrelations. Acts as instances of several traits. *Journal of Personality and Social Psychology,* 51, 371–81.

Bower, G., Black, J. & Turner, T. (1979). Scripts in text comprehension and memory. *Cognitive Psychology,* 11, 307–36.

Bowers, K.S. (1973). Situationism in psychology: An analysis and critique. *Psychological Review,* 80, 307–36.

Brewer, M.B., Dull,V. & Lui, L. (1981). Perceptions of the elderly: Stereotypes as prototypes. *Journal of Personality and Social Psychology,* 41, 656–70.

Briggs, S.R. & Cheek, J.M. (1986). The role of factor analysis in the development and evaluation of personality scales. *Journal of Personality,* 54, 106–48.

Bringle, R.G., Renner, P., Terry, R.L. & Davis, S. (1983). An analysis of situation and person components of jealousy. *Journal of Research in Personality,* 17, 354–68.

Brody, N. (1988). *Personality: In Search of Individuality.* San Diego, CA: Academic Press.

Burton, R.V. (1963). The generality of dishonesty reconsidered. *Psychological Bulletin,* 70, 481–99.

Buss, A.R. (1977). The trait-situation controversy and the concept of interaction. *Personality and Social Psychology Bulletin,* 3, 196–201.

Buss, D.M. (1983). Evolutionary biology and personality psychology. *Personality and Individual Differences,* 4, 51–63.

(1984). Toward a psychology of person–environment (PE) correlation: The role of spouse selection. *Journal of Personality and Social Psychology,* 47, 361–7.

(1985). The act frequency approach to the interpersonal environment. In: R. Hogan & W.H. Jones (eds.), *Perspectives in Personality* (vol. 1). Greenwich, CT: JAI-Press, pp. 173–200.

(1987). Selection, evocation, and manipulation. *Journal of Personality and Social Psychology,* 53, 1214–21.

Buss, D.M. & Craik, K.H. (1980). The frequency concept of disposition: Dominance and prototypically dominant acts. *Journal of Personality,* 48, 380–92.

(1981). The act frequency analysis of interpersonal dispositions: Aloofness, gregariousness, dominance and submissiveness. *Journal of Personality,* 49, 175–92.

(1983a). The act frequency approach to personality. *Psychological Review*, 90, 105–26.

(1983b). Act prediction and the conceptual analysis of personality scales: Indices of act density, bipolarity, and extensity. *Journal of Personality and Social Psychology*, 45, 1081–95.

(1983c). The dispositional analysis of everyday conduct. *Journal of Personality*, 51, 393–412.

(1984). Acts, dispositions, and personality. In: B.A. Maher & W.B. Maher (eds.), *Progress in Experimental Personality Research* (vol. 13). New York: Academic Press, pp. 241–301.

(1986). The act frequency approach and the construction of personality. In: A. Angleitner, A. Furnham, & G. v. Heck (eds.), *Personality Psychology in Europe* (vol. 2). Lisse: Swets & Zeitlinger, pp. 141–56.

(1989). On the cross-cultural examination of acts and dispositions. *European Journal of Personality*, 3, 19–30.

Butler, J.M. & Haigh, G.V. (1954). Changes in the relation between self-concepts and ideal concepts consequent upon client-centered counseling. In: C.R. Rogers & R.F. Dymond (eds.), *Psychotherapy and Personality Change*. University of Chicago Press, pp. 55–75.

Byrne, D. (1964). Repression-sensitization as a dimension of personality. In: B.A. Maher (ed.) *Progress in Experimental Personality Research* (vol. 1). New York: Academic Press, pp. 170–220.

Cantor, N. (1981). Perceptions of situations: Situation prototypes and person–situation prototypes. In: D. Magnusson (ed.). *Toward a Psychology of Situations*. Hillsdale, NJ: L. Erlbaum, pp. 229–44.

Cantor, N. & Mischel, W. (1979a). Prototypes in person perception. In: L. Berkowitz (ed.), *Advances in Experimental Social Psychology* (vol. 12). New York: Academic Press, pp. 4–52.

(1979b). Prototypicality and personality: Effects on free recall and personality impression. *Journal of Research in Personality*, 13, 187–205.

Cantor, N., Mischel, W. & Schwartz, J. (1982). A prototype analysis of psychological situations. *Cognitive Psychology*, 14, 45–77.

Carlson, R. (1971). Where is the person in personality research? *Psychological Bulletin*, 75, 203–19.

(1984).What's social about social psychology? Where's the person in personality research? *Journal of Personality and Social Psychology*, 47, 1304–9.

Carson, R.C. (1989). Personality. *Annual Review of Psychology*, 40, 227–48.

Cattell, R.B. (1950). *Personality*. New York: McGraw-Hill.

(1957). *Personality and Motivation Structure and Measurement*. Yonkers-on-Hudson, NY: World Book Company.

Champagne, B.M. & Pervin, L.A. (1987). The relationship of perceived situation similarity to perceived behaviour similarity: Implications for social learning theory. *European Journal of Personality Psychology*, 1, 79–91.

Chaplin, W.F. & Buckner, K.E. (1988). Self-ratings of personality: A naturalistic comparison of normative, ipsative, and idothetic standards. *Journal of Personality*, 56, 509–30.

Chaplin, W.F. & Goldberg, L.R. (1985). A failure to replicate the Bem and Allen study of individual differences in cross-situational consistency. *Journal of Personality and Social Psychology*, 47, 1074–90.

Cheek, J.M. (1982). Aggregation, moderator variables, and the validity of personality tests: A peer-rating study. *Journal of Personality and Social Psychology*, 43, 1254–69.

Cochran, L.R. (1978). Construct systems and the definition of social situations. *Journal of Personality and Social Psychology*, 36, 733–40.

Cohen, C.E. (1981). Person categories and social perception: Testing some boundaries of the processing effects of prior knowledge. *Journal of Personality and Social Psychology*, 40, 441–52.

(1983). Inferring characteristics of other people: Categories and attribute accessibility. *Journal of Personality and Social Psychology*, 44, 34–44.

Conger, A.J. (1983). Towards a further understanding of the intuitive personologists: Some critical evidence on the diabolical quality of subjective psychometrics. *Journal of Personality*, 51, 248–58.

Conley, J.J. (1984a). The hierarchy of consistency: A review and model of longitudinal findings on adult individual differences in intelligence, personality, and self-opinion. *Personality and Individual Differences*, 5, 11–26.

(1984b). Relation of temporal stability and cross-situational consistency in personality: Comment on the Mischel–Epstein debate. *Psychological Review*, 91, 491–6.

Costa, P.T. & McCrae, R.R. (1988). Personality in adulthood: A six-year longitudinal study of self-reports and spouse ratings on the NEO personality inventory. *Journal of Personality and Social Psychology*, 54, 853–63.

Dahlgren K. (1985). The cognitive structure of social categories. *Cognitive Science*, 9, 379–98.

Deluty, R.H. (1985). Consistency of assertive, aggressive, and submissive behavior for children. *Journal of Personality and Social Psychology*, 49, 1054–65.

Diener, E. & Larsen, R. (1984). Temporal stability and cross-situational consistency of affective, behavioral, and cognitive responses. *Journal of Personality and Social Psychology*, 47, 871–83.

Diener, E., Larsen, R.J. & Emmons, R.A. (1984). Person × situation interactions: Choice of situations and congruence response models. *Journal of Personality and Social Psychology*, 47, 580–92.

Dobson, K.S. (1983). A regression analysis of the interactional approach to anxiety. *Canadian Journal of Behavioral Science*, 15, 163–73.

Dolan, C.A. & White, J.W. (1988). Issues of consistency and effectiveness in coping with daily stressors. *Journal of Research in Personality*, 22, 395–407.

Donat, D.C. (1983). Predicting state-anxiety: A comparison of multidimensional and unidimensional trait approaches. *Journal of Research in Personality*, 17, 256–62.

Dworkin, R.H. (1979). Genetic and environmental influences on person–situation interactions. *Journal of Research in Personality*, 13, 279–93.

Dworkin, R.H. & Goldfinger, S.H. (1985). Processing bias: Individual differences in the cognition of situations. *Journal of Personality*, 53, 480–501.

Dworkin, R.H. & Kihlstrom, J.F. (1978). An S–R inventory of dominance for research on the nature of person–situation interactions. *Journal of Personality*, 46, 43–56.

Eckes, T. (1986). Eine Prototypenstudie zur natürlichen Kategorisierung sozialer Situationen. *Zeitschrift für Differentielle und Diagnostische Psychologie*, 7, 145–61.

Edwards, J.M. (1984). Situational determinants of behavior. In: N.S. Endler & J. McV. Hunt (eds.), *Personality and the Behavioral Disorders* (vol. 1). New York: Wiley, pp. 147–82.

Edwards, J.M. & Endler, N.S. (1983). Personality research. In: M. Hersen, A.E. Kazdin & A.S. Bellack (eds.). *The Clinical Psychology Handbook*. New York: Pergamon, pp. 223–38.

Edwards, L.A. & Klockars, A.J. (1981). Significant others and self-evaluations: Relationships between perceived and actual observations. *Personality and Social Psychology Bulletin*, 7, 244–51.

Ekehammar, B. (1974). Interactionism in psychology from a historical perspective. *Psychological Bulletin*, 81, 1026–48.

Ekehammar, B., Magnusson, D. & Ricklander, L. (1974). An interactionist approach to the study of anxiety. *Scandinavian Journal of Psychology*, 15, 4–14.

Ekehammar, B., Schalling, D. & Magnusson, D. (1975). Dimensions of stressful situations: A comparison between a response analytical and stimulus analytical approach. *Multivariate Behavioral Research*, 10, 155–64.

Emmons, R.A. & Diener, E. (1986). An interactional approach to the study of personality and emotion. *Journal of Personality*, 54, 371–84.

Emmons, R.A., Diener, E. & Larsen, R.J. (1985). Choice of situations and congruence models of interactionism. *Personality and Individual Differences*, 6, 693–702.

(1986). Choice and avoidance of everyday situations and affect congruence: Two models of reciprocal interactionism. *Journal of Personality and Social Psychology*, 51, 815–26.

Endler, N.S. (1975). A person–situation interaction model of anxiety. In: C.D. Spielberger & I.G. Sarason (eds.), *Stress and Anxiety* (vol. 1), Washington, DC: Hemisphere, pp. 145–64.

(1980). Person–situation interaction and anxiety. in: I.L. Kutash & L.B. Schlesinger (eds.). *Handbook of Stress and Anxiety*. San Francisco: Jossey-Bass, pp. 249–66.

(1981). Persons, situations, and their interactions. In: A.I. Rabin, J. Aronoff, A.M. Barclay & R.A. Zucker (eds.). *Further Explorations in Personality*. New York: Wiley, pp. 114–51.

(1982). Interactionism comes of age. in: M.P. Zanna, E.T. Higgins & C.P. Herman (eds.). *Consistency in Social Behavior. The Ontario Symposium* (vol. 2). Hillsdale. NJ: L. Erlbaum, pp. 209–49.

(1983). Interactionism: A personality model, but not yet a theory. In: M.M. Page (ed.). *Personality: Current Theory and Research*. 1982 Nebraska Symposium on Motivation. Lincoln, NB: University of Nebraska Press, pp. 155–200.

(1985). Origins of interactional psychology. In: A. Furnham (ed.), *Social Behavior in Context*. Boston: Allyn & Bacon, pp. 11–48.

Endler, N.S. & Hunt, J.Mcv. (1966). Sources of behavioral variance as measured by the S–R-inventory of anxiousness. *Psychological Bulletin*, 65, 336–46.

Endler, N.S., Hunt, J.McV. & Rosenstein, A.J. (1962). An S–R-Inventory of anxiousness. *Psychological Monographs*, 76, (Whole No. 536).

Endler, N.S., King, P.R., Edwards, J.M., Kuczynski, M. & Diveky, S. (1983). Generality of the interaction model of anxiety with respect to two social evaluation field studies. *Canadian Journal of Behavioral Science*, 15, 60–9.

Endler, N.S. & Magnusson, D. (eds.) (1976a). *Interactional Psychology and Personality*. New York: Hemisphere.

(1976b). Toward an interactional psychology of personality. *Psychological Bulletin*, 83, 956–74.

Endler, N.S., Magnusson, D., Ekehammar, B. & Okada, M. (1976). The multidimensionality of state and trait anxiety. *Scandinavian Journal of Psychology*, 17, 81–96.

Endler, N.S. & Okada, M. (1975). A multidimensional measure of trait-anxiety: The S–R inventory of general trait anxiousness. *Journal of Consulting and Clinical Psychology*, 43, 319–29.

Epstein, S. (1977). Traits are alive and well. In: D. Magnusson & N.S. Endler (eds.), *Personality at the Crossroads*. Hillsdale, NJ: L. Erlbaum, pp. 83–98.

   (1979). The stability of behavior: I. On predicting most of the people much of the time. *Journal of Personality and Social Psychology*, 37, 1097–1126.

   (1980). The stability of behavior: II. Implications for psychological research. *American Psychologist*, 35, 790–806.

   (1983a). The stability of confusion. A reply to Mischel & Peake. *Psychological Review*, 90, 179–84.

   (1983b). Aggregation and beyond: Some basic issues on the prediction of behavior. *Journal of Personality*, 51, 360–92.

   (1984). The stability of behavior across time and situations. In: R.A. Zucker, J. Aronoff & A.I. Rabin (eds.). *Personality and the Prediction of Behavior*. New York: Academic Press, pp. 209–68.

Epstein, S. & O'Brien, E.J. (1985). The person–situation debate in historical and current perspective. *Psychological Bulletin*, 98, 513–37.

Epting, F.R. & Landfield, A.W. (eds.) (1985). *Anticipating Personal Construct Psychology*. Lincoln, NB: University of Nebraska Press.

Eysenck, H.H. (1952). *The Scientific Study of Personality*. London: Routledge & Kegan Paul.

Fazio, R.H. & Williams, C.J. (1986). Attitude accessibility as a moderator variable of the attitude–perception and attitude–behavior relations. An investigation of the 1984 presidential election. *Journal of Personality and Social Psychology*, 51, 505–14.

Fenigstein, A., Scheier, M. & Buss, A. (1975). Public and private self-consciousness; Assessment and theory. *Journal of Consulting and Clinical Psychology*, 43, 522–7.

Fennell, G.R. (1975). What is a situation? A motivational paradigm. *The Journal of Psychology*, 91, 259–69.

Feshbach, S. (1984). The 'personality' of personality theory and research. *Personality and Social Psychology Bulletin*, 10, 446–56.

Fiske, D.W. (1978). *Strategies for Personality Research*. San Francisco: Jossey-Bass.

Flood, M. & Endler, N.S. (1980). The interaction model of anxiety: An empirical test in an athletic competition situation. *Journal of Research in Personality*, 14, 329–39.

Forgas, J.P. (1976). The perception of social episodes: Categorical and dimensional representations of two different social milieus. *Journal of Personality and Social Psychology*, 34, 199–209.

   (1978). Social episodes and social structure in an academic setting: The social environment of an intact group. *Journal of Experimental Social Psychology*, 14, 434–48.

   (1979a). *Social Episodes: The Study of Interaction Routines*. London: Academic Press.

   (1979b). Multidimensional scaling: A discovery method in social psychology. In: G.P. Ginsburg (ed.), *Emerging Strategies in Social Psychological Research*. New York: Academic Press, pp. 59–101.

(1981). Social episodes and group milieu: A study in social cognition. *British Journal of Social Psychology*, 20, 77–87.

(1982). Episode cognition: Internal representations of interaction routines. In: L. Berkowitz (ed.), *Advances in Experimental Social Psychology* (vol. 15). New York: Academic Press, pp. 59–101.

(1983a). Episode cognition and personality: A multidimensional analysis. *Journal of Personality*, 51, 34–48.

(1983b). Social skills and the perception of social episodes. *British Journal of Clinical Psychology*, 22, 195–207.

Forgas, J.P., Brown, L.B. & Menyhart, J. (1980). Dimensions of aggression: The perception of aggressive episodes. *British Journal of Social and Clinical Psychology*, 19, 215–27.

Forgus, R. & Shulman, B. (1979). *Personality – A Cognitive View*. Englewood Cliffs, NJ: Prentice-Hall.

Fransella, F. & Bannister, D. (1977). *A Manual for Repertory Grid Technique*. London: Academic Press.

Frederiksen, N. (1972). Toward a taxonomy of situations. *American Psychologist*, 27, 114–23.

Fridhandler, B.M. (1986). Conceptual note on state, trait, and the state–trait distinction. *Journal of Personality and Social Psychology*, 50, 169–74.

Funder, D.C. (1982). On assessing social psychological theories through the study of individual differences: Template matching and forced compliance. *Journal of Personality and Social Psychology*, 43, 100–10.

(1983). Three issues in predicting more of the people: A reply to Mischel & Peake. *Psychological Review*, 90, 283–9.

Funder, D.C. & Ozer, D.J. (1983). Behavior as a function of the situation. *Journal of Personality and Social Psychology*, 44, 107–12.

Furnham, A. (1981). Construing social situations. In: M. Argyle, A. Furnham & J.A. Graham, *Social Situations*, Cambridge University Press, pp. 256–66.

Furnham, A. & Argyle, M. (eds.) (1981). *The Psychology of Social Situations*. Oxford: Pergamon.

Furnham, A. & Jaspers, J. (1983). The evidence for interactionism in psychology: A critical analysis of the situation–response inventories. *Personality and Individual Differences*, 6, 627–44.

Gadlin, H. & Rubin, S.H. (1979). Interactionism: A nonresolution of the person–situation controversy. In: A.R. Buss (ed.), *Psychology in Social Context*. New York: Irvington, pp. 213–38.

Geis, F.L. (1978). The psychological situation and personality traits in behavior. In: H. London (ed.), *Personality – A New Look at Metatheories*. Washington: Hemisphere, pp. 123–52.

Gibson, E.J. (1979). *The Ecological Approach to Visual Perception*. Boston: Houghton Mifflin.

Golding, S.L. (1975). Flies in the ointment: Methodological problems in the analysis of the percentage of variance due to persons and situations. *Psychological Bulletin*, 82, 278–88.

(1977). The problem of construal styles in the analysis of person–situation interactions. In: D. Magnusson & N.S. Endler (eds.), *Personality at the Crossroads*. Hillsdale, NJ: L. Erlbaum, pp. 401–7.

Goldstein, K.M. & Blackman, S. (1981). Theoretical approaches to cognitive style. In: F. Fransella (ed.), *Personality*. London: Methuen, pp. 121–33.

Gormley, J. (1983). Predicting behavior from personality trait scores. *Personality and Social Psychology Bulletin*, 9, 267–70.

Gough, H.G. (1957). *Manual for the California Psychological Inventory*. Palo Alto, CA: Consulting Psychologists Press.

Graesser, A.C., Gordon, S.E. & Sawyer, J.D. (1979). Recognition memory for typical and atypical actions in scripted activites: Test of a pointer + tag hypothesis. *Journal of Verbal Learning and Verbal Behavior*, 18, 319–32.

Graesser, A.C., Wolls, S.B., Kowalski, D.J. & Smith, D.A. (1980). Memory for typical and atypical actions in scripted activities. *Journal of Experimental Psychology: Human Learning and Memory*, 6, 503–13.

Gruen, R.J., Folkman, S. & Lazarus, R.S. (1988). Centrality and individual differences in the meaning of daily hassles. *Journal of Personality*, 56, 743–62.

Guilford, J.P. (1959). *Personality*. New York: McGraw-Hill.

Hampson, S.E. (1982). *The Construction of Personality*. London: Routledge & Kegan Paul.

(1984). The social construction of personality. In: H. Bonarius, G. v. Heck & N. Smid (eds.), *Personality Psychology in Europe*. Lisse: Swets & Zeitlinger, pp. 3–13.

Harrison, J. & Sarre, P. (1976). Personal construct theory and the measurement of environmental images. *Environment and Behaviour*, 7, 3–58.

Harrison, R.H. (1986). The grouping of affect terms according to the situations that elicit them: A test of a cognitive theory of emotion. *Journal of Research in Personality*, 20, 252–66.

Hartshorne, H. & May, M.A. (1928). *Studies in the Nature of Character* (vol. 1: Studies in Deceit). New York: Macmillan.

Heck, G.L.M. van (1981). *Anxiety: The Profile of a Trait*. Diss. Tilburg.

Heilizer, F. (1980). Psychodigms of theory in personality and social psychology. *Psychological Reports*, 46, 63–85.

Hermans, H.J.M. (1988). On the integration of nomothetic and idiographic research methods in the study of personal meaning. *Journal of Personality*, 56, 785–812.

Hirschberg, N. (1978). A correct treatment of traits. In: H. London (ed.), *Personality – A New Look at Metatheories*. Washington, DC: Hemisphere, pp. 48–68.

Honikman, B. (1976). Construct theory as an approach to architectural and environmental design. In: P. Slater (ed.). *The Measurement of Interpersonal Space by the Grid Technique* (vol. 1: Explorations of Interpersonal Space). London: Wiley, pp. 167–81.

Houts, A.C., Cook, T.D. & Shadish, W.R. (1986). The person–situation debate: A critical multiplist perspective. *Journal of Personality*, 54, 52–105.

Howard, J.A. (1979). Person–situation interaction models. *Personality and Social Psychology Bulletin*, 5, 191–5.

Hoy, E. & Endler, N.S. (1969). Types of stressful situations and their relation to trait anxiety and sex. *Canadian Journal of Behavioural Science*, 1, 207–14.

Hyland, M.E. (1984). Interactionism and the person × situation debate. In: J.R. Royce & L.P. Mos (eds.), *Annals of Theoretical Psychology* (vol. 2). New York: Plenum Press, pp. 303–28.

Jackson, D.N. (1967). *Personality Research Form Manual*. Goshen, NY: Research Psychologists Press.

Jackson, D.N., & Paunonen, S.V. (1985). Construct validity and the predictability of behaviour. *Journal of Personality and Social Psychology*, 49, 554–70.

Jaspers, J.M. (1985). The future of social psychology: Taking the past to heart. In: A. Furnham (ed.), *Social Behavior in Context*. Boston: Allyn & Bacon, pp. 273–310.

Kahle, L.R. (1984). *Attitudes and Social Adaptation. A Person–Situation Interaction Approach*. Oxford: Pergamon Press.

Kelly, G.A. (1955). *The Psychology of Personal Constructs* (vol. 1). New York: Norton.

Kendall, P.C. (1978). Anxiety: States, traits – situations? *Journal of Consulting and Clinical Psychology*, 46, 280–7.

Kenny, D.A. & La Voie, L. (1984). The social relations model. In: L. Berkowitz (ed.), *Advances in Experimental Social Psychology* (vol. 18). Orlando, FL: Academic Press, pp. 141–82.

Kenrick, D.T. (1986). How strong is the case against contemporary social and personality psychology? A response to Carlson. *Journal of Personality and Social Psychology*, 50, 839–44.

Kenrick, D.T. & Dantchik, A. (1983). Interactionism, idiographics, and the social psychologial invasions of personality. *Journal of Personality*, 51, 286–307.

Kenrick, D.T. & Funder, D.C. (1988). Profiting from controversy: Lessons from the person–situation debate. *American Psychologist*, 43, 23–34.

Kenrick, D.T., Montello, D.R. & MacFarlane, S. (1985). Personality: Social learning, social cognition, or social biology? In: R. Hogan & W.J. Jones (eds.), *Perspectives in Personality* (vol. 1). Greenwich, CT: JAI–Press, pp. 201–34.

King,, G.A. & Sorrentino, R.M. (1983). Psychological dimensions of goal-oriented interpersonal situations. *Journal of Personality and Socical Psychology*, 44, 140–62.

King, P.R. & Endler, N.S. (1982). Medical intervention and the interaction model of anxiety. *Canadian Journal of Behavioral Science*, 14, 82–91.

(1989). Improving the assessment of situation perception with respect to anxiety. *Personality and Individual Differences*, 10, 1063–9.

Klein, G.S. (1954). Need and regulation. In: M.R. Jones (ed.), *Nebraska Symposium on Motivation*. Lincoln, NB: University of Nebraska Press, pp. 224–74.

Klirs, E.G. & Revelle, W. (1986). Predicting variability from perceived situational similarity. *Journal of Research in Personality*, 20, 34–50.

Koestner, R., Bernieri, F. & Zuckerman, M. (1989). Trait-specific versus person-specific moderators of cross-situational consistency. *Journal of Personality*, 57, 1–16.

Koffka, K. (1935). *Principles of Gestalt Psychology*. New York: Harcourt, Brace.

Koretzky, M.B., Kohn, M. & Jeger, A.M. (1978). Cross-situational consistency among problem adolescents: An application of the two-factor model. *Journal of Personality and Social Psychology*, 36, 1054–9.

Krahé, B. (in press). *Person–Situation–Interactions: Concepts, Methods, and Issues*. London: Sage.

Krauskopf, C. (1978). Comment on Endler and Magnusson's attempt to redefine personality. *Psychological Bulletin*, 85, 280–3.

Kreitler, H. & Kreitler, S. (1982). The theory of cognitive orientation: Widening the scope of behavior prediction. In: B.A. Maher & W.B. Maher (eds.), *Progress in Experimental Personality Research* (vol. 11). New York: Academic Press, pp. 101–69.

Kreitler, S. & Kreitler, H. (1983). The consistency of behavioural inconsistencies. *Archiv für Psychologie*, 135, 199–218.

Lamiell, J.T. (1981). Toward an idiothetic psychology of personality. *American Psychologist*, 36, 276–89.

(1982). The case for an idiothetic psychology of personality: A conceptual and empirical foundation. In: B.A. Maher & W.B. Maher (eds.), *Progress in Experimental Personality Research* (vol. 11). New York: Academic Press, pp. 1–64.

(1986). Epistemological tenets of an idiothetic psychology of personality. In: A. Angleitner, A. Furnham & G. v. Heck (eds.), *Personality Psychology in Europe* (vol. 2). Lisse: Swets & Zeitlinger, pp. 3–22.

(1987). *The Psychology of Personality: An Epistemological Inquiry*. New York: Columbia University Press.

Lamiell, J.T., Foss, M.A., Larsen, R.J. & Hempel, A.M. (1983). Studies in intuitive personology from an idiothetic point of view; Implications for personality theory. *Journal of Personality*, 51, 438–67.

Lamiell, J.T., Foss, M.A., Trierweiler, S.J. & Leffel, G.M. (1983). Toward a further understanding of the intuitive personologist: Some preliminary evidence for the dialectical quality of subjective personality impressions. *Journal of Personality*, 51, 214–35.

Lamiell, J.T. & Trierweiler, S.J. (1986). Interactive measurement, idiographic inquiry, and the challenge to conventional 'nomothetism'. *Journal of Personality*, 54, 460–9.

Lamiell, J.T., Trierweiler, S.J. & Foss, M.A. (1983) Detecting (in)consistencies in personality: Reconciling intuitions and empirical evidence. *Journal of Personality Assessment*, 47, 380–9.

Lanning, K. (1988). Individual differences in scalability: An alternative conception of consistency for personality theory and measurement. *Journal of Personality and Social Psychology*, 55, 142–8.

Lantermann, E.D. (1980). *Interaktionen – Person, Situation und Handlung*. Munich: Urban & Schwarzenberg.

(1982). Person–Umwelt–Interaktionen aus handlungspsychologischer Sicht. In: E.D. Lantermann (ed.), *Wechselwirkungen*. Göttingen: Hogrefe, pp. 42–54.

LaPiere, R.T. (1934). Attitudes versus actions. *Social Forces*, 13, 230–7.

Lazarus, R.S. & Launier, R. (1978). Stress-related transactions between person and environment. In: L.A. Pervin & M. Lewis (eds.), *Perspectives in Interactional Psychology*. New York: Plenum Press, pp. 287–327.

Lazzarini, A., Cox, T. & Mackay, C. (1979). Perceptions of and reactions to stressful situations: The utility of a general anxiety trait. *British Journal of Social and Clincial Psychology*, 18, 363–9.

Lerner, M.J. (1980). *The Belief in a Just World: A Fundamental Delusion*. New York: Plenum Press.

Levy, L.H. (1983). Trait approaches. In: M. Hersen, A.E. Kazdin & A.S. Bellack (eds.), *The Clinical Psychology Handbook*. New York: Pergamon, pp. 123–42.

Lewin, K. (1936). *Principles of Topological Psychology*. New York; McGraw-Hill.

Lobel, T.E. (1982). The prediction of behavior from different types of beliefs. *Journal of Social Psychology*, 118, 213–23.

Loevinger, J. (1987). *Paradigms of Personality*. New York: Freeman.

Loevinger, J. & Knoll, E. (1983). Personality: Stages, traits and the self. *Annual Review of Psychology*, 34, 195–222.

Lord, C.G. (1982). Predicting behavioral consistency from an individual's perception of situational similarities. *Journal of Personality and Social Psychology*, 42, 1076–88.

McCrae, R.R. (1982). Consensual validation of personality traits: Evidence from self-reports and ratings. *Journal of Personality and Social Psychology*, 43, 293–303.

Magnusson, D. (1971). An analysis of situational dimensions. *Perceptual and Motor Skills*, 32, 851–67.

(1974). The individual in the situation: Some studies on individuals' perception of situations. *Studia Psychologica*, 16, 124–36.

(1976). The person and the situation in an interactional model of behaviour. *Scandinavian Journal of Psychology*, 17, 253–71.

(1978). *On the Psychological Situation*. Reports from the Department of Psychology, The University of Stockholm, No. 544.

(1980). Personality in an interactional paradigm of research. *Zeitschrift für Differentielle und Diagnostische Psychologie*, 1, 17–34.

(ed.) (1981a). *Toward a Psychology of Situations*. Hillsdale, NJ: L. Erlbaum.

(1981b). Wanted: A psychology of situations. In: D. Magnusson (ed.), *Toward a Psychology of Situations*. Hillsdale, NJ: L. Erlbaum, pp. 9–32.

(1987). *Individual Development from an Interactional Perspective: A Longitudinal Study*. Hillsdale, NJ: L. Erlbaum.

Magnusson, D. & Allen, V.L. (eds.) (1983). *Human Development: An Interactional Perspective*. New York: Academic Press.

Magnusson, D. & Ekehammar, B. (1975). Perceptions of and reactions to stressful situations. *Journal of Personality and Social Psychology*, 31, 1147–54.

(1978). Similar situations – similar behaviors? *Journal of Research in Personality*, 12, 41–8.

Magnusson, D. & Endler, N.S. (eds.) (1977a). *Personality at the Crossroads*. Hillsdale, NJ: L. Erlbaum.

(1977b). Interactional psychology: Present status and future prospects. in: D. Magnusson & N.S. Endler (eds.), *Personality at the Crossroads*. Hillsdale, NJ: L. Erlbaum, pp. 3–35.

Magnusson, D. & Stattin, H. (1982). Methods for studying stressful situations. In: H.W. Krohne & L. Laux (eds.), *Achievement, Stress, and Anxiety*. Washington, DC: Hemisphere, pp. 317–31.

Maller, J.B. (1934). General and specific factors in character. *Journal of Social Psychology*, 5, 97–102.

Malloy, T.E. & Kenny, D.A. (1986). The social relations model: An integrative method for personality research. *Journal of Personality*, 54, 199–225.

Mervis, C.B. & Rosch, E. (1981). Categorization of natural objects. *Annual Review of Psychology*, 32, 89–115.

Michela, J.L. (1990). Within-person correlational design and analysis. In: C. Hendrick & M.S. Clark (eds.). *Research Methods in Personality and Social Psychology*. Newbury Park: Sage, pp. 279–311.

Miller, L.C., Berg, J.M. & Archer, R.L. (1983). Openers: Individuals who elicit intimate self-disclosure. *Journal of Personality and Social Psychology*, 44, 1234–44.

Mischel, W. (1968). *Personality and Assessment*. New York: Wiley.

(1973). Toward a cognitive social learning reconceptualization of personality. *Psychological Review*, 81, 252–83.

(1976). *Introduction to Personality* (2nd edn). New York; Holt, Rinehart & Winston.

(1977). On the future of personality measurement. *American Psychologist*, 32, 246–54.

(1978). Personality research; A look at the future. In: H. London (ed.), *Personality – A New Look at Metatheories*. Washington, DC: Hemisphere, pp. 1–19.

(1979). On the interface of cognition and personality. *American Psychologist*, 34, 740–54.

(1983). Alternatives in the pursuit of the predictability and consistency of persons: Stable data yield unstable interpretations. *Journal of Personality*, 51, 578–604.

(1984a). Convergences and challenges in the search for consistency. *American Psychologist*, 39, 351–64.

(1984b). On the predictability of behavior and the structure of personality. In: R.A. Zucker, J. Aronoff & A.I. Rabin (eds.), *Personality and the Prediction of Behavior*. New York: Academic Press, pp. 269–305.

(1986). *Introduction to Personality* (4th edn). New York: CBS.

Mischel, W. & Peake, P.K. (1982a). Beyond déjà vu in the search for cross-situational consistency. *Psychological Review*, 89, 730–55.

(1982b). The search for consistency: Measure for measure. In: M.P. Zanna, E.T. Higgins & C.P. Herman (eds.), *Consistency in Social Behavior – The Ontario Symposium* (vol. 2). Hillsdale, NJ: L. Erlbaum, pp. 187–207.

Mischel, W. & Peake, E. (1983a). Analysing the construction of consistency in personality. In; M.M. Page (ed.), *Personality – Current Theory and Research*. The 1982 Nebraska Symposium on Motivation. Lincoln, NB: University of Nebraska Press, pp. 233–62.

(1983b). Some facets of consistency: Replies to Epstein, Funder, and Bem. *Psychological Review*, 90, 394–402.

Moskowitz, D.S. (1986). Comparison of self-reports, reports by knowledgeable informants, and behavioral observation data. *Journal of Personality*, 54, 294–317.

(1988). Cross-situational generality in the laboratory: dominance and friendliness. *Journal of Personality and Social Psychology*, 54, 829–39.

Moskowitz, D.S. & Schwartz, J.C. (1982). Validity comparisons of behavior counts and ratings by knowledgeble informants. *Journal of Personality and Social Psychology*, 42, 518–28.

Mothersill, K.J., Dobson, K.S. & Neufeld, R.W. (1986). The interactional model of anxiety: An evaluation of the differential hypothesis. *Journal of Personality and Social Psychology*, 51, 640–48.

Murray, H.A. (1938). *Explorations in Personality*. New York: Oxford University Press.

Niedenthal, M., Cantor, N. & Kihlstrom, J.F. (1985). Prototype-matching: A strategy of social decision making. *Journal of Personality and Social Psychology*, 48, 575–84.

Olweus, D. (1977). A critical analysis of the 'modern' interactionist position. In: D. Magnusson & N.S. Endler (eds.), *Personality at the Crossroads*. Hillsdale, NJ: L. Erlbaum, pp. 221–33.

(1980). The consistency issue in personality psychology revisited – with special reference to aggression. *British Journal of Social and Clinical Psychology*, 19, 377–90.

Ozer, D.J. (1986). *Consistency in Personality: A Methodological Framework*. New York: Springer.

Ozer, D.J. & Gjerde, P.F. (1989). Patterns of personality consistency and change from childhood to adolescence. *Journal of Personality*, 57, 483–507.

Paunonen, S.V. (1988). Trait relevance and the differential predictability of behavior. *Journal of Personality*, 56, 599–619.

Paunonen, S.V. & Jackson, D.N. (1985). Idiographic measurement strategies for personality and prediction: Some unredeemed promissary notes. *Psychological Review*, 92, 486–511.

(1986). Nomothetic and idiographic measurement in personality. *Journal of Personality*, 54, 447–59.

Peake, P.K. (1984). Theoretical divergences in the person–situation debate. In: J.R. Royce & L.P. Mos (eds.), *Annals of Theoretical Psychology* (vol. 2). New York; Plenum Press, pp. 329–38.

Pervin, L.A. (1968). Performance and satisfaction as a function of individual–environment fit. *Psychological Bulletin*, 69, 56–68.

(1976). A free-response description approach to the analysis of person–situation interaction. *Journal of Personality and Social Psychology*, 34, 465–74.

(1978). Definitions, measurements, and classifications of stimuli, situations, and environments. *Human Ecology*, 6, 71–105.

(1981). The relation of situations to behavior. In: D. Magnusson (ed.), *Toward a Psychology of Situations*. Hillsdale, NJ: L. Erlbaum, pp. 343–60.

(1984a). Idiographic approaches to personality. In: N. Endler & J.M. Hunt (eds.), *Personality and the Behavioral Disorders*. New York: Wiley, pp. 261–82.

(1984b). Persons, situations, interactions, and the future of personality. In: J.R.Royce, & L.P. Mos (eds.), *Annals of Theoretical Psychology* (vol. 2). New York: Plenum Press, pp. 339–44.

(1984c). *Current Controversies and Issues in Personality*. (2nd edn). New York: Wiley.

(1985). Personality: Current controversies, issues, and directions. *Annual Review of Psychology*, 36, 83–114.

Pervin, L.A. & Lewis, M. (eds.) (1978). *Perspectives in Interactional Psychology*. New York: Plenum Press.

Peterson, D.R. (1979). Assessing interpersonal relationships in natural settings. In: L.R. Kahle (ed.), *Methods for Studying Person–Situation Interactions*. New directions for Methodology of Behavioral Science, 2. San Francisco: Jossey-Bass, pp. 33–54.

Phares, E.J. & Lamiell, J.T. (1977). Personality. *Annual Review of Psychology*, 28, 113–40.

Phillips, B.J. & Endler, N.S. (1982). Academic examinations and anxiety: The interaction model empirically tested. *Journal of Research in Personality*, 16, 303–18.

Phillips, E.M. (1989). Use and abuse of the repertory grid: A PCP approach. *The Psychologist*, 2, 194–8.

Plomin, R. (1986). Behavioral genetic methods. *Journal of Personality*, 54, 226–61.

Price, R.H. (1974). The taxonomic classification of behaviors and situations and the problem of behaviour–environment congruence. *Human Relations*, 27, 567–85.

Pryor, J.B. (1980). Self-reports and behavior. In: D.M. Wegner & R.R. Vallacher (eds.), *The Self in Social Psychology*. New York: Oxford University Press, pp. 206–28.

Pryor, J.B. & Merluzzi, T.V. (1985). The role of expertise in processing social interaction scripts. *Journal of Experimental Social Psychology*, 21, 362–79.

Romer, D., Gruder, C.L. & Lizzardo, T. (1986). A person–situation approach to altruistic behaviour. *Journal of Personality and Social Psychology*, 51, 1001–12.

Rorer, L.G. & Widiger, T.A. (1983). Personality structure and assessment. *Annual Review of Psychology*, 34, 431–63.

Rosch, E. (1975). Cognitive representation of semantic categories. *Journal of Experimental Psychology: General*, 104, 192–233.

Rosch, E. & Lloyd, B.B. (1978). *Cognition and Categorization*. Hillsdale, NJ; L. Erlbaum.

Rosenberg, S. & Gara, M.A. (1983). Contemporary perspectives and future directions of personality and social psychology. *Journal of Personality and Social Psychology*, 45, 57–73.

Ross, A.O. (1987). *Personality*. New York: Holt, Rinehart & Winston.

Rothbart, M. & Park, B. (1986). On the confirmability and disconfirmability of trait concepts. *Journal of Personality and Social Psychology*, 50, 131–42.

Rowe, D.C. (1987). Resolving the person–situation debate. *American Psychologist*, 42, 218–27.

Runyan, W.M. (1983). Idiographic goals and methods in the study of lives. *Journal of Personality*, 51, 414–37.

Rush, M.C. & Russell, J.E.A. (1988). Leader prototypes and prototype-contingent consenus in leader behavior descriptions. *Journal of Experimental Social Psychology*, 24, 88–104.

Rushton, J.P., Brainerd, C.J. & Pressley, M. (1983). Behavioral development and construct validity: The principle of aggregation. *Psychological Bulletin*, 94, 18–38.

Rushton, J. & Erdle, S. (1987). Evidence for an aggressive (and delinquent) personality. *British Journal of Social Psychology*, 26, 87–9.

Russell, J.A. & Pratt, G. (1980). The description of the affective quality attributed to environments. *Journal of Personality and Social Psychology*, 38, 311–22.

Sarason, I.G., Smith, R.E. & Diener, E. (1975). Personality research: components of variance attributable to the person and the situation. *Journal of Personality and Social Psychology*, 32, 199–204.

Schank, R. & Abelson, R. (1977). *Scripts, Plans, Goals, and Understanding: An Inquiry into Human Knowledge Structures*. Hillsdale, NJ: L. Erlbaum.

Schutte, N., Kenrick, D.T. & Sadalla, E.K. (1985). The search for predictable settings: Situational prototypes, constraint, and behavioral variation. *Journal of Personality and Social Psychology*, 49, 121–8.

Sears, D.O. (1986). College sophomores in the laboratory: Influences of a narrow data base on social psychology's view on human nature. *Journal of Personality and Social Psychology*, 51, 515–30.

Sechrest, L. (1976). Personality. *Annual Review of Psychology*, 27, 1–28.

Shaver, P., Schwartz, J., Kirson, D. & O'Connor, C. (1987). Emotion knowledge: Further exploration of a prototype approach. *Journal of Personality and Social Psychology*, 52, 1061–86.

Sherman, S.J. & Fazio, R.H. (1983). Parallels between attitudes and traits as predictors of behavior. *Journal of Personality*, 51, 308–45.

Shweder, R.A. (1975). How relevant is the individual difference theory of personality? *Journal of Personality*, 43, 455–84.

   (1982). Fact and artifact in trait perception: The systematic distortion hypothesis. In: B.A. Maher & W.B. Maher (eds.), *Progress in Experimental Personality Research* (vol. 11). New York: Academic Press, pp. 65–101.

Singer, J.L. & Kolligian, J. (1987). Personality: Developments in the study of private experience. *Annual Review of Psychology*, 38, 533–74.

Skinner, B.F. (1963). Behaviorism at fifty. *Science*, 140, 951–8.

Slater, P. (1977). *The Measurement of Interpersonal Space by the Grid Technique* (vol. 2: Dimensions of Interpersonal Space). London: Wiley.

Snyder, M. (1974). Self-monitoring of expressive behavior. *Journal of Personality and Social Psychology*, 30, 526–37.

Snyder, M. Ickes, W. (1985). Personality and social behavior. In: G. Lindzey & E. Aronson (eds.), *Handbook of Social Psychology* (vol. 2, 3rd edn). New York: Random House, pp. 883–947.

Spielberger, C.D. (1966). The effect of anxiety on complex learning and academic achievement. In: C.D. Spielberger (ed.), *Anxiety and Behavior*. New York: Academic Press.

(1972). Anxiety as an emotional state. In: C.D. Spielberger (eds.), *Anxiety: Current Trends in Theory and Research* (vol. 1). New York: Academic Press, pp. 23–49.

Spielberger, C.D., Gorsuch, R.L. & Lushene, R.E. (1970). *Manual for the State–Trait–Anxiety Inventory*. Palo Alto, CA: Consulting Psychologists Press.

Staats, A.W. & Burns, G.L. (1982). Emotional personality repertoire as cause of behavior: Specification of personality and interaction principles. *Journal of Personality and Social Psychology*, 43, 873–81.

Stebbins, R.A. (1985). The definition of the situation: A review. In: A. Furnham (ed.), *Social Behavior in Context*. Boston: Allyn & Bacon, p. 134–54.

Stringer, P. (1976). Repertory grids in the study of environmental perception. In: P. Slater (ed.), *The Measurement of Interpersonal Space by the Grid Technique* (vol. 1: Explorations of Interpersonal Space). London: Wiley, pp. 183–208.

Taylor, R.B. (1981). Perception of density: Individual differences. *Environment and Behavior*, 13, 3–21.

(1983). Conjoining environmental psychology with social and personality psychology: Natural marriage or shotgun wedding? In: N.R. Feimer & E.S. Geller (eds.), *Environmental Psychology*. New York: Praeger, pp. 24–59.

Taylor, S.E. (1981). The interface of cognitive and social psychology. In: J.H. Harvey (ed.), *Cognition, Social Behavior, and the Environment*. NJ: L. Erlbaum, pp. 189–211.

Taylor, S.E. & Crocker, J. (1981). Schematic bases of social information processing. In: E.T. Higgins, C.P. Herman & M.P. Zanna (eds.), *Social Cognition – The Ontario Symposium* (vol. 1). Hillsdale, NJ: L. Erlbaum, pp. 89–134.

Tellegen, A., Kamp, J. & Watson, D. (1982). Recognizing individual differences in predictive structures. *Psychological Review*, 89, 95–105.

Thomas, W.I. (1928). *The Child in America*. New York: Knopf.

Tolman, E.C. (1935). Psychology versus immediate experience. *Philosophy of Science*, 2, 356–80.

Tomkins, S.S. (1981). The rise, fall, and resurrection of the study of personality. *The Journal of Mind and Behavior*, 2, 443–52.

Valsiner, J. (1986). Between groups and individuals: Psychologists' and laypersons' interpretation of correlational findings. In: J. Valsiner (ed.), *The Individual Subject and Scientific Psychology*. New York: Plenum, pp. 113–51.

Vleeming, R. (1981). Some sources of behavioural variance as measured by an S–R inventory of machiavellianism. *Psychological Reports*, 48, 359–68.

Wakenhut, R. (1978). *Über die Einbeziehung von Situationen in psychologische Messungen*. Frankfurt-am-Main: Lang.

West, S.G. & Graziano, W.G. (1989). Long-term stability and change in personality: An introduction. *Journal of Personality*, 57, 175-93.

Wicker, A.W.'(1969). Attitudes versus actions: The relationship of verbal and overt behavioral responses to attitude objects. *Journal of Social Issues*, 4, 41-78.

Wilson, J.P. & Petruska, R. (1984). Motivation, model attributes, and prosocial behavior. *Journal of Personality and Social Psychology*, 46. 458-68.

Wilson, T.D. & Capitman, J.A. (1982). Effects of script availability on social behavior. *Personality and Social Psychology Bulletin*, 8, 11-19.

Wish, M., Deutsch, M. & Kaplan, S. (1976). Perceived dimensions of interpersonal relations. *Journal of Personality and Social Psychology*, 3, 409-20.

Witkin, H.A., Dyk, R.B., Faterson, H.F., Goodenough, D.R. & Karp, S.A. (1962). *Psychological Differentiation*. New York: Wiley.

Wittgenstein, L. (1953). *Philosophical Investigations*. New York: Macmillan.

Woodruffe, C. (1984). The consistency of presented personality: Additional evidence from aggregation. *Journal of Personality*, 52, 307-17.

(1985). Consensual validation of personality traits: Additional evidence and individual differences. *Journal of Personality and Social Psychology*, 48, 1240-52.

Woody, E.Z. (1983). The intuitive personologist revisited: A critique of dialectical person perception. *Journal of Personality*, 51, 236-47.

Wymer, W.E. & Penner, L.A. (1985). Moderator variables and different types of predictability: Do you have match? *Journal of Personality and Social Psychology*, 49, 1002-15.

Wysor, M. (1983). Comparing college students' environmental perceptions and attitudes: A methodological investigation. *Environment and Behavior*, 15, 615-45.

Zavalloni, M. & Louis-Guerin, C. (1979). Social psychology at the crossroads: Its encounter with cognitive and ecological psychology and the interactive perspective. *European Journal of Social Psychology*, 9, 307-21.

Zevon, M.A. & Tellegen, A. (1982). The structure of mood change: An idiographic/nomothetic analysis. *Journal of Personality and Social Psychology*, 43, 111-22.

Zuckerman, M., Koestner, R., DeBoy, T., Garcia, T., Maresca, B.C. & Sartoris, J.M. (1988). To predict some people some of the time: A reexamination of the moderator variable approach in personality theory. *Journal of Personality and Social Psychology*, 54, 1006-19.

Zuroff, D.C. (1982). Person, situation, and person-by-situation interaction components in person perception. *Journal of Personality*, 50, 1-14.

(1986). Was Gordon Allport a trait theorist? *Journal of Personality and Social Psychology*, 51, 993-1000.

Author index

Abelson, R.P. 13, 80, 87, 88, 90, 118, 119, 137
Ackerman, C.A. 64
Acock, A.C. 9
Adams-Webber, J. 30, 123
Ajzen, I. 5, 8, 9, 92
Alker, H.A. 52
Allen, A. 26, 92, 114, 115, 159, 165, 170
Allen, B.P. 60
Allen, V.L. 57
Allport, G.W. 3, 12, 15, 16, 17, 22, 34, 38, 176, 182
Amato, P.R. 79, 83
Anderson, C.A. 89
Andrews, K.H. 9
Archer, R.L. 54, 57
Argyle, M. 5, 6, 52, 67, 72, 73
Aronoff, J. 68
Asendorpf, J.B. 108, 109
Athay, M. 32, 33

Backteman, G. 45
Ball, D.W. 77
Bandura, A. 17, 18, 28, 31
Bannister, D. 123, 126, 144
Baron, R.M. 5, 9, 11, 76
Battistich, V.A. 79
Baumeister, R.F. 9, 73, 92
Beail, N. 30
Bem, D.J. 4, 16, 24, 26, 33, 57, 92, 93, 97, 99, 100, 101, 113, 114, 120, 159, 165, 170
Berg, J.M. 54, 57
Bernieri, F. 92
Bishop, D.W. 57
Black, J. 88
Blackman, S. 29
Blass, T. 5, 8, 9, 10, 114
Block, J. 24, 25, 38, 39, 45, 98, 180
Block, J.H. 45
Borkenau, P. 94
Boudreau, L.A. 5, 11, 76
Bower, G. 88
Bowers, K.S. 17, 19, 20, 51

Brainerd, C.J. 9, 92
Brewer, M.B. 85
Briggs, S.R. 49
Bringle, R.G. 57
Brody, N. 17, 21, 23, 27, 93, 109, 178
Brown, L.B. 83
Buckner, K.E. 107
Burns, G.L. 57
Burton, R.V. 15
Buss, A.R. 10, 44, 93
Buss, D.M. 5, 10, 22, 45, 67, 94, 95, 96, 97, 103n
Butler, J.M. 98
Byrne, D. 28

Campbell, A. 73
Cantor, N. 13, 28, 34, 80, 84, 85, 86, 99, 118, 136
Capitman, J.A. 89
Carlson, R. 7, 8, 10, 114
Carson, R.C. 4, 67
Cattell, R.B. 23, 24
Champagne, B.M. 33, 47
Chaplin, W.F. 107, 113, 170
Cheek, J.M. 25, 49
Cochran, L.R. 123
Cohen, C.E. 85, 86
Conger, A.J. 104
Conley, J.J. 4, 33, 45, 113
Cook, T.D. 112, 113
Costa, P.T. 45
Cox, T. 62
Craik, K.H. 22, 93, 94, 95, 96, 97, 103n
Crocker, J. 85

Dahlgren, K. 85
Dantchick, A. 5, 7, 10, 11, 20, 176
Darley, J.M. 32, 33
Davis, S. 57
Deluty, R.H. 24
Deutsch, M. 78
Diener, E. 45, 51, 55, 56, 57, 68, 113
Diveky, S. 64
Dobson, K.S. 65, 66
Dolan, C.A. 47, 106

Donat, D.C. 62
Dull, V. 85
Dworkin, R.H. 43, 52, 67, 75, 76, 77, 89

Eckes, T. 86, 87
Edwards, J.M. 17, 41, 64, 72
Edwards, L.A. 25
Ekehammar, B. 39, 40, 43, 47, 49, 60,
    113, 122, 131, 132n, 136, 137, 138,
    140
Emmons, R.A. 55, 56, 57, 58
Endler, N.S. 5, 6, 17, 32, 40, 41, 43, 44,
    48, 51, 53, 57–64, 66, 67, 73, 121,
    122, 126, 127, 130, 131, 150
Epstein, S. 4, 15, 17, 23, 24, 25, 33, 40,
    46, 92, 113, 176
Epting, F.R. 30
Erdle, S. 92
Eysenck, H.J. 23

Fazio, R.H. 5, 9, 92, 114
Fenigstein, A. 10
Fennell, G.R. 73
Feshbach, S. 4, 11
Fiske, D.W. 51
Flood, M. 62
Folkman, S. 114
Forgas, J.P. 81, 82, 83, 84, 118, 119, 134
Forgus, R. 3
Foss, M.A. 103, 104
Fransella, F. 123, 126, 144
Frederiksen, N. 73
Fridhandler, B.M. 60
Funder, D.C. 4, 7, 20, 25, 28n, 33, 97,
    99, 101, 113, 123
Furnham, A. 5, 52, 53, 67, 72, 73

Gadlin, H. 69
Gara, M.A. 5, 8n
Geis, F.L. 77
Gibson, E.J. 76
Gjerde, P.F. 45, 176, 179, 180
Goldberg, L.R. 113, 170
Goldfinger, S.H. 43, 75, 76, 77, 89
Golding, S.L. 29, 50, 51, 52
Goldstein, K.M. 29
Gordon, S.E. 88
Gormly, J. 93
Gorsuch, R.L. 58
Gough, H.G. 95
Graesser, A.C. 88
Graham, J.A. 5, 67, 72, 73
Graziano, W.G. 176
Gruder, C.L. 57
Gruen, R.J. 114
Guilford, J.P. 23

Haigh, G.V. 98

Hampson, S.E. 25, 28
Harrison, J. 123
Harrison, R.H. 73
Hartshorne, H. 9, 12, 15, 16, 17, 176
Heck, G.L.M. van 123
Heilizer, F. 5
Hempel, A.M. 105
Hermans, H.J.M. 107, 109
Hirschberg, N. 21, 22, 26
Honikman, B. 123
Houts, A.C. 112, 113
Howard, J.A. 44
Hoy, E. 62
Hunt, J.McV. 48, 51
Hyland, M.E. 44n, 68, 89

Ickes, W. 3, 9, 26, 72

Jackson, D.N. 4, 95, 104, 105, 109, 110,
    120
Jaspers, J.M. 52, 53, 73
Jeger, A.M. 24

Kahle, L.R. 10
Kamp, J. 113
Kandel, D.B. 9
Kaplan, S.J. 78
Kelly, G.A. 12, 14, 28, 29, 30, 123, 125,
    126, 144
Kendall, P.C. 60, 61, 62
Kenny, D.A. 9, 51, 53, 54, 68
Kenrick, D.T. 4, 5, 7, 8, 10, 11, 20, 25,
    28n, 67, 73, 86, 87, 176
Kihlstrom, J.F. 52, 86, 99
King, G.A. 78
King, P.R. 64
Kirson, D. 85
Klein, G.S. 28
Klirs, E.G. 47, 106, 122
Klockars, A.J. 25
Knoll, E. 4
Koestner, R. 92
Koffka, K. 39
Kohn, M. 24
Kolligian, J. 10, 28
Koretzky, M.B. 24
Kowalski, D.J. 88
Krahé, B. 6, 93
Krauskopf, C. 44n
Kreitler, H. 29, 35, 36, 37
Kreitler, S. 29, 35, 36, 37
Kuczynski, M. 64

Lamiell, J.T. 4, 17, 18, 46, 93, 101, 102,
    103, 104, 105, 109, 120, 176, 178
Landfield, A.W. 30
Lanning, K. 74, 75
Lantermann, E.D. 51, 68

LaPiere, R.T. 9
Larsen, R. 45, 55, 68, 104, 113
Launier, R. 65
La Voie, L. 53
Lazarus, R.S. 65, 114
Lazzarini, A. 62
Leffel, G.M. 104
Lerner, M.J. 10
Levy, L.H. 21, 24, 26
Lewin, K. 39
Lewis, M. 57
Little, B.R. 6, 52
Lizzardo, T. 57
Lloyd, B.B. 84
Lobel, T.E. 36
Loevinger, J. 4, 17
Lord, C.G. 97, 99, 100, 106
Louis-Guerin, C. 77
Lui, L. 85
Lushene, R.E. 58

McCrae, R.R. 24, 45, 93
MacFarlane, S. 67
Mackay, C. 62
Magnusson, D. 5, 6, 32, 40–9, 57, 60, 72,
    73, 77, 78, 79, 113, 122, 131, 132n,
    136, 137, 138, 140, 177
Maller, J.B. 15
Malloy, T.E. 51, 53, 54, 58
Mancuso, J.C. 30, 123
May, M.A. 9, 12, 15, 16, 17, 176
Menyhart, J. 83
Merluzzi, T.V. 89
Mervis, C.B. 84, 85
Michela, J.L. 152
Miller, L.C. 54, 57
Mischel, W. 4, 9, 13, 16, 17, 18, 19, 21,
    24, 25, 28, 31–5, 37, 40, 42, 45, 57,
    80, 84, 85, 86, 110, 113, 136, 139,
    157, 176, 178, 182
Montello, D.R. 67
Moskowitz, D.S. 92, 93, 162
Mothersill, K.J. 66
Murray, H.A. 39

Neufeld, R.W. 66
Niedenthal, P.M. 86, 99

O'Brien, E.J. 15, 113
O'Connor, C. 85
Okada, M. 48, 59, 60
Olweus, D. 45, 50, 51, 57
Ozer, D.J. 20, 46, 51, 176, 179, 180

Park, B. 27
Paunonen, S.V. 4, 92, 104, 105, 109,
    110, 120

Peake, P.K. 4, 25, 31n, 32, 33, 35, 45,
    69, 113, 157, 178
Pearce, P. 83
Penner, L.A. 113, 170
Pervin, L.A. 4, 31, 33, 34, 44, 47, 50, 57,
    69, 72, 106, 109, 178
Peterson, D.R. 53, 68
Petruska, R. 57
Phares, E.J. 4, 18
Phillips, B.J. 63
Phillips, E.M. 123
Plomin, R. 50, 67
Potkay, C.R. 60
Pratt, G. 79
Pressley, M. 9, 92
Price, R.H. 73
Pryor, J.B. 89, 162

Renner, P. 57
Revelle, W. 47, 106, 122
Ricklander, L. 49
Romer, D. 57
Rorer, L.G. 4, 27
Rosch, E. 84, 85, 86
Rosenberg, S. 5, 8n
Rosenstein, A.J. 48
Ross, A.O. 102
Rothbart, M. 27
Rowe, D.C. 50, 67
Rubin, S.H. 69
Runyan, W.M. 106
Rush, M.C. 86
Rushton, J.P. 9, 92
Russell, J.A. 79
Russell, J.E.A. 86

Sadalla, E.K. 73, 86, 87
Sarason, I.G. 51
Sarre, P. 123
Saunders, J. 79, 83
Sawyer, J.D. 88
Schalling, D. 43, 49
Schank, R. 13, 87, 88, 119
Scheier, M. 10
Schutte, N. 73, 86, 87
Schwartz, J.C. 80, 85, 86, 93, 136
Scott, W.J. 9
Sears, D.O. 11
Sechrest, L. 5
Shadish, W.R. 112, 113
Shaver, P. 85
Sherman, S.J. 5, 9, 114
Shulman, B. 3
Shweder, R.A. 25, 28n
Singer, J.L. 10, 28
Skinner, B.F. 17
Slater, P. 30, 123

Smith, D.A. 88
Smith, R.E. 51
Snyder, M. 3, 9, 26, 72, 83
Sorrentino, R.M. 78
Spielberger, C.D. 25, 58, 61
Staats, A.W. 57
Stattin, H. 42
Stebbins, R.A. 71, 77
Stringer, P. 123

Taylor, R.B. 5, 79
Taylor, S.E. 5, 85
Tellegen, A. 106, 107, 113, 182
Terry, R.L. 57
Thomas, W.I. 77
Thompson, E.G. 79
Tice, D.M. 9, 73, 92
Tolman, E.C. 39
Tomkins, S.S. 4
Trierweiler, S.J. 103, 104, 105
Turner, T. 88

Valsiner, J. 17, 46, 176
Vleeming, R. 57

Wakenhut, R. 43, 49
Watson, D. 113
West, S.G. 176
White, J.W. 47, 106
White, P. 73
Wicker, A.W. 9
Widiger, T.A. 4, 27
Williams, C.J. 92
Wilson, J.P. 57, 68
Wilson, T.D. 89
Wish, M. 78
Witkin, H.A. 28
Witt, P.A. 57
Wittgenstein, L. 57
Wolls, S.B. 88
Woodruffe, C. 24, 93, 162
Woody, E.Z. 104
Wymer, W.E. 113, 170
Wysor, M. 123

Zavalloni, M. 77
Zevon, M.A. 106, 107, 182
Zuckerman, M. 92, 113, 181
Zuroff, D.C. 57

Subject index

Act frequency approach 22, 93ff., 101
  and modal human tendencies 45
  measurement of act trends 22, 95, 96
Affect *see* emotions
Anxiety 13, 49, 57ff.
  interaction model 58, 60, 66, 68, 121,
    126, 127, 143
  multidimensional model *see* interaction
    model
  -provoking situations 5, 13, 14, 47ff.,
    57ff., 122, 130, 137, 143 ff., 162ff.
    idiographic sampling of xii, 123ff.,
      162, 173
  state 25, 58ff., 120
    unidimensional vs. multidimensional
      60
  trait 25, 58ff., 120
    ambiguous 59ff., 127, 129, 130
    facets of 59ff., 120
    interpersonal 59ff., 127, 129,130
    multidimensional 58, 59, 61, 62
    physical danger 59ff., 127, 129, 130
    social evaluation 59ff., 127, 129, 130
    unidimensional 58, 61
Ascription rules 27, 28
A-state *see* anxiety, state
A-trait *see* anxiety, trait
Attitude 8, 9
  – behaviour consistency 9, 10
  traits and 8, 9

Behaviour
  and reinforcement 17, 18
  consistency 4, 11, 15, 25, 35, 38, 92,
    106
  discriminativeness 8, 31, 69
  equivalence classes 16
  functional meaning 16, 38
  generality vs. specificity 40, 50
  genetics 50, 67
  measures of 14, 131ff., 149ff., 161ff.
  observation of 21, 33, 51, 52, 54, 180,
    181
  patterns of 21, 27, 38, 42, 51, 87, 92,
    119
  prediction of 9, 10, 15, 23, 34, 36, 38,
    42, 86, 96, 97, 100, 109, 118

  self-report measures of 25, 33, 45, 52,
    98, 162, 180
  situation specificity 15, 17, 20, 50
  variability 31, 33, 34, 46, 69, 75, 87,
    113, 117
Behavioural intentions 36, 89
Belief in a just world 10
BRQ (Behavioral Reactions Questionnaire)
  62

California Personality Inventory *see* CPI
Carlton Behavior Study 33
Cluster analysis 45, 48, 179
Cognition 12
  definition of 29
  of situations *see* situation, cognition
  social 5, 10
Cognitive control 28
Cognitive prototypes 13, 34, 80, 84ff.,
    118, 119, 124, 132ff., 142ff., 163ff.,
    181
  characteristic features 87, 133, 148,
    163
  consensual feature lists 85ff.
  index of feature overlap 136, 137, 151,
    166
  of situations 86ff.
  shared features 86, 90
Cognitive scripts *see* scripts
Cognitive styles 28, 29
Coherence 5ff., 34ff., 56, 80, 111ff., 117ff.,
    140, 142ff., 152ff., 172ff.
  cross-situational xii, 5ff., 14, 42, 79,
    90ff., 110, 138, 153, 178
  intraindividual 14, 57, 114, 177
  level of analysis 6, 13, 49, 138, 159,
    168
  model 14, 57, 124, 131, 140, 158, 173
  of situation cognition and behaviour 68,
    87
Congruence *see* coherence
Congruence response model 55
Consistency xii, 4, 9, 13, 16, 24, 47, 50,
    66, 91, 104, 105, 121, 129
  absolute 5, 6, 31, 37, 111, 117
  controversy xi, 6ff., 15ff., 56, 71, 112,
    114, 117, 176ff.

cross-situational 3, 5, 11ff., 21, 26, 31, 33, 74, 75, 102ff., 176ff.
  debate *see* controversy
  in personality 3, 26
  intraindividual xii, 3, 6, 17, 39, 66, 93, 97, 100, 105
  lack of 16, 18, 31, 38, 117, 140
  paradox 24, 38, 104
  relative 5ff., 19, 23, 31, 37, 66, 111, 117, 176
  self-rated 26, 159, 160, 170, 171
  temporal 18, 21, 33, 34, 45, 46, 178ff.
Correlations
  and modern interactionism 45, 48, 50
  and the trait approach 20, 21, 142
  intraindividual 46, 47, 124, 137ff., 142, 152ff., 168ff., 179
  within-subject *see* intraindividual
  z-transformed 138, 139, 154, 171
Covariation
  hypothesis 120, 142, 152, 160, 161.
  of perceived and behavioural similarity 6ff., 30, 47, 68, 100, 106, 111, 118, 124, 137ff., 142ff., 166ff., 178
  of situation cognition and behaviour xii, 12, 34, 43ff., 81, 84, 91, 112, 117ff., 173, 174
CPI (California Personality Inventory) 95, 96

Delay of gratification 32, 99
Dispositions *see* traits
Dissonance theory 99
Drop-out rates 143, 160

Emotions 50, 55ff., 65, 106, 182
Euclidean distance 136, 151
Experiment 8ff.
  and situationism 18ff., 71

Factor analysis 48ff., 59, 106
Field dependence 28
Fuzzy sets 34, 85, 94

Generalisability theory 51

Idiographic xi, xii, 13ff., 30ff., 42, 47, 50, 84, 87, 91ff., 105ff., 140, 162
  reconciliation of idiographic and nomothetic strategies 13, 14, 101, 102, 112, 159, 176, 182
Idiothetic approach 93, 101ff., 108
  and act frequency approach 103n
  dialectical reasoning 104
Impression formation 34, 85
Inconsistency *see* consistency, lack of; behaviour, discriminativeness; behaviour, variability

Individual-centred approach 5, 7, 12, 14, 30, 50, 81ff., 105, 110ff., 117ff., 129, 134ff., 143ff., 160, 161, 180ff.
  process/content distinction 120, 121, 178
  role of subjects in 37, 182
Individual difference paradigm 3, 10, 11, 18, 19, 23, 26, 34, 43, 50, 59, 71, 83, 93, 95, 104, 105, 120, 123, 176
Interaction
  meanings of 40, 44, 50, 53, 56, 111

Learning history 31ff.
Longitudinal studies 45

Mediating variables 41, 42
Modern interactionism xi, 4ff., 32, 38ff., 71, 73, 92, 104, 111, 121, 176ff.
  analysis of variance model 50, 54
  ANOVA paradigm 50, 68
  critical appraisals 39, 66ff.
  general postulates 40
  generalisability studies 51
  ideological foundations 69
  role of situation variables 43, 67, 69
  variance components strategy 37, 50, 51, 53
Mood *see* emotions
Multidimensional scaling 79, 82, 103

Nomothetic xi, 13ff., 17, 47, 56, 78, 87, 92, 96, 100, 104ff., 113, 114, 129, 131, 137, 139, 153, 156, 181
Norm-centred *see* nomothetic

Omega^2 index 51

PARQ (Present Affect Reactions Questionnaire) 60, 131, 136, 137, 142, 150ff., 160
Personal construct psychology 28, 39, 40, 125
  dichotomy corollary 144
  fundamental postulate 30
  individuality corollary 30
  organisation corollary 30
Personality
  and emotions 55
  coefficient 113, 139
  -cognition interface 34
  cognitive view 3, 12, 28, 34, 37
  definition 3, 50
  dynamic view of 37
  genetic bases 67
    see also behaviour, genetics
  interaction-centred theory of 32, 33
  psychology vs. differential psychology
Research Form *see* PRF

Personality (*cont.*)
  role of the situation in 4, 39, 67, 71
  -social psychology interface 5ff., 80, 114
  theory xi
Personality measurement 48
  aggregation 9, 27, 33, 57, 92, 93, 103,
    106
  and differential psychology 102
  ipsative 108
  moderator variables 9, 92, 93, 155, 181
  multiple-act criteria 9, 22, 92, 94
  peer ratings 24, 33, 93, 98, 162
Personality psychology
  crisis of confidence 4, 9, 40, 102
Person-centred *see* individual-centred
    approach
Person–situation debate *see* consistency,
    controversy
Person–situation interaction 4, 12, 14, 45,
    49ff., 66, 68, 70, 75, 77, 84, 100,
    104, 178
  see also modern interactionism
Physiological arousal 4, 58, 156
  see also PARQ
PRF (Personality Research Form) 95, 96
Prisoner's dilemma game 99
Prototypes *see* cognitive prototypes
P × S approach *see* modern interactionism

Q-sort 98, 99, 179
  California 98

R-data 24
Reaction variables 41, 42
Repertory grid technique 14, 30, 123,
    126, 144
  construct pole 144, 148
  contrast pole 144, 148
  emergent pole 144
  implicit pole 144
    see also personal construct psychology;
      situation, Grid
Repression-sensitization 28

Scripts 13, 80, 87ff., 118, 119, 124, 132,
    134ff., 142ff., 163ff., 181
  elements of 88
  strong vs. weak 88
S-data 25
Self-disclosure 54ff.
Self-esteem 10
Self-monitoring 9, 83
Self-perception theory 99
Self-presentation theory 99
Similarity
  behavioural 6, 49, 80, 106, 118, 136
    global ratings of 118, 151ff., 163ff.
  matrices 132

perceived 6, 47, 49, 79, 80, 86ff., 100,
    118, 126, 132, 141
  global ratings of 124, 131, 137, 141,
    147ff., 163ff.
situational 13, 84, 91, 114, 118, 136,
    141, 179
Situation choice model 55
Situationism 11, 12, 16ff., 24, 25, 28, 40,
    51, 71, 176
  and causal explanation 19
Situation(s)
  analysis of 4, 41
  anxiety-provoking *see* anxiety
  chosen vs. imposed 56
  cognition xii, 5ff., 29, 34, 42f., 65, 68,
    71ff., 118, 146
  cognitive representation of xii, 5ff., 31,
    33, 43, 68, 71ff., 111, 123, 140,
    173, 177
  dimensions of 45, 78, 79, 82, 83, 90
  Experience Questionnaire 127ff.
  Grid 124, 125, 129, 130, 134, 142ff.,
    161ff.
    constructs 125, 134
    elements 125, 137, 144
    titles 126
  objective definition of 5, 12, 13, 30ff.,
    38, 47, 72ff., 113
  psychological xi, 5, 6, 12, 13, 42, 56,
    67, 71, 79, 101, 141, 158
  scalability of 74, 75
  stressful 47, 59ff., 65, 141
  subjective definition of 5, 12, 13, 30ff.,
    38, 47, 72ff., 113
  taxonomies 41, 48, 50, 67, 73ff., 86
  units of analysis 72
Social episodes 13, 80ff., 90, 118, 119,
    124, 132, 134ff., 142ff., 163ff., 181
  episode space 82
  individual differences in episode
    cognition 82, 84
Social learning theories 17ff., 28, 31
  cognitive 17, 31ff.
  person variables in 31, 32, 41
Social relations model 53, 54
S–R GTA (S–R Inventory of General Trait
    Anxiousness 59, 61ff.
S–R inventories 48, 50, 52, 53, 68
Stability *see* consistency, temporal
STAI (State–Trait–Anxiety Inventory) 58,
    61
Stimulus–response (S–R) links 19
Stress 13, 57

T-data 26, 27
Template matching 93, 97ff., 104, 106
  contextual 100
  Q-set 100

S-set 100
Theory of cognitive orientation 35ff.
Thomas theorem 77
Traits 4ff., 15ff., 39, 41, 51, 71, 75,
    176
  and causal explanation 21, 23, 26
  as cognitive categories 11, 25, 28, 34
  behavioural indicators of 21ff., 34, 38,
    94, 109
  conscientiousness 23, 33, 75, 100
  dishonesty 15, 16, 38
  dispositional view of 21, 23, 26
  dominance 23, 95, 96

extraversion 55, 83
friendliness 21, 33, 75, 94
impulsivity 55
introversion 34
metatraits 9
neuroticism 34
shyness 108, 109
sociability 55, 76, 89
summary view of 21ff., 26, 93

Variables 19
  dependent 20, 44, 51, 67
  independent 19, 44, 51, 67, 73, 74

LaVergne, TN USA
23 September 2010
198093LV00002B/8/P

9 780521 154987